Mother's
Bedside Book

Mother's Bedside Book

EDITED BY

ERIC DUTHIE

HEINEMANN

LONDON MELBOURNE TORONTO

William Heinemann Ltd

LONDON   MELBOURNE   TORONTO

CAPE TOWN   AUCKLAND

THE HAGUE

First published 1960

Printed in Great Britain
by The Windmill Press Ltd
Kingswood, Surrey

Contents

CONTENTS

PART THREE

BELOW STAIRS

PART FOUR

SUCCESS STORIES FOR MOTHER

PART FIVE

IT'S YOUR FATHER ALL OVER: a Procession of Husbands

[vi]

CONTENTS

PART SIX

BEAUTY AND THE BEAST

PART SEVEN

A NEST IN THE COUNTRY

Foreword

Mother's Bedside Book and *Father's Bedside Book* will explain themselves. They are made for those of us to whom twenty, or thirty, or fifty years ago seems now more than ever like yesterday, and whose sense of humour, if no longer quite that of the Fourth Form, has, happily, not yet outgrown the Sixth. But no humour, perhaps, outgrows the Sixth.

On the level of simple entertainment these pieces give one a sense of the welter and diversity of life. Many of them are like the flowers of the fields – works of nature rather than of art. Most of them are not so memorable that you will never forget them, but having half-forgotten them you will find them very re-readable.

If the writers have anything in common it is that they are enjoying themselves. They are life-greedy people, of an age to take pleasure in things past and not a few delighting to re-create with the bloodshot eye of experience what they lived through sentimentally, when young and tender. Wondering why I had chosen so many 'first-person' pieces (for I was not deliberately doing so) I supposed it was because I wanted the books to be good company. Not only must there be humour and high spirits but plenty of friendliness as well. Writers in the first person who write about themselves give off this feeling spontaneously. Unlike the biographer (who remains off-stage), the autobiographer puts on his own show. It is an intimate one, for he has chosen to talk to you; and whether he is laughing at himself or boasting of what a fine fellow he is or using his 'poet's eye' to show you what his world is like or telling you things about himself his mother never knew, or merely – as often happens here – clowning a bit to amuse you, he is always in some sense *making himself known to you*. A collection of such writings can hardly help being a friendly gathering. You pass from vitality to vitality, and before long you are thinking: Life is its own justification!

To make a man's book is natural; to make a collection for women may seem a little bold. In the men's book there is more humour and horseplay; in the women's, rather more sentiment and family life. As I have never known a time when the products of the Fashion Puss and the Women's Editor did not cause more laughter than approval at the breakfast table, I have come to accept that whatever interests intelligent men is likely to interest women too. So I put in the Women's Book what pleased myself, being hopeful that mothers over forty have minds both masculine and feminine. (If you say: 'What about battle, cricket, interplanetary communication and the higher mathematics?' – okay, I play safe – I cut them out.)

So you will find much that could have been in either book, and mature persons of any age and either sex can swap the volumes with mutual benefit: there are pieces – nay, whole sections – in Father's book that he can read aloud to amuse Mother, and, although there is virtually an armistice in the sex war, there are no doubt pieces in Mother's book that she can read aloud to annoy Father. What could be more complementary?

Eric Duthie.

IN proportion as the years both lessen, and shorten, I set more count upon their periods, and would fain lay my ineffectual finger upon the spoke of the great wheel. I am not content to pass away 'like a weaver's shuttle'. Those metaphors solace me not, nor sweeten the unpalatable draught of mortality. I care not to be carried with the tide, that smoothly bears human life to eternity; and reluct at the inevitable course of destiny. I am in love with this green earth; the face of town and country; the unspeakable rural solitudes, and the sweet security of streets.

– Charles Lamb.

Acknowledgements

For arrangements made with various authors, their representatives and publishing houses by which copyright material was permitted to be reprinted in this book, and for the courtesy thus extended by them, the following acknowledgements are gratefully made:

To Messrs Barrie Books, Ltd. and Lady Cynthia Asquith for 'First Season' from *Remember and Be Glad*.

To The Bodley Head, Ltd. and Adrian Bell for 'Country Notebook' from *A Suffolk Harvest*.

To Messrs Jonathan Cape, Ltd. and the Authors for 'Mother and Son' from *Museum Pieces* by William Plomer; and for 'Mrs Wrench' from *A Thatched Roof* by Beverley Nichols.

To Messrs Cassell and Company, Ltd. and Aage Thaarup for 'Aage Thaarup Makes Hats' from *Heads and Tales*.

To Messrs Chatto and Windus, Ltd. and Alfred A. Knopf, Inc. for 'Father Hires a Cook' from *Life with Father* and for 'Father Brightens the Sick Room' from *Life with Mother*, both by Clarence Day.

To Messrs William Collins, Sons and Company, Ltd. and the Authors for 'My Birds' from *Birds as Individuals* by Len Howard; for 'The Opened Door' from *The Only Child* by James Kirkup; and for 'On Brensham Hill' from *Brensham Village* by John Moore.

To Messrs Constable and Company, Ltd. and the Authors for 'Europe, Here We Come' from *Our Hearts were Young and Gay* by Cornelia Otis Skinner and Emily Kimbrough.

To Messrs Peter Davies, Ltd. and Ann Davison for 'Ann Davison Sails the Atlantic' from *My Ship is so Small*.

To Messrs J. M. Dent and Sons, Ltd. and Mrs Robert Henrey for 'Childhood in Paris' from *The Little Madeleine*.

To Messrs André Deutsch, Ltd. and Elizabeth Hamilton for 'Let Me Go Free' from *A River Full of Stars*.

ACKNOWLEDGEMENTS

To Messrs Eyre and Spottiswoode (Publishers) Ltd. for 'Miss Tennant Steps Out' from *The Autobiography of Margot Asquith* by Lady Oxford and Asquith.

To Messrs Faber and Faber, Ltd. and Alison Uttley for 'Farmer's Girl' from *Ambush of Young Days* and 'Scented Memories' from *Here's a New Day*; and to Henry Williamson for 'Fox in the Moonlight' from *Tales of a Devon Village*.

To Rowene Farre for 'The Music Lover' from *Seal Morning*.

To Messrs Victor Gollancz, Ltd., Charles Scribner's Sons, and Rose C. Feld for 'Eventide à la Française (Card up her Sleeve) from *My Aunt Lucienne* © 1955 Rose C. Feld; and to Messrs Victor Gollancz, Ltd. and Simon and Schuster, Inc. for 'Groucho' from *Groucho* by Arthur Marx. Also to the same Publisher and the Author's Executors for 'Hatching Eggs' from *Personal Pleasures* by Rose Macaulay.

To Messrs Hamish Hamilton, Ltd. and the Authors for 'A Sequence of Servants' © James Thurber (from *The Thurber Carnival*, Hamish Hamilton, London) and for 'Lord Fortinbras and the English Aristocracy' from *Noblesse Oblige* by Nancy Mitford.

To The Harvill Press, Ltd. and Virginia Graham for 'Country Etiquette for Mother' from *Say Please*.

To Messrs Rupert Hart-Davis, Ltd. and the Authors for 'Doing the Rounds at Belvoir' from *The Rainbow Comes and Goes* by Lady Diana Cooper; for 'The Durrells in Corfu' from *My Family and Other Animals* by Gerald Durrell; for 'Young and Tender' from *To Be Young* by Mary Lutyens; and for 'No Tears, No Good' from *My Sister Eileen* by Ruth McKenney.

To Messrs William Heinemann, Ltd. and the Authors for 'Married Daughters' from *Pin a Rose on Me* © by Josephine Blumenfeld 1958; for 'Cartwright and the Need for Sleep' from *My Husband Cartwright* by Olivia Manning; for 'Bicycles Built for Two' from *Over the Bridge* by Richard Church; and for 'Noël Coward Produces *The Vortex*' from *Present Indicative* by Noël Coward.

To the same publisher and the Author's Executors for 'The Virtuoso?' from *And Even Now* by Sir Max Beerbohm.

To Messrs William Heinemann, Ltd. and Little Brown and Company for 'Miss Paddleford' from *Gulf Coast Stories* by Erskine Caldwell; and for 'Elsa Maxwell Throws a Party' from *I Married the World* by Elsa Maxwell. To the same publisher and the Thomas Y. Crowell Company and the Authors for 'Fun with the Gilbreths' from *Cheaper by the Dozen* by Frank Gilbreth and Ernestine Gilbreth Carey.

ACKNOWLEDGEMENTS

To The Hogarth Press, Ltd. and Laurie Lee for 'A Country Brood' from *Cider with Rosie*.

To Messrs Hutchinson and Company, Ltd. and the Authors for 'The Edwardian Kitchen' from *The Elegant Edwardian* by Ursula Bloom; for 'Things My Nanny Taught Me' by Eileen Baillie from *The Shabby Paradise*; and for 'My African Cats' from *With Lions by my Side* by Paulette Lloyd Greame. To the same publisher, to the J. P. Lippincott Company, and to the Author for 'Zora Starts to Walk' from *Dust Tracks on a Road* by Zora Neale Hurston. Copyright 1942 by Zora Neale Hurston.

To Messrs Hurst and Blackett, Ltd. and Rebecca Warren for 'Lamb's Tale' from *A Lamb in the Lounge*.

To Messrs Michael Joseph, Ltd. and the Authors for 'Victorian Garden' from *The Country Heart* by H. E. Bates, and for 'Monica Dickens Practises Nursing' from *One Pair of Feet* by Monica Dickens. To the same publisher and Harper and Brothers for 'The Whipping' from *A Genius in the Family* by Hiram Percy Maxim.

To Messrs Longmans, Green and Company, Ltd. and Alfred A. Knopf, Inc. for 'The General's Tomboy' from *Impressions That Remained* by Dame Ethel Smyth.

To Messrs Methuen and Company, Ltd. for 'Fear' from *The Blue Lion* by Robert Lynd.

To Messrs Frederick Muller, Ltd. and Wendy Wood for 'Dear Back of Beyond' from *Mac's Croft*.

To Messrs Phoenix House, Ltd. and Sid Chaplin for 'Period Piece (What Katie Did)' from *The Leaping Lad*.

To The Oxford University Press and Mrs Angela Thirkell for 'Kensington Child' from *Three Houses*.

To The Society of Authors and the Public Trustee for 'Uncle William' from the Preface to *Immaturity* by Bernard Shaw.

PART ONE

When We Were Girls

Zora Starts to Walk

ZORA NEALE HURSTON

My sister Sarah was my father's favourite child, but that one girl was enough. Plenty more sons, but no more girl babies to wear out shoes and bring in nothing. I don't think he ever got over the trick he felt that I played on him by getting born a girl, and while he was off from home at that. A little of my sugar used to sweeten his coffee right now. That is a Negro way of saying his patience was short with me. Let me change a few words with him – and I am of the word-changing kind – and he was ready to change ends. Still and all, I looked more like him than any child in the house. Of course, by the time I got born, it was too late to make any suggestions, so the old man had to put up with me. He was nice about it in a way. He didn't tie me in a sack and drop me in the lake, as he probably felt like doing.

People were digging sweet potatoes, and then it was hog-killing time. Not at our house, but it was going on in general over the country, like being January and a bit cool. Most people were either butchering for themselves, or off helping other folks do their butchering, which was almost just as good. It is a gay time. A big pot of hasslits cooking with plenty of seasoning, lean slabs of fresh-killed pork frying for the helpers to refresh themselves after the work is done. Over and above being neighbourly and giving aid, there is the food, the drinks and the fun of getting together.

So there were no grown folks close round when Mama was taken ill. She sent one of the smaller children to fetch Aunt Judy, the midwife, but she was gone to Woodbridge, a mile and a half away, to eat at a hog-killing. The child was told to go over there and tell Aunt

[3]

Judy to come. But nature, being indifferent to human arrangements, was impatient. My mother had to make it alone. She was too weak after I rushed out to do anything for herself, so she just was lying there, sick in the body, and worried in mind wondering what would become of her, as well as me. She was so weak, she couldn't even reach down to where I was. She had one consolation. She knew I wasn't dead, because I was crying strong.

Help came from where she never would have thought to look for it. A white man of many acres and things, who knew the family well, had butchered the day before. Knowing that Papa was not at home, and that consequently there would be no fresh meat in our house, he had decided to drive the five miles and bring a half of a shoat, sweet potatoes, and other garden stuff along. He was there a few minutes after I was born. Seeing the front door standing open, he came on in, and hollered: 'Hello, there! Call your dogs!' That is the regular way to call in the country because nearly everybody who has anything to watch has biting dogs.

Nobody answered, but he claimed later that he heard me spreading my lungs all over Orange County, so he shoved the door open and bolted on into the house.

He followed the noise and then he saw how things were, and, being the kind of a man he was, he took out his Barlow knife and cut the navel cord, then he did the best he could about other things. When the midwife, locally known as a granny, arrived about an hour later, there was a fire in the stove and plenty of hot water on. I had been sponged off in some sort of a way, and Mama was holding me in her arms.

As soon as the old woman got there, the white man unloaded what he had brought, and drove off cussing about some blankety-blank people never being where you could put your hand on them when they were needed.

He got no thanks from Aunt Judy. She grumbled for years about it. She complained that the cord had not been cut just right, and the belly-band had not been put on tight enough. She was mighty scared I was going to have a weak back, and for many years I did.

The next day or so a Mrs Neale, a friend of Mama's, came in and reminded her that she had promised to let her name the baby in case it was a girl. She had picked up a name somewhere which she thought was very pretty. Perhaps she had read it somewhere, or somebody back in those woods was smoking Turkish cigarettes. So I became Zora Neale Hurston.

There is nothing to make you like other human beings so much as doing things for them. Therefore, the man who grannied me was back next day to see how I was coming along. Maybe it was pride in his own handiwork, and his resourcefulness in a pinch, that made him want to see it through. He remarked that I was a God-damned fine baby, fat and plenty of lung-power. As time went on, he came infrequently, but somehow kept a pinch of interest in my welfare. It seemed that I was spying noble, growing like a gourd vine, and yelling bass like a 'gator. He was the kind of a man that had no use for puny things, so I was all to the good with him. He thought my mother was justified in keeping me.

But nine months rolled around, and I just would not get on with the walking business. I was strong, crawling well, but showed no inclination to use my feet. . . . Then I was over a year old, but still I would not walk. They made allowances for my weight, but yet, that was no real reason for my not trying.

They tell me that an old sow-hog taught me how to walk. That is, she didn't instruct me in detail, but she convinced me that I really ought to try.

It was like this. My mother was going to have collard greens for dinner, so she took the dishpan and went down to the spring to wash the greens. She left me sitting on the floor, and gave me a hunk of cornbread to keep me quiet. Everything was going along all right, until the sow with her litter of pigs in convoy came abreast of the door. She must have smelled the cornbread I was messing with and scattering crumbs about the floor. So she came right on in and began to nuzzle around.

My mother heard my screams and came running. Her heart must have stood still when she saw the sow in there, because hogs have been known to eat human flesh.

But I was not taking this thing sitting down. I had been placed by a chair, and when my mother got inside the door I had pulled myself up by that chair and was getting around it right smart.

As for the sow, poor misunderstood lady, she had no interest in me except my bread. I lost that in scrambling to my feet and she was eating it. She had much less intention of eating Mama's baby than Mama had of eating hers.

With no more suggestions from the sow or anybody else, it seems that I just took to walking and kept the thing a-going. The strangest thing about it was that once I found the use of my feet, they took to wandering. I always wanted to go. I would wander off in the woods all alone, following some inside urge to go places. This alarmed my mother a great deal. She used to say that she believed a woman who was an enemy of hers had sprinkled 'travel dust' around the doorstep the day I was born. That was the only explanation she could find. I don't know why it never occurred to her to connect my tendency with my father, who didn't have a thing on his mind but this town and the next one. That should have given her a sort of hint. Some children are just bound to take after their fathers in spite of women's prayers.

I used to take a seat on top of the gate-post and watch the world go by. One way to Orlando ran past my house, so the carriages and cars would pass before me. The movement made me glad to see it. Often the white travellers would hail me, but more often I hailed them, and asked: 'Don't you want me to go a piece of the way with you?'

They always did. I know now that I must have caused a great deal of amusement among them, but my self-assurance must have carried the point, for I was always invited to come along. I'd ride up the road for perhaps a half-mile, then walk back. I did not do this with the permission of my parents, nor with their foreknowledge. When they found out about it later, I usually got a whipping. My grandmother worried about my forward ways a great deal. She had known slavery and to her my brazenness was unthinkable.

'Git down offa dat gate-post! You li'l sow, you! Git down! Setting up there looking dem white folks right in de face! They's gowine to lynch you yet. And don't stand in dat doorway gazing out at 'em either. Youse too brazen to live long.'

Nevertheless, I kept right on gazing at them, and 'going a piece of the way' whenever I could make it. The village seemed dull to me most of the time. If the village was singing a chorus, I must have missed the tune.

But I had one person who pleased me always. That was the robust, grey-haired white man who had helped me get into the world. When I was quite small, he would come by and tease me and then praise me for not crying. When I got old enough to do things, he used to come along some afternoons and ask to take me with him fishing. He said he hated to bait his own hook and dig worms. In between fishing business, he would talk to me in a way I liked – as if I were as grown as he. He would tell funny stories and swear at every other word. He was always making me tell him things about my doings, and then he would tell me what to do about things. He called me Snidlits, explaining that Zora was a hell of a name to give a child.

'Snidlits, don't be a nigger[1]', he would say to me over and over. 'Niggers lie and lie! Any time you catch folks lying, they are skeered of something. Lying is dodging. People with guts don't lie. They tell the truth and then if they have to, they fight it out. You lay yourself open by lying. The other fellow knows right off that you are skeered of him and he's more'n apt to tackle you. If he don't do nothing, he starts to looking down on you from then on. . . . You'll get 'long all right if you do like I tell you. Nothing can't lick you if you never get skeered.'

My face was all scratched up from fighting one time, so he asked me if I had been letting some kid lick me. I told him how Mary Ann and I had started to fighting and I was doing fine until her older sister Janie and her brother Ed, who was about my size, had all doubleteened me.

'Now, Snidlits, this calls for talking. Don't you try to fight three kids at one time unlessen you just can't get around it. Do the best you can, if you have to. But learn right now not to let your head start more than your behind can stand. Measure out the amount of

1 The word 'nigger' used in this sense does not mean race. It means a weak, contemptible person of any race.

[7]

fighting you can do, and then do it. When you take on too much and get licked, folks will pity you first and scorn you after a while, and that's bad. Use your head!'

'Do de best I can,' I assured him, proud for him to think I could.

'That's de ticket, Snidlits. The way I want to hear you talk. And while I'm on the subject, don't you never let nobody spit on you or kick you. Anybody who takes a thing like that ain't worth de powder and shot it takes to kill 'em, hear?'

'Yessir.'

'Can't nothing wash that off but blood. If anybody ever do one of those things to you, kill dead and go to jail. Hear me?'

I promised him I would try, and he took out a peanut bar and gave it to me.

– From *Dust Tracks on a Road*.

Kensington Child

ANGELA THIRKELL

I

It Was Always Afternoon

I have only to turn my eyes into my mind and there I find the Old Kensington of my youth.

Our day nursery looked out on the street. In winter the window was kept tightly shut and sausages of red baize filled with sand were laid along the openings to exclude the death-dealing fresh air. If it was freezing and the panes were covered with fronds and leaves and stars, Nanny would put a saucer of milk out for us overnight on the window sill. Next morning we would be allowed to eat the smutty congealed mixture.

Just opposite us lived a family of about our own ages, and when we were all shut up in our respective nurseries with colds, we used to communicate across the street by breathing on the pane and writing a message backwards. A lengthy business – but time had no value then. Both nurseries liked to watch the lamp-lighter. When the early darkness had fallen we would lift a corner of the window curtain to watch for his coming and an answering gleam of light would come from the other side of the road, till the Nannies called us away from the draught and both curtains fell again. . . .

In spring our nursery window was as good as a dress circle seat for seeing what went on in the Square. On the first of May Jack-in-the-Green still came in his bower, accompanied by chimney sweeps dressed in gay colours who danced in the streets for the pennies we threw down. On the same day all John Barker's horse-vans were drawn up in the Square before starting on their rounds, each horse with its tail and mane intricately plaited and bound up in ribbons and bright rosettes. Wherever we were on May Day we met charming horses all bedizened and gay, up and down the streets of Kensington. Then there were a number of itinerant musicians whom we knew by sight. The Highlander with his Highland lass in tartans, playing the bagpipes, the girl frightening my brother dreadfully by picking him up and kissing him. The weekly German band, very clean and respectable, in uniform and peaked caps, each man with his little piece of music in a clip at the end of his instrument. The Italian organ-grinder with a monkey, in a red jacket and a little cap with a feather, who would take your penny and put it in his pouch. The man who was a walking orchestra; he had a hat covered with bells, a drum behind him which he beat with his elbows, strings attached to his feet with which he twitched cymbals, pan pipes strapped under his chin, and his hands free for five or six other instruments. The Frenchman who brought a mild bear called Joséphine walking on her hind legs, ready for buns or fruit which she managed to eat through her muzzle. These and many more were our spring entertainers.

On the west side of the Square a white house with bright window-boxes was the home of Mrs Patrick Campbell. My parents and grandparents loved and admired her, and to us she was 'Auntie Stella'. My father had made a special translation of *Pelléas and Mélisande* for her. We were all much in and out of each other's houses then. She would descend upon Young Street with a swish of silk and a froth and fluff of lace demanding nursery tea, or suddenly require a bed in a darkened room as it was impossible for her to rest in her own house. Sometimes I was sent for to keep her company in the curtained room. She dressed her little Stella, who was not much older than I, like a fairy princess, and I used to inherit pinafores made of the finest silk woven with gold and frocks of shimmering stuffs.

Going to her house was always an adventure because you never knew who was there or what might happen. Auntie Stella might receive me in bed with curtains drawn, lamentably moaning that she was an old woman and would never be nice to look at again. Or she might be trailing about the house in a long-tailed lace wrapper alternately scolding and caressing whoever came within reach, lavishing affection on Pinky Ponky Poo, her adored dog, companion for many years. One might find Mr Yeats upstairs and M. Henri Bernstein downstairs while, neglecting them both, Auntie Stella might insist on taking me for a drive in a hansom and reciting *Mélisande* in French (she was going to act with Sarah Bernhardt) begging her most incompetent companion to criticise her French accent.

There was constant intercourse between Young Street and the Grange, my grandfather's house in North End Road. . . .

Sunday breakfast took its leisurely course till eleven o'clock or so when we had to go upstairs and be cleaned and dressed for Sunday lunch with our grandparents. Perhaps the golden haze is needed when we come to Sunday clothes, for they were a little inhuman compared with the freedom of to-day. My brother may have been let off comparatively lightly with blue blouse and knickerbockers, a holland smock, brown shoes and socks, and a sailor hat whose elastic was always too tight or too loose; but for me there was the ordeal of starch. Button-holes starched so stiffly together that one couldn't force the buttons into them; starched petticoats which were rather fun to put on because they crackled so, as you pulled the folds apart, but had complications of starched tapes at the neck which needed Nanny's relentless fingers; white piqué frocks with full sleeves standing up like crinolines and all the hooks ironed flat so that Nanny had to lever them open with the nursery nail scissors; white pinafores with frills round the neck; white cotton gloves, well stiffened, into which one's hot hands were with difficulty thrust; black shoes and long stockings and then the straw hat with a wreath of flowers and the inevitable elastic. How it hurt when it was half an inch too short and how inelegant it looked when Nanny had tied a knot in the middle to shorten it.

At last we were ready and set out with our father and mother for North End Lane, Fulham. . . . We went up Young Street from Kensington Square, past the old shops at the corner, past John Barker's little drapery establishment, and got into a red horse bus opposite the church. Six on each side inside and fourteen outside – how small it sounds now. The table of fares, hand-painted, with its convention of a wiggly line connecting stopping-places and fares did not hold more than a dozen names. On we went, past the old brick houses standing back on both sides of the road then, past the leafage of Holland Park, past more terraces of old houses and over the railway bridge. No buses went down North End Lane and we walked along past early eighteenth-century houses, each in its own garden of elms and cedars and mulberries. The air was warm, the sun shone on the blossoming trees hanging over the brick walls, and so we came to the Grange.

On Sunday my grandparents, the Burne-Joneses, kept open house. Two or three extra places were laid at lunch for any friends who might drop in, but whoever came, I sat next to my grandfather. I was allowed to blow into the froth of his beer 'to make a bird's nest', or to have all the delicious outside from the mashed potatoes when they had been browned in the oven. If, disregarding truth, I said that my toast was always buttered on both sides, my statement was gravely accepted and the toast buttered accordingly. There can have been few granddaughters who were so systematically spoiled as I was and it is a legend that the only serious difference of opinion which ever arose between Gladstone and Burne-Jones was as to which of them spoiled an adored grandchild the more.

After lunch my grandfather often settled down to a game of draughts, which was a good moment for my brother and myself to escape and do a little exploring.

As soon as we were out of the house we might have been in the country. Gardens surrounded us on all sides and only a few years earlier there had been fields behind the little orchard which bounded the farther end. Ugly brick houses had been built since then, but they were hidden by the long white rough-cast studio which stood between the orchard and the road. It was called the Garden Studio, and here my grandfather worked on his larger canvases.

On the grass, among the pear trees and apple trees, we played for endless hours while people came and went with jingling and clip-clopping of hansoms between The Grange and other hospitable houses. The men played bowls on the lawn and smoked and talked, and the women paced the gravel walk by the long flower-bed or joined them under the trees. Though we had been at The Grange for immemorial space, there was always time for further pleasures in those days when it was always afternoon. We might be put into a hansom and taken to other gardens with studios in them, where our parents would talk and pace the paths and we would play among rose trees and apple trees and the very sooty creeping ivy peculiar to London gardens. All through the long afternoons the gardens waited for us. Draycott Lodge, where the Holman Hunts lived, Beavor Lodge and the Richmonds, the Vale, home of the De Morgans – all bricks and mortar now. Melbury Road, even then only a ghost of its old self where the Prinseps used to have their friends in a yet more golden age and where Watts still lived. Grove End Road with Tadema's stories which were so difficult to understand until his own infectious laugh warned you that he had reached the point; the agate window and the brazen stairs. Hampstead, Chelsea, Hammersmith, gardens were waiting for us everywhere and people who made noble pictures and were constant friends.

At last the long afternoon came to an end. A final visit to the kitchen regions to talk to Robert the parrot and examine the hatch for the hundredth time and the hansom was at the door. Then a drive home in the cool of the day and the little girl was allowed to sit up to supper in her dressing-gown and have baked potato with a great deal of butter till she was half asleep and was carried upstairs in her father's arms while he sang – very slowly, so that the nursery should not be reached before the song was ended:

> My grandfather died, I cannot tell you how,
> He left me six horses to gang with the plough. . . .

One more long happy Sunday had joined the pale golden Sundays that are gone. Better – to us at any rate – than Sundays now. . . .

II

At the Seaside

The most tremendous amount of dressing took place before we were allowed to paddle. In those days no one had thought of anything better than heavy blue serge for little girls to wear at the sea. Our cuffs were unbuttoned and turned up to the elbows, our skirts were gathered into a handful behind and twisted like a rope and rammed into our voluminous serge knickerbockers, which must have given us a curiously bunchy look, and we were allowed to take our shoes and stockings off and put sand-shoes on. Then the legs of our knicker-bockers were rolled up as high as they would go and with awful warnings against getting wet we were let loose with spades and buckets. What happened to the younger children I don't remember. Certainly the Nannies wouldn't have trusted them to us and equally they would never have spoilt their morning's chat – 'talking about Him and Her' we used to call it – by escorting their young charges to the water. I can only suppose that the babies played with pebbles or banged their pails on the stones for sheer joy of the noise till someone stopped them.

If it was a lucky morning the tide was low so that we could dig in the wet sand and explore the rocks, and just on the turn so that we could bathe later on when the grown-ups came down.

And now everything was in train for bathing. That science had made but little progress since the days of Leech's drawings of pretty ladies coming out of the canvas hoods of bathing machines and horrible old bathing women with bonnets, apparently walking about in the sea all fully dressed. On the beach above high-water mark was a row of bathing machines, little houses with pointed roofs and a door at each end with a flight of steps to let down. When the tide was right for bathing the boatmen used to push them down the shingly slope to the water's edge and it was our great ambition to get into the machines and go down to the sea in triumph. . . .

I always shared a machine with Lily Ridsdale who could brave the stormiest seas and had me under her charge. Inside the little house it was deliciously snug. There was a seat along each side and a little window with a wooden shutter that one could pull across. I can still smell the damp seaweedy smell and feel the wet sandy floor under my bare feet. The machine was like a door into a different world. You had gone up a ladder from a beach full of friends, with boats and cliffs and everything safe; you emerged through the farther door upon a waste of waters which were already lapping round the foot of your ladder. It needed some courage to make the first strokes in that cold tossing sea, but with Lily one was quite safe and could swim out to the end of the pier and back. How one kept afloat at all in the dresses one had to wear then I can't imagine. My grandmother had brought me a particularly fashionable one from Paris. It was of heavy dark blue serge in two pieces. The knickerbocker part was very baggy and buttoned just above the knee; the tunic part had a very full skirt knee length, puffed sleeves, a high neck and enormous collar or cape embroidered with daisies. I don't know why I wasn't pulled down by the sheer weight to a fishy death, but it was the thing and one accepted it. On the shore my mother would sit, watch in hand, anxiously counting the minutes, and the moment our time was up she waved a white handkerchief and we had to come in.

And now came the most exciting part of the morning. Far above us on the cliff was a capstan from which long wire ropes, over which everybody tripped, hung down to the beach. A hook at the end of this rope was attached to the bathing machine and a donkey began to walk round and round the capstan hauling us up. It was delirious joy to feel the little house beginning to move, to hear first the swish of the waves against the side and then the scrunch of wheels on shingle as the donkey pursued his round and we went higher and higher up the beach. Then we were unhooked and a small, damp, dishevelled, sandy figure precipitated herself down the steps with her bundle. Those serge bathing dresses were beyond human power to wring out unaided and a very horny-handed boatman, or sometimes Mr Trunky Thomas himself, who owned the machines, if he happened to be doing nothing particular on the beach at the moment, used to twist them into ropes and hang them out to dry. Then there were warm buns to eat while Nanny dried and brushed my hair.

III

Christmas at Rottingdean

It was a point of honour to wake very early on Christmas morning and on that one day Nanny relaxed her stringent (and well-advised) rules about lighting candles ourselves and I was allowed to grabble for the matches when I woke and light my own candle and look at my stocking. There was something unspeakably satisfying about the feel of a well filled stocking stuffed with lumps of all sizes and shapes. Cubic lumps, spherical lumps, lumps in crinkly tissue paper, lumps that might be penknives and sometimes a dormouse curled up all stiff and cold. Dormice were a recurring Christmas gift because last year's usually got lost. One dormouse, woken by the unaccustomed warmth of Christmas Day, came alive, leaped from my hand and disappeared. I was disconsolate and another dormouse was got to replace it and weeks afterwards the original dormouse was found curled up asleep, quite well, under a heavy pile of blankets in the linen-cupboard. Another dormouse escaped – my own fault alas! I forgot to put his water-tin back and he squeezed out through the hole – and drowned himself in the nursery slop-pail. I cried bitterly till my grandparents let me bury him in the garden among the lilies of the valley and my father drew me a picture of his little form with wings flying to Paradise, with earth spread out far below, and I coloured it with the nursery chalks and my grandfather had it framed in a carved and gilded frame – or at least it looked like that. But livestock was on the whole a rarity and the lumps were mostly inanimate, and always in the toe of every stocking was a tangerine orange. Nothing else would do.

The ritual of the morning was that my brother and I should bring our stockings into our grandmother's bedroom and examine them there. Her bedroom was over the drawing-room and had a big window facing east like the window in the room below. Through it she could see the sun rise over the brow of East Hill until elms growing taller on the other side of the green made a jagged edge where once the line of the downs had stood out clear against the dawn. But we were with her long before the winter sunrise, climbing on to her bed, an oak four-post bed with curtains of the most delicate Madras muslin, soft enough to go through a wedding ring and so exquisitely patterned that one of her grandchildren wore dresses made from them twenty years later. In my remembrance she always used very fine cashmere sheets against the cold, and even in bed had lace on her head and the softest shawls pinned with a paste brooch. It was so cold getting out of one's own bed by candlelight in front of a black fire-place, that one could hardly wait to put on dressing-gown and slippers, and then we dashed into our grandmother's room where the fire had been kept in all night and my brother got in beside her with his sock, while I made a nest for myself at the foot of the bed with my stocking. I usually brought with me a couple of gingernuts which I had taken to bed the night before to make them soft and malleable. On any other morning it would have been my pleasure to roll them into sausages, or mould them into balls, or into a likeness of the human face, but this morning there were better things to do.

How delicious it was to plunge one's hand deeper and deeper into the stocking, pull out the presents, tear off the tissue paper and gloat on the reindeer gloves with fur lining, the necklace, the little fan, the tiny Prayer Book with print that no human eye could read and Sir Joshua Reynolds' angels stamped in silver on the cover (how perfectly beautiful one thought it then), the pastels, the box of round chocolates sprinkled with sugar, and always at the end the tangerine, so cool to the touch, so sweet to the mouth, and even after you had eaten it, still useful for fireworks. You pinched a piece of the peel sharply, very near the candle and little spurts of oil from it caught fire for a moment and flashed through the flame.

After so much emotion there were sausages for breakfast as if it were Sunday, as indeed it sometimes was, and – we must have been an extremely lucky nursery – heaps of presents on the dining-room table. All the things that were too big to get into our stockings, things like books and engines and bricks and a real carriage-clock of one's own and always something very magnificent from Uncle Phil like a Punch and Judy Show that we could work ourselves, or a fort with a drawbridge, fully garrisoned, or one's favourite poet (Longfellow that year, Browning next), bound in blue or green morocco with one's name in gold on the cover, or quires of notepaper from Asprey's with monograms in gold and silver and all colours.

This second wave of emotion carried us on to church time. As far as I can remember we never went to church in London, except the Abbey, which is different, but always in the country because of not hurting the Vicar's feelings, so on Christmas day the family, represented by the women and children, turned up in full force. I had on a green woollen frock from Liberty's with an embroidered yoke, a brilliant red woollen jacket, a blue tam-o'-shanter, and my new reindeer gloves which it took me the whole length of the service to get properly buttoned. How we enjoyed singing in the church and how delightful Lily Ridsdale's voice sounded and how infinitely more we admired the peacock yell of Miss White, the village laundress, and how nobly Mr Sanders the carpenter demeaned himself on the organ. Then there was the fun of saying 'Happy Christmas' to every one, lunch, the turkey with its gilded claws and general repletion.

– From *Three Houses*.

Things My Nanny Taught Me

EILEEN BAILLIE

I ran to her when I was in trouble, I turned to her in all my many problems. On her 'days off' I felt strange, lonely, and always faintly apprehensive for fear she might never come back at all. (Oh, the blessed relief of waking up next morning to see, in the dim light of dawn, the reassuring hump of Nanny's sleeping form in the other bed!) Indeed, I suffered from a perpetual lurking suspicion that she was going to be taken away from me, and once I believed her lost to me for ever. This occurred when my tonsils had to be removed. I was not warned of my ordeal beforehand, and one day, without a word of explanation, I was kept in bed and given hardly any breakfast. Since I felt perfectly well, I became frightened and suspicious, waiting miserably upon events while I wondered what on earth they could be going to do to me. Even Nanny, although fondly comforting, would not enlighten me; and one of my cousins added to my growing terror by putting her head round the door to gloat sadistically over my plight.

'I *am* sorry for you!' she remarked suggestively, and disappeared.

By the time two strange men and a nurse had arrived, addressing me with a horrible false heartiness and bringing with them an unpleasant piece of apparatus, I was in much the same state of near-panic as a bullock being driven to the *abattoir* when he first scents the blood of his unfortunate predecessors. Worst of all, everyone, including Nanny, was sent out of the room; and when the sinister trio gathered closely round my bed, I was prepared for any ghastly fate.

'Do you like scent?' the younger man inquired fatuously, while the elder, venerable, grey-haired, and attired, I fancy, in a morning coat, beamed ghoulishly at his elbow.

Strictly on the defensive, I replied with caution: 'Only Cherry Blossom,' having bought a bottle of this innocuous perfume at the Church Bazaar.

'Then here's something very much nicer!' exclaimed the anæsthetist, coming out in his true colours by clapping over my face a metal mask rather like a large coffee-strainer, on to which he shook something out of a bottle.

The gloves were off now with a vengeance. I was choking, I was being murdered. 'Nanny! Nanny!' I yelled despairingly. Had I but known it, Nanny was listening outside the door, weeping bitterly. I kicked and fought and used all the words I heard on the Poplar trams, which I knew were very wicked. The nurse attempted to hold my legs, but with a final effort, I kicked her violently in the stomach. . . . The first word I uttered on my return to consciousness, before being extremely sick into a basin, was a feeble 'Nanny!'

Nanny grew to love Poplar and made many friends there. From time to time we paid them visits, which made a welcome interruption in the monotony of our daily walks. There was an excitable lady who seemed quite unable to stop talking, who would tell our fortunes by cards, tea-leaves, or palmistry, according to your fancy. In a dismal basement-kitchen lived a mournful person who took in washing, and whose husband had a deplorable habit of getting drunk on Saturday nights and pelting her with her own flat-irons. I am not at all sure that he did not also beat her – a normal occurrence in Poplar, regarded as reprehensible, but exciting no special comment. We would be expected to commiserate, even to examine the bruises; and while the recital of her dreary griefs droned on, punctuated by Nanny remarking: 'Fancy!' or 'Tut-tut!' at suitable moments, I would sit in the window, gazing up entranced at the passing legs and feet seen from this unusual angle: the shapeless, broken boots of the down-and-outs, the thick-soled, heavy boots of workmen, the more stylish shoes of the rent-collector and the insurance agent; the carpet-slippers, slit open to relieve a painful bunion, of old women creeping to the pub for a jug of supper-beer.

Here, too, with a suitable shade of hesitation, Nanny would accept 'just a cup of tea, then – so refreshing!' The kettle would sing softly on the shining black range, hot cinders fell out with a crash, too near for comfort to the old, sleeping tabby-cat curled up in a ball inside the polished fender. There was a smell of fresh ironing and fresh-made tea, superimposed on the rich, ancient aroma of a thousand meals, a hundred wash-days.

Usually, of course, we were at home for tea, especially in the winter, when we would hurry along the dry, ringing pavements in the frosty air, with the sun already setting red behind the railway station. The warmth of the nursery would be comforting and Nanny, poking the banked-up fire into a yellow blaze, would soon produce that most tempting of all meals when you are hungry – nursery tea. A lightly-boiled egg, perhaps, a plate of freshly-cut, crusty bread and butter which, after the first two slices you could spread with jam or a sprinkle of brown sugar; sponge fingers, rock-cakes (Mrs Packer's could have had no truer appellation), and a mug of milk with a dash of tea to make you feel 'grown-up'.

In the street outside the lamp-lighter came by, his long stick tipped with fire over his shoulder, leaving in his wake the shining lamps of Ullin Street and St Leonard's Road. The fog was closing down on the River, for ships were blowing hoarsely in a distant, confused chorus, and somewhere down by Custom House a railway-engine was whistling anxiously. It would be time for Nanny to draw the curtains, so that the leaping flames glowed warmly on the great pink and crimson cabbage-roses with which they were patterned; and the two of us would sit companionably in the quiet nursery, silent save for the loud tick of an old alarm-clock on the mantelpiece and the rustling of the fire behind its high wire guard.

This was the hour when, to my joy, Nanny might suggest a 'sing-song'. Once you could persuade her to begin, she would go on and on until the inexorable guillotine of bed-time cut short the entertainment; for an entertainment it most certainly was. Nanny, blessed with a good ear and a clear, true voice, had an extensive repertoire. The Boer War was still so comparatively recent that its songs lived in people's memories: songs such as 'Soldiers of the Queen' and 'Good-bye, Dolly, I must leave you', and a splendid ditty in which some luckless child received at its christening the names of every general and battle of the South African campaigns. Then there were the latest hits of the day, 'Yip-i-addy' and 'She sells sea-shells by the seashore' which caused endless hilarity in the nursery.

Best of all, in my estimation, were the songs that made you feel sad. With what sentimental warmth Nanny and I together would sing 'Clementine' and 'Swanee River' – I could easily have wept over those poor, exiled darkies – and that prime favourite, 'Just a Song at Twilight'!

As an educationalist Nanny was superb, the equal, I should imagine, of any highly-trained young lady with a 'system'. For one thing, she was a mine of fascinating information, of those saws, sayings, and expedients that in later life one takes for granted. When your store of worldly knowledge is still quite small, there is all the charm of novelty, the wonder of newly-acquired wisdom, in being told that new shoes squeak because you haven't paid for them; that the north wind doth blow, then you will have snow; and that tea can be defined as 'the cup that cheers but not inebriates'. It was Nanny who introduced me to that mysterious Mr Manners, for whom one always left something on the plate. . . .

It was Nanny who taught me – in addition to the 'three R's' – to say my prayers, to hem, buttonhole and feather-stitch, to sew on buttons firmly – not 'with a hot needle and thread' as the shop-people did – and to set in a sleeve. It was Nanny who showed me how to make paste for my scrap-album out of flour and hot water, and how to grow mustard-and-cress on damp flannel in the nursery window-boxes. It was Nanny who covered my ill-used and tattered story-books neatly in brown paper and wrote on them their titles in her beautiful, clear and flowing hand which is as firm today at the age of eighty as it was fifty years ago. It was Nanny who nursed me through all the minor ailments, Nanny who allayed my panic fears when the nursery ceiling fell down in a cloud of plaster, and on another terrible occasion when the nursery chimney caught fire with an angry roar; Nanny who, when we encountered a herd of bullocks in a narrow, high-hedged Devonshire lane, realised that I was wearing *red*, and with the utmost presence of mind backed my go-cart into a gateway and threw a dark blanket over until the danger was past. An experience that impressed indelibly upon my mind the alarming possibilities of the countryside as opposed to those in towns.

And it was Nanny who collected gradually, over a period of months, the 'presentation plates' of Christmas Annuals, coloured illustrations from magazines and catalogues, from grocers' calendars and discarded nursery books, to make my 'picture-screen'. When she considered that she had enough material, the virgin screen, already neatly covered with sheets of stout brown paper, would be laid upon the nursery floor, and Nanny, on her hands and knees, to the accompaniment of unrestrained excitement, would perform the tremendous task of 'laying-out' and then 'pasting-on', the odd corners being filled with 'scraps' – little coloured drawings of flowers, fruit, animals and fairies that one could buy for a few pence a sheet at Mr Seager's.

The screen stood round my bed; and over the years of childhood and adolescence I have studied it so often that I need only shut my eyes to see again those bright, familiar pictures: the elegant Edwardian ladies in motoring-hats and waisted fur-coats; the fleet of big yachts racing off Cowes; a nauseatingly skittish little girl in a very *décolleté* dress tying her own sun-bonnet on to the head of a long-suffering spaniel; a painting called 'Dignity and Impudence' which represented with indifferent art an enormous bloodhound, chin on paws, being annoyed by a Skye terrier; a Christmas scene, all red sunset, white snow, and cottages with lamplit windows; some of Kate Greenaway's illustrations to *John Gilpin*, rescued before the book disintegrated under heavy nursery pressure; a bunch of daffodils, very lifelike, from a calendar, with the date, 1907, across the top. How time was flying! I was already well into my fifth year! The screen, if I possessed it now, would evoke with perfect clarity the sentiments, the opulence, the faint condescension, and perhaps the first stirrings of that new century and age that were agitating already the heavy drapes of Victorian hypocrisy and Gladstonian *laisser faire*.

Nanny at that time was indisputably the pivot upon which my limited world revolved. Nanny was all-sufficing, constant, stable as a rock in a world of uncertainties. Even today, a very old lady, she still inspires the same confidence, convinces me that she still knows what is best to do in any eventuality. She is, as ever, sensible, reassuring, eminently realistic, a mistress of understatement.

'Fancy,' she observes when one makes some perturbing pronouncement, and proceeds to debate the most practical solution to the problem. Nothing seems to ruffle or excite her. I have a feeling that, should I tell her: 'Nanny! Nanny! The end of the world has come!' she would reply 'Fancy!' in that flat, unemotional tone of hers, thus reducing the whole cataclysm to the manageable level of a nursery *contretemps*.

– From *The Shabby Paradise*.

Farmer's Girl

ALISON UTTLEY

At the farm there were unending pleasures for a child, little circus scenes which appeared to be performed for one's own benefit, so that I had only to stand by the stile, or to clamber on a low wall to watch.

Two calves butting one another with lowered knobby heads; a horse rolling on the grass-plat, his great hooves splashing the air, his neck arched, then grunts and squeals and springing to his feet, with shakes and quivers of his body, and the happy settling to his eating again; a pig running, squealing, with body shaking and feet asplay; a lamb leaping in the air; all these things were my early delight.

I liked watching people, too, for they also went through antics which I found enchanting as a peep-show. I liked my father shaving, his broad handsome face lathered with soap, so that he looked like a strange snow-covered giant, his mouth pulled sideways, twisted, as he drew the razor across his cheek, and peered at himself in the little mirror which he set up against the oaken spoon-box to catch the light. Our looking-glasses with their dim shadows and odd reflections were particularly unsuited for shaving. I remember feeling alarm as I gazed at him, transfigured with the soap, although I knew perfectly well who it was, and when he kissed me, dabbing my cheek with white, I shrieked, partly with fear, and partly with joy.

Every day I watched the servant boy stir the bran mash. As the hot water swished down into the centre of the bucket, the smell made me wrinkle my nose with delight; but the most interesting of the food preparations was the cooking of thousands of little potatoes in the brewhouse copper, and the mashing of them for pig food in the tub.

[25]

I stood at the door, not three years old, long before my brother was born, and I watched the wooden masher being moved up and down in a great tub of smoking sweet-smelling hot potatoes. As the masher moved with rhythmical thuds, somebody chanted this song to me:

> Rub-a-dub-tub, three men in a tub,
> The brewer, the baker, the candlestick-maker,
> They all jumped out of a rotten potato.

I waited expectantly, with my eyes glued on the tub, looking for three little men to leap from it. The song, the smell of the 'tatoes, the warmth and steam, all blend together, and I look up to see a face singing through the curls of steam, grinning broadly at my bewilderment and wonder.

For threepence one could buy a tiny bottle of scent, a miniature affair holding a few drops of White Heather, or Jockey Club. A servant presented me with a bottle, which was one of my most treasured possessions for many a year. I found that the empty bottle retained its smell, and whenever I was unhappy I sniffed the fragrant emptiness, and all my sorrows fled away.

I had a valentine, too, a beautiful mystery with paper lace which opened out to disclose a picture of lilies, gummed on a sweetly-scented pad. Greedy for more of the smell, I opened the pad and was disappointed to find only cotton wool inside. I had expected something wonderful, the essence of valentines, a packet of precious ointment such as Mary Magdalene had when she anointed the feet of Jesus.

When I was seven I explored a hay-chamber where I had seldom been, in the oldest part of the farm. There I found a collection of bottles of all sorts and sizes, many of them small and ancient, queer-shaped, odd things with evil smells. They had been there for many years, forgotten in the lumber. I washed them with a bit of rag in the horse-trough, and started on a profession by which I hoped to earn my living when the time came. I decided to be a scent-maker!

I gathered all the sweet-smelling things I could find, basketfuls of rose-petals dropped from the roses which covered the house and farm buildings, for roses grew in many odd places, on pigsty and cowhouse and barn. I got rose-petals from the bushes which grew along one side of the kitchen garden, and roses from the little borders in the grass-plat. I gathered lavender and lad's-love, camomile, honeysuckle, rosemary. I soaked these in spring water, and bottled the result. Although I was indefatigable in my attempts, repeating my experiments with every kind of scented flower, going into the fields and hedges, varying the amounts of water, leaving the flowers in sun and in shade, the only result was a drab ill-smelling liquid which even an optimistic child could not truthfully call scent. I was not disappointed, for the task of collecting the rose-petals and sweet herbs gave me pleasure, and, like the ancients who sought for the philosopher's stone. I expected that if I could hit upon the right formula, the correct blend of rose-petals, I should discover the true secret of Attar of Roses. So every day after breakfast I rushed out to the garden with new zest to seek for flowers, and to gather my red and white wealth from the grass under the trees. I never destroyed a rose, such a thing would have shocked me, but when the petals once dropped they were mine for the scent bottle.

I was filled with devotion for the servant boy, who was the earliest friend I remember. Willie Miller had fair sun-baked hair, candid blue eyes, and a freckled face with rosy cheeks. His kindly ways and good manners made him a delightful companion and nurse. I was safe with him, and I spent all my time following him to the farm buildings, trotting after him like a dog, to stable and pigsty, asking innumerable questions, whilst he held the stalk of a primmy-rose or daisy between his white teeth, and gave me satisfactory if incorrect answers on the subjects of Jesus and horses and stars.

His brown hands held aside the bushes and showed me the nests of robin and thrush. He lifted out the delicate blue eggs from the black-bird's nest and slipped them for a moment into my small hands. I held these jewels, warm smooth exquisite gems from the hedges, whilst he impressed on me that I must never keep them for myself, or the mother bird would mourn. His clear bright eyes laughed as he talked, and he walked up the lane behind the cart, stopping here and there to show me some treasure, robin's pincushion or sticky burr, or gay butterfly . . .

When Willie went to the stable to fettle the mare, I went after to hear him hiss as he groomed her legs. To me the sound of that ss-ss-ss was music, and I left everything to run and hear it again. He set me on the mare's back and I rode along the path in front of the house, looking in at the dining-room windows to see if I was observed, as we went to the watering. The strong smell of the mare's flesh and skin, the feeling of the coarse hair under my fingers, and the warm body under my kicking legs was rapture. I thought of the Queen of England, and felt mightier than she.

At Christmas we invited the schoolmaster and his wife to spend the evening with us. The dairy and pantry were full of delicacies, cakes and iced buns, honey and cream, great home-cured hams, roasted chickens, glass dishes of potted meats, jellies, pork-pies, pastries, for we had killed the pigs and there was good cheer for everyone. There was even a box of chocolates, the first I had ever seen, a large flat pink box full of tiny dark balls, each with a centre of cream, a present from a kind friend, which my mother felt she must share with company.

The house was gay with its green holly and mistletoe, with wreaths and garlands of ivy and yew, with scarlet, black and ivory berries, and flags and Chinese lanterns. I was proud that the schoolmaster should see my lovely home, but I was also alarmed lest he should tell my mother how often I had to be caned for lateness and talking.

They arrived, muffled in great coats, carrying lanterns and slippers. I stood in the hall, where the lamp shone like a star under its many-coloured shade, and the oak bureau gleamed with polish. I held out my hand, very shy, and to my utter astonishment Mrs Allen, the schoolmaster's wife, stooped and kissed me. I was overcome with amazement, for I expected to be scolded for some naughtiness. I felt at once there was a secret compact between us – she wouldn't tell my parents of my faults, and I wouldn't remember the ruler which stung my fingers, or the ink and chalk and dust of school. We both forgot that often she told me I was enough to aggravate a saint. We were transformed into celestial beings, nothing everyday about us. I was a good little girl in my cashmere smocked-frock and my red silk sash, and she was a charming lady with curled hair and a velvet dress. The schoolmaster too, cast off his sternness, and changed into an affable man who laughed and joked with my father, and ate the rich and varied fare with evident enjoyment.

They looked at our carved old oak, admired the grandfather clock and the chairs, and were in raptures over the old silver and china which decked the table. They were human beings to whom one talked freely, who ate and drank and lived like us, gods come down to earth, and entertained by mortals. I decided that when a favourable opportunity arose I would ask a few of the many questions which I dare not ask at school.

After tea, when the farm work was finished and my father was free, we all sat round the dining-room fire. I played a couple of 'pieces', 'The Mocking-bird' and 'Home Sweet Home with variations', on the piano, which had migrated to that room for the winter out of the coldness of the parlour . . .

Mr Allen adjusted his eyeglass and listened to me attentively. Mrs Allen said I played very nicely, and she hoped I would perform at the next concert, whilst I inwardly prayed to be spared from that ordeal, for my hands were already trembling with fright. Then, my duty over, I returned to my place by the fire.

I brought out my collection of fossils and stones, and my little brother, who had not started school, showed his toys. I asked a carefully disguised question about the age of the Earth, and the schoolmaster hesitatingly suggested about 4,000 years. Afterwards I verified this in the notes in the family Bible, and was much relieved.

'That is the age of man,' he explained. 'The rocks go back millions of years, when the prehistoric life was on earth.' The conversation drifted away, for my mother wasn't interested in the age of the Earth, but my father brought down his precious book, *The World's Birthday*, and we all looked at the pictures of the moon and her craters, asking questions about that luminous orb, one side of which nobody had ever seen.

Next I asked about the echo, what it was, and how it came about, for I was convinced an invisible person in our fields answered my call.

'It is simply a reflection of sound,' answered Mr Allen, and I was just as much puzzled, for the term 'reflection of sound' meant nothing to me, and our echo lived in the air, first in one field and then in another.

I waited a while before I posed my next and most important question, a vital question for my happiness.

'What is there above the sky?' I asked.

For some time Mr Allen could not understand my difficulty. There was nothing above the sky, said he. The sky was air, which dwindled into space.

'The *blue* sky,' I demanded. 'What is there above the *blue* sky? What is there on the other side?'

'It isn't blue, it is colourless air, which becomes nothing, space, emptiness.'

'But . . .' I stammered, 'the floor of heaven. Isn't it up there? Isn't it in the blue sky? What is the blue made of?'

He tried to explain the nothingness to me, and as he talked the sky retreated a billion miles, leaving me cold and naked and lost, as if I had no mother, no home and no bed. Was there nothing above us, but just a deep pit going on for ever? I was filled with dismay to find there was no floor to heaven, particularly as I had intended to ask him about heaven's roof, and what was beyond that again. Was there another sky above heaven's roof, and how did it end? That question was not posed. Soft filmy sapphire-blue floor, and crystal roof of heaven disappeared in a twinkling, God's throne had nothing to stand upon, and my angels were left homeless, whilst I had nowhere to go when I died.

The schoolmaster went on talking of the vast distances of space. My mother and father listened with interest; they had their faith, which nothing could shake, and heaven was secure for them, but I was lost. It was a blow to the structure of religion.

The conversation was moved from these high altitudes, and we passed round the pink chocolate box, admiring the lace papers which divided the rows, and the broad pink ribbon round it. The world seemed more secure as I nestled closer to my mother, and touched her silk dress and warm comforting hand, so that when it was nine o'clock and the pony and trap came round to the front gate to take our visitors home, I ran out to the cold freezing air, convinced that heaven was hiding somewhere, undiscovered by our clever guests.

Some weeks later I found a little red octagonal-shaped tract, and in it I read more about the vasty deeps of the sky. I sat alone with this innocent-looking little book, which set forth these stupendous figures in order to show the glory of God, but to me they brought horror. I caught my breath and my hair seemed to stand on end as I read. So the schoolmaster was right, there was no floor, and the stars went on for ever, millions of them which I couldn't see, which no one saw. I was so very much upset that my first thought was to keep the terrible truth from my parents. They should never know. They should be shielded from the cruel reality, and I would keep the appalling knowledge to myself.

I hid the little book, lest my mother's heaven should be lost, too, and I pondered these figures about express trains running for ever before they reached the nearest star, and cannon balls speeding at miraculous rates towards the sun. Nobody must know, neither the clergyman who preached in the same old way, nor the congregation that listened so unconcernedly, and went home to Sunday dinner. Life would never be the same, for my home might fall off into that great chasm above me, everything might fall and be lost in space.

But life went on, nothing happened, and as long as the little book was hidden at the back of the bookcase, I felt happier. I should have burnt it, but my curiosity made me return to its hateful truths. Gradually my fears were allayed, the peace of my world calmed me, the quiet of the fields, and the security and eternity of my home. I felt once more anchored to earth. Everything had been and would be, and I was part of the continuity of life.

– From *Ambush of Young Days.*

Childhood in Paris

MRS ROBERT HENREY

The year 1909 ended for my mother with the birth of a son who was to be her last child. He came into the world in the new apartment at Clichy and his arrival that Christmas constitutes my earliest memory. My maternal grandmother had come specially from Blois, dressed entirely in black and carrying an immense umbrella and a wicker basket in which a dozen pots of home-made gooseberry jam were wrapped up in a linen napkin smelling of lavender. As soon as the cover was removed from one of these jars, all the delicious evocations of a sunny garden in the Loire filled the room. The colour and taste of the fruit charmed the little girl that I was.

My baby brother had red hair, my mother's rather sad beauty, and was quite adorable when being bathed in the washtub. I recall equally the gentle hours we spent watching him asleep in his cot, my mother with a lace blouse between her delicate fingers and I, sitting on a low stool beside her with fragments of lace I had picked up from the floor trying to sew without pricking my fingers, not daring to cry when I did so for fear of waking my brother. Occasionally my mother would sing softly, with a little catch in her voice in the sentimental parts, the romances she had learnt at Blois from the seamstresses in her apprentice days. There were passages which the little girl found passionately unintelligible but which she interpreted as she could, helped by an already strong imagination, unhappy love, children without fathers, patriotic songs of the war of 1870 in which figured the tricolour, lilac in bloom, and the woods of Meudon. I learnt early to play without making a noise, most often at being haberdasher with my mother as the customer who bought

[32]

everything, paying with buttons, patiently lending me her scissors to cut out tiny designs from her lace. These were indeed gentle hours! The baby would wake up, whereupon my mother would lift him up out of the cot addressing him in a language of her own. Then taking the pins from her corsage she would proudly give him the breast. All was calm. One listened to the tiny creature feeding, and kneading with plump fingers the milk-heavy bosom.

I remember also Émile coming home one evening with a young fox-terrier which had followed him in the street. Dogs and children were attracted by the loud authority in his voice and they alone, perhaps, perceived his deep hidden goodness. He called the terrier Follette. Knocking me over, she showed her friendliness and gratitude at being given a home by pawing and barking, but my mother was resentful, saying that there was no place for a dog in an apartment of one room and a kitchen and in which there were two children. No dog could have kept quieter in the daytime than Follette who intelligently sensed my mother's antagonism. She was anxious, in these circumstances, to remain unnoticed and scarcely emerged from her hiding-place even for food, but at night, hearing Émile's footsteps long before my mother did, she would run to the door, sniff and yelp, and when Émile arrived her happiness would have touched any woman less embittered by life than my mother. She, I think, saw in the animal's joy merely the waking of her son in the cot, and often her husband caressed the dog before he spoke to her. I have a clear picture of him at these times putting down the heavy sack in which he brought back for our stove wood salvaged from some demolished house or picked up from under the carpenter's bench. When we had all been kissed he would go out again, with the dog at his heels, and for long we would hear the animal's delirious barking as they went along the street.

My mother laid supper on the round table covered with an oil-cloth and in the centre of which she placed, on winter evenings, the lamp with its yellow flame that I likened to a mermaid in a mysterious sea. This mermaid became, at my will, a fairy, a sleeping princess, a fair damsel imprisoned in a glass tower. Then came the evening soup after which Émile would take the wood out of his sack and a pleasant odour of resin and tar would fill the room. When a piece was too large for the stove he would split it with a hatchet against a plank balanced on his knees, and when a splinter flew across the carpet Follette, her tail wagging, would bring it back in her mouth and drop it at the feet of her master, certain that she would be patted and sometimes, even, given a lump of sugar. After this ceremony Émile took a foot-bath, which would be removed by my mother, holding it by the two handles, her young body and narrow waist bent under the weight, obedient and lovely like a Roman slave, whilst I knelt down with the slippers. He went to bed almost immediately, and within a minute or two was fast asleep, for his day began at five. His snoring was echoed by that of his dog. My mother put out a clean pair of socks, a clean shirt, the money for the subway train, and a thick slice of bread spread with dripping or hard pork sausage which he carried in his haversack to eat at midday. The remains of the evening soup she poured into a saucepan for him to heat it up before going to work. He liked to dip a piece of bread in it and always shared this early meal with the dog.

After a hard winter the Seine, in 1910, began suddenly to overflow its banks and everybody watched the stone figure of the zouave which, with its back against the central arch of the Alma bridge, is invariably used as a yardstick on such occasions. The water quickly covered the zouave's feet, rose above his gaiters, and in a few days reached his chin. Then panic took hold of those who lived nearest the river. These are my first clear-cut memories of the outside world.

Our street had become a tributary of the Seine during the night and the water continued to rise. The doorkeepers left their lodges and arranged new quarters for themselves on the first floor. As the cellars were flooded there was no coal for heating, and in ours Émile had put a cask of wine which somebody had sent him from the south of France, and this cask, half empty, had been raised by the water, and thus floating on the summit of the waves bumped so loudly and continuously against the roof of the cellar, which was also the floor of our room, that we had the impression all night of a visitation by a ghost . . .

Still the Seine rose; sewer rats swam along the streets. People started to talk about a plague. A house not far from ours caught fire and firemen arrived in a punt, their shining hats reflected in the muddy water.

Then, as happened to Noah, the water suddenly fell. Émile found his cask of wine dented but in tolerable condition. His potatoes had become mixed up with his coal, and the subsiding waters had left three dead rats on the infamous heap. Our neighbours turned their attention to the coming carnival. Reopened shops decorated their windows with masks, false noses, and confetti. A new picture is now printed on my mind – the queen of the carnival on a throne surrounded by her princesses. A monkey dressed as a zouave played tricks at the end of a string. The brass bands made me cry with soldier-loving emotion. Clowns rode on elephants. Thousands of people threw confetti.

That summer little girls, older than I, played diabolo in the street; others spun coloured tops under the very wheels of the drays and horse-cabs. The cry of the creamy cheese vendor came, through the open window, into our stifling room. Her earthenware jar full of fresh cream was wrapped up in a damp napkin of the purest linen, and when, at the request of a customer, she ladled the cream on a heart-shaped cheese, the whiteness of the cream contrasted with the whiteness of the cheese, the whole handed for freshness on a leaf in an osier heart. My mother, putting a few halfpence in one tiny hand and a salad bowl in the other, sent me with much trepidation to buy two for her lunch and mine. Soon I accompanied her to the baker, often hiding in the cages in which the long French loaves were placed. I remember the bakeress pulling me out, giving me a kiss on my forehead, and placing in my hand a *croissant* still warm from the oven. . . .

I was on the point of being taught the Christmas hymns at school when I was taken with a sore throat, and then a headache and a fever. Émile went in the middle of the night to fetch a four-wheeler beyond the gate in the fortifications, and when I had been wrapped up in a blanket I was taken to the Hérald Hospital suffering from diphtheria.

For several days I was in danger. I used to see the whiteness of my mother's face through the glass partition, her eyes red with crying. her brave but unconvincing smile. Émile also had a whiteness about his skin, and his long moustaches could not keep still. He was made to put on a surgeon's white coat and this new manner of dressing intrigued me. My small brother on these visits was left in the care of the hospital porter. After a few moments my parents blew me a last kiss and departed, leaving some small gifts which a nurse would later bring and put on my bed, and the fun of opening these things repressed the tears which usually started to well up at the sight of their emotion and sad going away.

I was later moved to a room which faced the kitchens, and as I was better and consequently thought only of food I had the satisfaction of watching the cooks, dressed in blue blouses, stacking the red copper cauldrons full of hot soup on the trolleys for distribution in the wards. Our meals were arranged in this way. Our usual nurse would place an empty plate in front of each patient. One of the blue-coated cooks would then put into it a full ladle of raw horse-flesh, minced fine, upon which a second cook would pour the soup. There were mashed potatoes also which, if I remember accurately, came later as a separate course . . .

The Sunday after my return home, Marie-Thérèse, her husband, and Rolande came to lunch and I was much petted. Life appeared to me new and wonderful, and during the ensuing week my mother, laying aside her blouses, occasionally took us for a walk which she had never done up to now. Another Sunday had not passed, however, before my small brother, feeling listless and not inclined to play, became at the approach of night feverish, and my parents, leaving me asleep in bed, hurried him to the Bretonneau Hospital where they learned that the serum he had been given at the time of my first illness not having taken, he now had diphtheria with complications.

There followed a series of pitiful visits to see him behind his glass partition. Meningitis set in and the ward sister exclaimed to my mother: 'Ah, madame, he is very young for two such serious illnesses!' But soon pneumonia arrived also. When, after this, my mother came back from seeing him, she said tearfully that his forehead was full of bleeding wounds from throwing his poor head against the iron bars of the cot.

We were in December. My mother's birthday was on the twelfth and with her still beautiful waist and magnificent red hair she was only twenty-six. That morning she hurried up the stairs of the hospital, anxious, hoping. A hand was placed gently on her arm and she was led to a bare room where her son lay dead on a marble slab. He had died in the night far from her.

My grandmother from Blois came for the funeral, and as my little brother had died at the Bretonneau he was buried in the vast cemetery of St Ouen.

My mother's resignation had been strained beyond her capacity to bear, and when she left the funeral service her revolt was immense. Her suffering was so acute that it is a wonder she did not die. I became a silent witness of it when for entire afternoons she would howl with pain, like a she-wolf barking, or again, her head in her hands, her whole frail body would shake with heaving sobs. Every day we found something fresh to increase her misery. My brother's grey cat, the stray he had befriended, miauling for him, not knowing he was dead. There were nails, stolen from Émile, he had clumsily but strongly hammered into chairs or furniture, pieces of clothing, tiny trousers whose pockets revealed pebbles and bits of string, a purse with a halfpenny in it, and, of course, worst of all, the rabbit with the red eyes.

My mother burned the rabbit but devoutly put away the sailor's cap with the red tuft which he had so often worn. How dreadful for the little girl who remained, who neither dared to cry nor to play but was obliged to look on silently at all this early sorrow!

Every Thursday afternoon my mother took me to the Boulevard Haussmann to deliver her blouses to Mme Gaillard . . . For me the Boulevard Haussmann was an enchantment. The Magasin du Printemps gave away coloured balloons and similar toys to the children of their customers every Thursday afternoon. It was for this reason, I think, that my mother chose this particular day to deliver her work to Mme Gaillard and she was able to qualify as a customer by buying at this magnificent store the many yards of fine net which she needed to line her blouses as well as the mother-of-pearl buttons with which to finish them.

The following Thursday we were informed by our friend the porter that Mme Gaillard had gone to bury her husband in the Auvergne. The next Thursday she was not yet back, and as my mother had finished all the work in hand she decided to take advantage of this lull in her sewing to wash a great many things, and on the Saturday night, having tied up all the dirty linen in the largest bed-sheet, we went together, for by now I accompanied her everywhere, to the famous public wash-house in the Boulevard Victor-Hugo.

A number was attached to the bundle, its counterpart being given to the owner, and the attendant, armed like a halberdier with a tall pole, then threw the bundle into the centre of an immense copper in which the linen bubbled and boiled. The next day the bundle, plainly numbered, would be found on an iron trolley, and then my mother would take her place in the long line of kneeling women who, their sleeves rolled up, their bodies moving rhythmically, scrubbed and soaked in the limpid water.

I loved this wash-house because we walked on planks under which the water lapped and gurgled. Women of all worlds came here, from the most vulgar to the most respectable, who quickly struck up wash-house acquaintanceship. Waiters from the neighbouring cafés moved deftly amongst us selling buttered rolls, *croissants*, hot coffee, and glasses of rum, but those who did the briskest business were the fortune-tellers who interpreted the future in the lines of wet palms that smelt agreeably of soap and disinfectant. These fortune-tellers were never for a moment idle. Even those women who pretended not to believe in them soon gave way. One would see them getting up from the water with loud laughs or nervous tittering, wiping their hands on their rough aprons before going over to the gipsies, and then believing everything they were told. There were other ambulating vendors who passed through this picturesque crowd giving the place the colour and movement of an Eastern Bazaar, dark-skinned men who sold scrubbing brushes, iron handles, beeswax, and even toilet soap and cheap perfumes. When the linen was rinsed one would make up the clean bundle, pushing it on the iron trolley to the drying-machine, where for a penny one could get rid of the water, or at least a good deal of it, which made the bundle much lighter to carry home. Later when the linen was hung up in our yard I would love to run between the sheets, playing at being the little girl lost or pursued in an imaginary city of white towers.

– From *The Little Madeleine*

No Tears, No Good

RUTH McKENNEY

My sister Eileen and I, movie fans when we were five and six respectively, would have scorned Mickey Mouse in our youth; we preferred Theda Bara to Fatty Arbuckle, and that was the acid test.

We saw our first movie shortly after we saw our first aeroplane. The aeroplane was very nice, of course, and we had a school half-holiday to celebrate the glorious moment when an air machine first put landing gear on the dreary soil of Mishawaka, Indiana. That was the early spring of 1918, and aeroplanes were very patriotic and thrilling; but in spite of the glamorous fellow who ran the queer machine, we liked the movie better than the aeroplane. The movie lasted longer.

Our first film was Chapter 3 of a serial which had to do with bandits, high cliffs, and pistols. Eileen was so small she was able to sneak under the ticket-seller's high box and get in free. The serial was shown that spring daily, not weekly, in a made-over garage not far from our schoolhouse. Chapter One of the adventures of, say, Death-Defying Desmond started on Monday at four o'clock sharp, and the last instalment ended at the Friday afternoon matinée, amid the hoarse cheers of the excited audience. Admission price was a nickel, but no self-respecting child in our fairly prosperous neighbourhood would have thought of stumbling down the dark aisles and throwing himself into a creaking wooden seat unless he were equipped with a bag of peanuts, price also five cents.

The peanuts were not merely for the inner man; the shells were used by the large and energetic audience to enliven the dull stretches in the scenario. To us, even the liveliest Western had a good many sleepy sequences, and, indeed, the whole audience could be bored into mass fidgets at the mere sight of a long sub-title, for few, if any, of the paying customers at those four o'clock matinées could read – not, at least, with any ease. Nobody in the theatre had the slightest idea of what the film was about, and nobody cared. We came to see the fights, and the horse races over the mountains, and the jumping across chasms. Our attention wandered as soon as the scene shifted indoors, and two sub-titles in a row were enough to start a peanut fight.

Thus, when the heroine began to plead with the villain for the hero's life, Benny Burns, a big boy in the third grade, would rise and shoot a peanut shell at his old enemy, Freddie Meriman. Freddie would respond in kind, and soon the darkened theatre would be the scene of a fine free-for-all battle, with both sides eventually running out of peanut shells and resorting to books, hats, apples, and other deadly weapons. Piercing screams could sometimes be heard all the way out to the street, and the howls of the wounded would sooner or later seriously annoy the bored movie operator, upstairs in his booth. He and the ticket-seller were the only attendants, for in those days there were no laws about matrons, and for a nickel we did not have the dubious pleasure of hearing the regular pianist. In the midst of the joyous battle, then, the lights would suddenly go on, the heroine disappear from the screen, and the racket diminish slightly while the operator bawled: 'Shut up, you brats, or I'll throw you all out.'

'Ya-a-ah,' we would all scream, Eileen's five-year-old shriek rising above the rest, 'come on and do it!'

He never tried, though. He waited for comparative quiet, dimmed the lights, and put the heroine back on the screen, this time perhaps pleading, in one of those lightning developments, for her own life. The peanut battles were apparently more exciting than the serials. I remember little of that first spring movie season except a train wreck, but that train wreck will live in my memory as one of the more piquant experiences of my life.

In the film, a motor-car, a Model T Ford, was racing down a country road, pursued by something – I think it was a lot of bandits in another car. Just as the motor-car approached the crossing, a train appeared around a convenient bend. All this was old stuff; we were used to seeing motor-cars and trains fight it out on the tracks.

But suddenly the camera switched from the general view of the automobile and the train, and on the screen appeared a huge pair of wheels – the train wheels. They grew larger and larger, revolving furiously. We were awed and horrified. The wheels were coming right for us; apparently the motor-car was not to be run over – we were. Suddenly my sister Eileen screamed, and began trying to climb across the tense legs of the little boys in our row.

'Let me out, let me out!' she howled. 'Ruth! Mamma! Help! It's coming!'

In the silence of the darkened movie house, Eileen's screams made a sensation. Other small girls burst into nervous sobs. Boys, even big boys in the third grade, began to whine dismally. On the screen the wheels were now rolling faster and faster, and the whole train loomed up, apparently about to descend upon us. In those days, when a cameraman had a good shot, he gave it plenty of footage, to let it sink in. Eileen's agonised howls and cries for help were now being drowned out by the panic-stricken roar of the whole audience. There was a tremendous din, and the scuffle of dozens of frightened children trying to stumble out into the aisles and run for home and mother. At this point the lights went on and the train, wheels and all, disappeared from the screen.

'For Christ's sake!' bawled the infuriated movie operator from his booth. The attention of the horrified audience was now shifted from the thought of escape to horror at hearing a bad word, a swear word, shouted so baldly from above. This was a polite neighbourbood.

'This ain't real,' the movie operator continued in his stentorian tones. 'Nobody's going to get hurt. It's just a movie.'

You could hear the soft rustle of everybody saying 'Oh' to his neighbour, the diminishing sniffles, the blowing of noses, the regaining of creaking wooden seats. But before the lights went down the ticket-seller, a mean-looking lady of what we thought was vast age, with side puffs over her ears, walked down the aisle.

'Who started this?' she demanded sternly. A dozen fingers pointed to my fat, tear-stained sister. Eileen tried to hide under her seat, but in vain. She was ordered out to the aisle.

'How old are you?' the ticket-seller demanded, in front of everybody.

'Theven,' Eileen lied, in her most unfortunate lisp. A dozen voices contradicted her. 'She's only in kindergarten,' various old pals shouted gleefully.

'Little girls in kindergarten aren't allowed to come to the movies,' the ticket-seller said grimly, and grabbed Eileen's chubby arm. Weeping dismally, my poor sister was ignominiously led out, with me tagging sorrowfully along behind. Unfortunately, this event made such a scandal that our mother heard of it, via other little girls' mothers, and we were forbidden to attend movies until we were older.

Older was next year, after we had moved to Cleveland. There were three movie houses within walking distance of our new home, and we settled down to delightful years of Saturday and Sunday afternoon film orgies.

Nobody censored our movie fare except ourselves. Mother had no idea of what grim and gripping pictures we were seeing, for she never went to the movies herself. She was something of an intellectual, and back in 1919 and 1920 people who had pretensions to culture, at least in the Middle West, wouldn't have been caught dead in a movie house. Mother thought the films were exclusively for children and morons, like the comic strips in the newspapers. . . .

'Don't sit through it more than twice!' she would shout from the front porch as we skipped off, hand in hand, to the movies. We would return, hours later, exhausted from the hard seats and emotional duress.

We saw some bright and cheerful pictures, but I don't remember many of them. There was Fatty Arbuckle, of course, and two wonderful children who threw dishes at each other – the Lee sisters. We worshipped them. But most of the pictures we saw were, to us anyway, grim and awful tragedies. If there were happy endings, we never noticed them. Some of the pictures were so unbearably sad we could hardly stay to see them twice. We did, though.

We wore large round hats with ribbons for these excursions to the movies. Once settled down in our seats, we held on anxiously to the hats. At the least sign of trouble on the screen, we put the hats in

[43]

front of our eyes. . . . Of course, since we saw every film twice, in spite of our hat system of censorship we generally got the thread of the plot on the second time round. If we still couldn't quite make out what had happened, we stayed for the third show and were late for dinner.

We had no favourite movie stars at first, for the truth was that we hadn't really believed that movie operator. For a long time we thought the movies were real, and that the tragedies we saw were photographed, mysteriously, from real and horrible life. I gradually came to understand that the suffering heroine was only an actress, and I used to reassure Eileen loudly as she wept. 'Don't cry,' I would bawl through my own tears. 'It's only a movie.'

At last, though, we grew out of this primitive stage of movie response and developed into Wally Reid and Lon Chaney fans. Mr Chaney, of course, we admired in a rather backhanded way. Each Chaney film was, for us, a terrible ordeal, through which we suffered and bawled and wept. As we staggered out of the theatre, our pug noses swollen to red beets, we swore never to set eyes on the man again. But the next time we were back, groaning in our seats, fascinated and horrified. Finally *The Hunchback of Notre Dame* came along and very nearly finished me off. Even now, Eileen refuses to discuss that gruesome movie. Mr Chaney was the hunchback, of course, and he suffered a peculiarly realistic and horrible beating in that old silent film. Eileen and I put our arms around each other and howled steadily throughout the entire beating.

Mr Reid, who came along a little earlier than the horror man, was a slightly more cheerful influence on our childhood, although his tragic death became, oddly enough, a family scandal. Our passion for Mr Reid was shared by a young aunt of ours, who admired that jaunty actor with rather more enthusiasm than detachment. Now, my mother cared nothing for Mr Reid but she was deeply attached to her only brother and she called him, as Mr Reid's devoted fans called their idol, Wally.

Imagine her horror, then, one evening, when my young aunt called up and wept over the phone, in broken accents: 'Maggie, Maggie, Wally's dead!'

'Dead?' shouted my mother, electrifying everybody at our dinner table. 'No! No! It isn't true!'

My aunt said, amid her tears, that it was true, alas. My mother began, naturally enough, to cry. My father, white and shaken, rushed to the phone, tenderly pushed his wife aside while she sobbed 'Wally's dead,' and picked up the receiver.

'How did it happen?' Father began, in that sombre tone of voice you use for these trying occasions. Then we heard him roar: 'What! You're crazy!' He hung up with a frightful bang and shouted: 'It's Wally Reid, the film actor!'

Eileen and I began to howl at once. We didn't know our uncle very well, but we certainly knew Wally Reid, and felt perfectly terrible about his death. We simply couldn't understand Mother's callous revival when she heard the good news that her brother still lived. That famous telephone conversation started a family feud that lasted for years. Mother never forgave her young sister, and my aunt stated freely and frankly that she thought Mother was a perfect idiot for not knowing that Wally Reid had been ill for days. People took their movies seriously those days, if they took them at all . . .

The Big Parade was the last picture belonging to the idyllic, or honeymoon, stage of the movies for us. After that our high-school beaux began to buy our movie tickets, and for many years, alas, the beaux took up more of our attention than the movies. By the time we had recovered from the shock of not paying our own way in, we were living in New York City and reading the *Times* moving-picture reviews. And somehow the movies have never been the same for us as they were in the days when we saw them in snatches from behind our big round hats.

– From *My Sister Eileen*.

Hatching Eggs

ROSE MACAULAY

Actually, I do not know that hatching is the right word, for I never, by human warmth, delivered any chicken from its shell. Neither would 'sitting on' be correct, for that was not the method adopted. I suppose incubating is the word. Anyhow, the pleasure lay in hope and dreams, never in consummation. We carried our eggs on the person by day, under the pillow by night. Only one at a time, and when it broke we began on another. They were mostly laid by hens, but once I found a duck's egg in the road, huge and pale green. How far it might already be advanced towards the duckling stage, I had no means of knowing; but I adopted it forthwith and stowed it away in the front of my sailor frock, the largest and proudest of the eggs on the persons of a family at the moment a prey to acute eggomania. There it lay, in that repository designed by heaven for carrying about oranges, books, rabbits, and kittens, so that the wearing of sailor suits, male and female, made a family inclined to thinness bulge in front as if they had been reared on some rich health food. My egg lay, I think, alone, and handkerchief-enwrapped; when tree or rock climbing was indulged in, it was removed and carefully laid in some snug cache.

For how many days I nursed this greenish and pregnant treasure, this shrine of a fluffy golden being who should emerge in the fullness of time, who should owe its happy waddling life to me, I know not. They were glorious days, if few. I walked and gingerly ran, dream-wrapped; I was with duckling, and must walk warily. When in the slippery paths of youth with heedless steps I ran, the bouncing against my bosom of my duck-to-be recalled me to the cautiousness of prospective motherhood.

How I would love it! It would be my dandling, my nestlechick, my pet. With my own hands I would teach it to swim, to run, to jump (for we were accustomed to organise hurdle races for our pets, of whatever species). Mine would be the swiftest duck e'er entered for the stakes. It would accompany me everywhere, sitting on my lap at meals, at lessons, bathing with me in the sea. How, too, it would love me! Why does the duckling love her so, people would ask, as of Mary's lamb? Well, she loves the duck, you see, they would reply. And was I not giving it life, tending it, sacrificing for it other pleasures? Should it not, when it came to perception, gratefully quack, with Joseph Addison,

> Unnumber'd comforts to my soul
> Thy tender care bestow'd,
> Before my infant heart conceived
> From whom those comforts flow'd?

Thus I mused in my maternal meditations, moving delicately about houses, shore, road, hill-side, my hands often crossed over my breast as in some holy picture. I felt safe, guarded, protected, with my dear and perilous burden; a thousand liveried angels lackeyed me, and I knew that this time a duck would be born. I would often take out the egg and put my ear to it as to a shell, to listen for faint cheepings, which I sometimes fancied that I heard. I wondered what would happen if it should hatch by night, beneath my pillow. . . . Suppose that I were to wake one morning and find a smothered duckling, whose cries had failed to wake me? But we had been told that chickens and ducklings usually hatched by day, so this chance seemed remote.

The end came, as usual. The liveried angels went off duty, and with heedless steps I ran across the slippery stone floor of a room, and fell prone on my chest. A horrid smash, and my pet flowed away, sticky, addled, smelling of the corruption of all mortality, and past return were all its dandled days.

In the ensuing mess and bitterness of baulked hope, my one and chilly comfort was that there had never, it seemed, been duck life in that shell. I had not been with duckling, only with egg; and with stale and ancient egg of date incalculable. My nestlechick had been but a fluffy golden vision, conceived in the pregnant rovings of my brain, never by duck and drake in sweet communion linked. It had been the child of my doting dreams alone. But, while they lasted, what doting and what dreams!

– From *Personal Pleasures.*

The General's Tomboy

DAME ETHEL SMYTH

We lived in those days at Sidcup, then quite a country place, selected by my father as not too far from Woolwich, where, on his return to England after the Indian Mutiny, he took up the command of the Artillery Depot. The Indian forces to which he belonged were then in course of fusion with the regular army, and being very popular, and having served with distinction, he was considered the right man for a task requiring both tact and common sense. I can see him now, starting for the daily ride to his office mounted on his 18-hand charger Paddy, who later filled the parts of hunter, brougham horse, and coal-cart horse with good humour and propriety. I have even ridden him myself, and an old friend once told us his first sight of me was wrong end upwards, suspended by the foot on Paddy's off side with my long hair sweeping the grass, the saddle having slipped round in Bramshill Park. As a tiny child I firmly believed the horse-radish served with the Sunday joint was plucked from the white saddle-marks on Paddy's high withers, and for this reason had an aversion to horse-radish sauce years after I knew the truth about it.

Sidcup Place, in the parish of Foots Cray, Kent, was originally a small, square, Queen Anne house, separated from the main road by a high wall covered with ivy, between the two a strip of garden. A wing had been added later, along the first storey of which, facing the real garden which was at the back, ran what seemed to me then an endless gallery, the most ideal of places for children to rush up and down and yell in. . . .

There were roomy stables and a big old-fashioned granary mounted on stone pillars, yet none the less infested, so they told us, by rats – a useful legend. The grounds were charming; on one side of the croquet lawn was the most enormous acacia I have ever seen, the bloom of which never failed, and on the other a fine cedar. Beyond was a walled kitchen garden with flowery borders and rose patches, and the object of our lives was to mount the walls, unobserved, from the far side in quest of forbidden fruit. Once I remember the gardener, who had stealthily removed the ladder, suddenly appearing with a long switch; we flew along the top, he at the bottom of the wall, calling out as we reached the spot where the ladder should have been: 'Now I've got yer, yer little warmints,' and I am glad to say I followed Johnny's lead and took a flying leap down into safety, a drop of eight or nine feet – not a mean performance for a child of less than that number of years. . . .

Fringed with disreputable-looking willows was a duck pond, on which we used to put forth in wine boxes and tubs; and hard by an old elm tree, in which Alice, Johnny, and a friend of his built one of the many descendants of the Tree House in *The Swiss Family Robinson*. It had a floor, and heaps of shelves and hooks, and we were allowed to have tea up there when we had been very good. As milk warm from the cow figured among our treats I pretended to love it, but really was rather nauseated, and privately thought milking an improper sight. It seemed cruel, too, to maul the poor cows like that, and when the gruff cowman said they liked it, he was not believed.

I have two special farmyard recollections, one being the occasion on which young Maunsell B—— a school friend of Johnny's who spent most of his holidays with us and considered himself engaged to Mary – promised me sixpence if I would ride a slim black pig called Fairylight round the yard. For some reason or other we were dressed in clean, open-work, starched frocks, and when, after being shot off on to the manure heap, I was dragged into my father's study by our infuriated nurse, it was easy to see he could hardly keep his countenance. The other incident was my bribing the cowman (again with sixpence) to let me see a pig killed – conduct which deeply shocked and horrified Johnny who considered such sights a male privilege. The terrific scolding that followed was unnecessary, since for months afterwards I turned green whenever I heard a pig squealing.

At last even the nurse pitied me and would say: 'Bless your heart he's only squealing for his dinner,' which I hope was true. Otherwise I am quite sure I was not a cruel little girl, except perhaps later on in the donkey days, when dreadful things were done with the butt end of a whip; but anyone who has had to do with donkeys will make allowances . . .

At each Church Festival the donkey cart was piled up with whatever might be the appropriate fruits of nature, and off we started to decorate the church, the great point being lunch with a kind old neighbour close by. As a tiny child I was terrified of churchyards, but at this time they must have had a morbid attraction, or perhaps it was under the influence of *Hamlet* that I loved to watch the sexton at work and 'think of graves and worms and epitaphs' as the young will – as the old won't. It may be remembered, too, that in order to increase the agony of love I would cheerfully consign my 'passions' to an early grave, but as regards myself terrors of Death haunted me throughout my youth, and it was perhaps with some vague idea of conjuring the spectre that I persuaded the sexton to give me a human bone, which I hid among my collars and handkerchiefs. But this relic left me no peace, for I knew its possession was sacrilegious, and at last in floods of tears confessed all to my mother. I think she was a good deal taken aback, but explained quite gently that it would never do, when the Day of Judgment comes, for people's limbs to be scattered about in different places. Evidently she had never read, or did not go with, a work called *The Last Day*, from which Mr Gosse quotes, in his book *Father and Son*, the following remarkable verse:

> Now charnels rattle, scattered limbs, and all
> The various bones, obsequious to the call,
> Self-mov'd advance – the neck perhaps to meet
> The distant head, the distant legs the feet.

Meanwhile she undertook to have the bone put back in the place it came from and later informed me that all was well, the sexton having assured her it was a sheep's bone, and that he never would have dreamed of giving me human remains. I often wonder if this was a legend invented by her to soothe my inflamed and suffering imagination, or whether the sexton, afraid of getting into trouble, really hazarded this improbable yarn . . .

I think on the whole we were a naughty and very quarrelsome crew. My father once wrote and pinned on the wall: 'If you have nothing pleasant to say, *hold your tongue*': an adage which, though excellent as a receipt for getting on in society, was unpopular in a nursery such as ours, for words lead to blows and we happened to love fighting. There was one terrific battle between Mary and myself in the course of which I threw a knife that wounded her chin, to which she responded with a fork that hung for a moment just below my eye, Johnny having in the meantime crawled under the table.

Then again there was a loft in which queer old swords and pistols looted by my father in his Indian campaigns were stored away, together with hideous discarded family portraits, to stab which was of course irresistible. But the strange thing is that we often fought with these weapons among ourselves, not infrequently in anger, and yet did each other no serious damage. It was in the loft that our first smoking essays took place. Some people say this is an acquired taste; if so, someone acquired mine for me before I was born, for we often smoked bits of my father's broken canes, as well as tea rolled inside brown paper, and I can truthfully say the thing came as naturally to me as eating pear-drops, nor was I ever the worse for it.

Of course we merited and came in for a good deal of punishment, including having our ears boxed, which in those days was not considered dangerous, and my mother's dramatic instinct came out strongly in her technique as ear-boxer. With lips tightly shut she would whip out her hand, hold it close to one's nose, palm upwards, for quite a long time, as much as to say: 'Look at this! You'll feel it presently' – and then . . . smack!

I think I am the only one of the six Miss Smyths who has ever been really thrashed; the crime was stealing some barley sugar, and though caught in the very act, persistently denying the theft. Thereupon my father beat me with one of grandmama's wooden knitting needles, a thing about 2½ feet long with a knob at one end. He was the least cruel of men, and opponents of corporal punishment will say its brutalising effect is proved by the fact that when I howled he merely said: 'The more noise you make the harder I'll hit you.' Hit hard he did, for a fortnight later, when I joined Alice, who had been away all this time at an aunt's, she noticed strange marks on my person while bathing me, and was informed by me that it came from sitting on my crinoline.

– From *Impressions That Remained.*

Young and Tender

MARY LUTYENS

In the best tradition of the girls' schools I fell in love with our very
pretty games mistress, Miss Kershaw, and got into the netball team
so as to see more of her. To attract her attention I used to pretend
to have fits after a hard game, when I would gasp like an asthma
sufferer, but she soon put a stop to this nonsense by telling me that
I would not be allowed to play at all if I had so little stamina. Miss
Kershaw also taught us botany, and again in a bid for her notice I
would behave like a delinquent moron in class only to come out
top in the end-of-term exam. This ruse succeeded better than the
fits. She seemed really puzzled by it and kept me back after class to
tax me with the discrepancy. I am sure she believed I had managed
to cheat in some way . . .

But the climax of my relationship with Miss Kershaw (if anything
so one-sided can be called a relationship) came when I met her at
tea one afternoon at the house of a fellow-member of the netball
team. She kissed this girl and her sister when she arrived, and then,
turning to me, said with a look of great distaste: 'I suppose I shall
have to kiss you too.' In spite of her obvious reluctance to touch me
I did not for several days wash my cheek where her lips had brushed
me. I wonder whether she had the slightest inkling of my feelings for
her. She left to get married soon after this and I have never been in
love with a woman since.

It was about this time that the Doll's House which Father had
designed for Queen Mary was being constructed in our drawing-
room. Furnishings of all sorts were arriving every day for it – linen,
glass, china, books, pictures, curtains, chandeliers, wine bottles,
golf clubs, motor-cars – as well as the fittings and furniture which
Father had designed. I went into the drawing-room at all times to

watch its progress and came to look upon it almost as my private possession. So much of the furniture was familiar to me. The bed in the Princess Royal's room was a perfect miniature of the beds Father had designed for my sisters Barbie and Ursula; the chandelier in the nursery was a copy of the one he had made for Barbie's new nursery, while the kitchen cupboards were reproductions of our own. I realised that this was the house we would have lived in if Father had been rich enough to build it for himself. It was his own dream house, and because I was imbued with his taste it was my dream house too. It took no effort of imagination to see us living in it.

No wonder Father did not like coming away with us for holidays to the schools or rectories which Mother rented. We spent the summer holidays of 1922 in a school at Hemel Hempstead. I had a tea party for my birthday at which I must have been showing off as usual because Mother said very sharply to the assembled company, which included some school friends who were staying with me: 'You can see Mary is still a baby although she is fourteen to-day.' This snub in front of my friends went to the quick. I could not remember another occasion in the whole of my life when Mother had snubbed me, but instead of being grateful for being spared so long, I was all the more resentful of this single snub which had spoiled my birthday . . . When I went to bed that night I vowed I would never forgive her.

Was it being told that I was still a baby that urged me that summer to indulge in experimental kisses with a charming young man to the strains of *Avalon*, *The Japanese Sandman*, *Say it with Music*, and *I'm Forever Blowing Bubbles*? I found that kissing was a most delightful occupation and that the feelings it produced linked up with sensations in the past which I had not realised had any connection with love-making. In other words I discovered for myself that I had had sexual feelings ever since I could remember, for I recognised my sensations for what they were, something quite different from the emotion of love. Kissing a young man I was fond of was a pleasure of the senses, whereas being in the same room as the person I was in love with was a joy of the whole being. To kiss the man one loved must be an ecstasy I could not even imagine.

– From *To Be Young*.

First Season

CYNTHIA ASQUITH

Like most young people, I liked my clothes to be 'exciting' or 'amusing' rather than correct or fashionable. I had an abiding love for golden and silver materials, imbued, I expect, by descriptions in fairy tales of the raiment worn by princesses. It was some time before I learned to appreciate the merits of perfectly plain tailormade clothes which I condemned as dull – just as well for my overdraft, for then as now, they were very expensive.

My favourite dressmaker was Madame Marie, who specialised in the sheening ball-gowns we called our 'fish-dresses' – lovely skin-tight sheaths of gold, silver or sea-coloured tissue.

Many of our clothes were far from comfortable or convenient. Country tweeds were long and trammelling. Imagine the discomfort of a walk in the rain in a sodden skirt that wound its wetness round your legs and chapped your ankles. Even our lawn-tennis dresses, usually like nursemaid's wear, made of white piqué, were so long that it was impossible to take a step back without treading on them. Walking about the London streets trailing clouds of dust was horrid. I once found I had carried into the house a banana skin which had got caught up in the unstitched hem of my dress! Our vast hats which took the wind like sails were painfully skewered to our heads by huge ornamental hatpins, greatly to the peril of other people's eyes.

My opaque stockings, never other than black, brown or white, were darned, darned, darned. My underclothes were unglamorously sensible. I seem to remember some terribly grim inherited nightgowns made, squalor of squalor, of flannel – with pockets! Cardigans, a

crying need in the then arctic climate of most country houses, had
not yet been introduced, and to keep your tweed jacket on indoors
was considered an uncivil reflection on the temperature in which
you were being entertained.

The chief convention was the indispensability of a chaperon in
any public place. To be seen at a theatre, a picture gallery, a restaurant
or in a hansom cab alone with a young man was tantamount to
announcing your engagement to him, or openly advertising that you
had decided to throw your cap over the windmill.

The qualifications that constituted a chaperon always seemed to
me comically arbitrary. No spinster, however mature and sober,
counted as one, whereas any flighty chit of eighteen years automatically
acquired this status directly a gold ring encircled her fourth finger.

Some débutantes were not even allowed to have a young man to
tea unchaperoned. My friends and I were, but quite a few mothers
considered the practice definitely what was then called 'fast'. Is that
quaint word ever used to-day? Imagination boggles as to what sort
of behaviour could earn it.

What *do* I remember of that first season?

I see striped awnings, linkmen with flaring torches; powdered,
liveried footmen; soaring marble staircases; tiaras, smiling hostesses;
azaleas in gilt baskets; white waistcoats, violins, elbows sawing the
air, names on pasteboard cards, quails in aspic, macédoine, straw-
berries and cream, tired faces of cloakroom attendants, washed
streets in blue dawns, sparrows pecking about the empty pavements,
my bedroom curtains being drawn apart to let in the late morning
light; a breakfast tray approaching my bedside; bandboxes, tissue
paper . . .

Springing each morning from my bed right into the middle of the
room, I would first rush to look into the mirror. 'How are you to-day?'
I would ask anxiously and yet detachedly, as though the reflection
I scanned were not my own but someone else's – someone, however,
with whom I was very closely concerned. Next I would rush to the
window to see what kind of a day awaited the two of us – that face
and me. Having a colour that came and went, I was uneasily aware of
being very *journalière*. When I knew I was too pale I would pinch

my cheeks to make them pink – a measure temporarily successful, but betrayed only a few minutes later by two tell-tale patches of red standing out in the surrounding whiteness. I used to rub my lips, too, until they were quite sore. Another besetting anxiety was whether my nose was shiny, for at that date a girl would no more have powdered her face in public than a man would lather his for shaving. Squinting at my reflection in a spoon, I sometimes furtively applied a leaf of papier poudré – a not very effective makeshift which I could conceal in my pocket handkerchief. Once when I particularly wanted to look my best and knew I was dead pale, desperation drove me to dab pink tooth powder on my cheeks. Another time I borrowed someone else's red lipstick (my own was white) and bedizened my face.

In those days dancing was real exercise. Faces crimsoned. Some dancers were classified as 'Two collar' or 'Three collar men'. Balls usually began very sedately, but as the room thinned, the dancing became wildly Corybantic. Elaborate variations were improvised. Disengaging ourselves from our partners in the Merry Widow valse fashion, we would sway round the room in fantastic *pas seuls;* now rippling our arms like – so we flattered ourselves – Maud Allan; now flinging ourselves about like Apaches, or dancing the Cake Walk. Threading their separate ways through the maze of dancers, disunited partners would put the utmost distance between one another; then converging from the opposite ends of the ballroom, join up together again to spin furiously round and round until at long last the two halves of the teetotum reeled apart. Kitchen Lancers (why Kitchen?) were riotously rowdy – in fact positively dangerous. Our favourite figure – Ladies to the Centre – converted us into a living Giant's Stride. The girls were all lifted right off their feet and swung by their four partners who with arms interlocked revolved in a ring. Higher and higher we were swirled, until our legs hurtled through the air on a level with our partners' shoulders. I once saw the tiara knocked clean off an onlooker's head by the whirring heels of a swung girl; another time my own hefty feet caught an unfortunate man in the diaphragm, so completely winding him that he was obliged to lie on the floor for several minutes.

And don't forget there were then no artificial stimulants. Cocktails didn't exist. A glass of champagne was permissible, but, if I remember rightly, unusual . . .

As I repicture the girls who thronged the ballrooms of my first season, what strikes me so poignantly is their one common denominator – that shiny dewy look of youth on all their faces – those expectant faces I was so soon – for we were dancing close to the brink – to see frozen into grief or, cruel turn of the screw, blank from the too early realisation that grief, like life itself, comes to an end – 'O last regret, regret can die!'

As I write, sounds, as well as images, rise out of the long ago. I hear the tender yearning strains of the Viennese valses to which we danced. Especially insistent, irresistibly inviting, the billowing lilt of the Merry Widow surges in my ears. Is this, of all valses, to me the most evocative of early youth? Even more dominantly, I hear tearing at my heart the strong, triumphant swing of the Blue Danube, at whose imperious command lovers of so many generations, impelled rather than consciously moving, have swirled, swooped, glided and revolved. I hear the whisper of their shuffling feet, and through the defiant strains of the music, thread-like but relentlessly clear, I seem to hear the words:

> 'All lovers young, all lovers must
> Consign to thee and come to dust.'

– From *Remember and Be Glad*.

Europe, Here We Come!

CORNELIA OTIS SKINNER AND
EMILY KIMBROUGH

It was settled we could meet in Montreal at whatever hotel it is that isn't the Ritz. I, clutching and occasionally kissing our steamship passage, was arriving from New York, Emily from Buffalo. That is, I hoped Emily was arriving. Some weeks previous she had sent me a rhapsodic letter which ended with the alarming words: 'I live for the moment when our boat pushes out from that dock in Winnipeg.' . . .

Mother, despite my nineteen years and a lamentable determination to look like Theda Baera, still persisted in calling me 'Baby'. She kept reminding me to put my purse in my pillow, never to speak to any strange men, always to spread paper on 'the seat' and to wire her if I arrived there safely. I quite expected her to pin my ticket on my blouse, tip the porter and tell him to make sure her little girl got off at Montreal.

Upon arrival in Montreal my emotions were indeed those of a little girl. It was my first experience of registering alone at a hotel and, far from feeling emancipated and like Theda Bara, I felt frightened and forlorn.

The clerk verified my misgivings about myself by assigning me a room so high up under the eaves I half expected pigeons to fly out of the dresser . . .

When Emily says she'll arrive around noon it can get so far around, it merges into noon of the following day. The time dragged along. I wrote some letters, studied bits of Baedeker and every fifteen minutes made certain my passport and letter of credit hadn't been stolen.

This last activity involved the opening up of a little contraption so humiliating that the memory of it even now makes me turn my attention rapidly to something else. Mother had harnessed about my person an incredible object known as a 'safety-pocket'. This was a large chamois purse that dangled at the knees in the manner of a sporran and was attached in a sort of block and tackle system of tape and buckle to an adjustable belt around the waist. It was worn. supposedly inconspicuously, under skirt and slip and I daresay in Mother's youthful and voluminously-clad day which engendered this prudent accessory, it flapped away subtly beneath yards of broad-cloth, watered-silk and batiste, and nobody was the wiser. But in my youthful and more skimpy day, everybody was not only the wiser but the more bewildered. The discovery that Emily, too, was the victim of the same motherly precaution heartened me a good deal . . .

At long last, Emily burst into the room. We were still at an age when girl friends upon meeting after a long absence, did a good deal of shrieking, and the sounds of our greeting made ring whatever the welkin is. A bellboy, barely discernible under Emily's mountain of luggage, looked on with disgust until Emily became aware of his presence and with the grand manner of royalty bestowing Maundy money, doled him out a tip. His expression deepened from one of disgust into the epitome of sullen persecution and with a suppressed snarl, he strode from the room. As he turned, I caught a glimpse of the coin Emily had handed him: 'Do you never tip more than a penny?'

'A penny? I gave him the largest coin I had.'

'Yes. And it was an English penny. Two cents in America.' Grabbing up her purse she rushed from the room crying 'Wait! I didn't mean it!' after the bellboy who by now had vanished past a turn in the corridor. It was some time before she returned. Knowing Emily and knowing that she attracts incident as blue serge attracts lint, I grew apprehensive. When finally she returned her face was the colour of bortsch before they add the sour cream. It seems that after making good with the bellboy, she had wandered back counting her change, opened a door she for some vague reason thought was ours, and had acidly remarked 'Well, I hope you feel better now' to what when she looked up proved to be an elderly gentleman completely nude. I assured her that this was just one more proof of how broadening travel could be.

She told me that what really had addled her had been the shock not so much of English money as the sight of me in that baby blue sports outfit. As a matter of fact her own travelling costume was not without its element of originality. It, too, was tweed . . . that flecked variety known as 'pepper and salt'. She had designed it herself and her mother's dressmaker had run it up. There was a skirt which was innocuous enough; with it, however, went not a jacket but a loose, rather billowing cape of the same material, lined with orange taffeta. What topped everything off, and in more ways than one, was her hat, which was also of the same tweed cloth and also run up by local talent. It had a small brim and a soft, folded crown that was meant to fit snugly to the head. Through some oversight the folds hadn't been stitched together and as a result, at the slightest breeze or toss of her head, the crown would open out like a collapsible drinking cup and rise to its full length of a good yard in the air. And there it would stay unless I found a chance to whisper to her: 'Your hat's up again . . .' Emily, who usually looked neat and chic, in this cape and Robin-Good-fellow hat seemed curiously Shakespearean and that was the last effect she'd had in mind when she designed the ensemble.

Next morning we woke up in a state of elation. June 10th had actually dawned and the world hadn't come to an end. Somehow we got to the dock and there moored alongside, smoke pouring from her smokestack, the blue peter fluttering at her mainmast, was the *Montcalm*, a real live ship, not just the paper diagram we'd been mulling over for six months. Oblivious to the jostling crowd, we stood gazing at the prosaic decks of the modest cabin-class liner, dewy-eyed, clutching each other, dropping things and holding up a line of less sensitive passengers.

The Fields saw us on board, George continuing to elucidate to Emily matters of maritime education. At last they bade us Godspeed and went ashore and not long after that the gangplank was hoisted clear. The foghorn let forth its shattering but beautiful bark and then slowly, proudly, unbelievably the little steamer moved from the dock, backed into the St Lawrence, turned her nose toward the east and headed for England.

It was a heavenly day. The engines chugged soothingly, the air was balmy and beyond the railing, hazy and serene, the tidy shores of the St Lawrence slipped past like a water colour on an endless scroll. The books in our hands sank supine on our stomachs and our eyes became glazed.

We were roused by the blast of a bugle played cacophonously in our ear.

'Our life preservers are in our cabin, aren't they?'

'Yes,' I said. 'Why?'

'Why? Didn't you hear that trumpet? It means something, doesn't it?'

'Certainly,' I answered. 'It means the First Service for lunch is ready.' And I yawned to show what an old sea-dog I was.

Two days before we were to land was the night of the ship's concert. I had been asked to participate and had agreed with alacrity. Those were the happy days when with that confidence of a Bernhardt which is vouchsafed only to the amateur I would recite at the drop of a hat and if nobody dropped a hat I'd recite anyway.

The morning of the concert dawned, and I woke to the realisation that my enthusiasm had lost some of its brightness. My throat was scrapy, my nose stopped up and it was all too apparent that I was giving birth to a fine young cold. I blamed it on the fog of the past three days and tried curing myself by lying in the sun on the top deck, where a series of vicious draughts played on my most vulnerable parts, and the smokestacks showered upon me a gentle rain of soot. By mid-afternoon my throat felt like something dangling from a hook in a butcher's shop. Towards evening I began to feel better, if slightly light-headed. I gulped down a cup of soup, dressed and put on a semblance of a make-up. That was one of the features of my dramatic display in those days. Whenever I recited, even if in a small living-room, I went on the theory that a full theatrical make-up was requisite. On this occasion I noticed that my eyes were somewhat glazed and that my cheeks didn't need much rouge, but I attributed this to excitement. The hour for the concert was announced by a boy banging a gong, and I went to the main saloon. My act wasn't due till towards the end of the programme, and for the first half I sat at one side behind the temporary stage. It was one of those routine ship's concerts. I listened in a daze, alternately burning with heat and shivering with chill. There was a high sea outside and the boat was doing a lot of pitching and tossing, which made things slightly awkward. My turn was drawing near, and Emily and I both began growing pretty nervous. Just before I went on, that conscientious drinker from Princeton brought me a hooker of straight brandy and that did the trick.

I have absolutely no memory of what I did, but it was apparently a hit. The brandy and that mixture of medicine had freed me of all inhibitions and I acted with a fine abandon. There was considerable applause and I was in a flush of what I mistook for success. The concert was followed by a gala dance with confetti and favours and those paper hats middle-aged people, if they're drunk, think are funny. The dance floor was crowded and we were never off it. I knew by now that I was ill but I didn't care. Mine was the 'tomorrow we die' spirit. I felt like the Dame aux Camélias and as if a breath would blow me away. With my hectic flush I didn't look much like the Dame aux Camélias and the only breath blowing was my brandy-laden own. I danced madly with everybody. It is like a kaleidoscopic delirium to me now but I can dimly remember the orchestra playing the 'Blue Danube' and my whirling in a dizzy waltz with Joe Aub and thinking I was pretty *Alt Wien*. I also have a distinct recollection of going out on deck with that Pride of Princeton and letting him kiss me. Girls didn't kiss much in those days. Those who did were considered 'fast'. We still had ringing in our consciences the maternal admonition that 'boys would lose all respect for us if we did'. Whenever I fell from grace in this fashion (which was whenever I had the slightest opportunity) I'd go through an aftermath of abject penitence, accusing myself of being a Magdalen. That night my abandon was so complete I felt no remorse. As a matter of fact I was incapable of feeling anything beyond a sore throat and a perpetual dry heat-wave.

I have no memory of ever getting to bed but I certainly remember waking up in the early morning and thinking I had a sprinkling of small-pox. I was much too ill to move. My breathing came with effort and a sound like a threshing machine. I moaned and lay staring at the ceiling waiting for the Fatal Reaper. Emily woke and looked at me and it was clear she was scared. She dressed and went forth to summon the ship's physician, then prompted by some fortuitous inner hunch, decided it might be wiser to get hold of one of our doctor friends. She found Joe Aub and in a frenzy yanked him down to the cabin. He looked me over, listened to my lungs and punched my stomach which, with the memory of our recent 'Blue Danube' whirl bright within me, at once embarrassed and rather pleased me. Then he told me to say 'Ah' and after I had he looked extremely grave.

'Have you ever had measles?' he asked.

'Measles? Why, no.'

'Well, my dear girl,' he said, 'you're coming down with a hell of a case.'

'Measles!' I couldn't believe him. 'But I thought I was past the age for such things.'

'Adults *can* have measles,' he said. 'And when they do it's pretty serious.'

Paul White came down and verified Joe's diagnosis, and then came the problem of what to do. If it became known I had measles they'd never let me land. The ship, after a day or two in Southampton, was to go on to Hamburg and I'd be sent in all probability to a German quarantine hospital. The prospect was too awful. I lay back on the pillows and amid a torrent of tears wailed that I didn't want to go to Germany and be nursed by a walkyrie.

The three of them went up on deck and into a huddle behind a lifeboat, where they made a solemn agreement. Emily would not report my contagious condition to the ship's doctor and neither would Paul or Joe. They might be disbarred or unfrocked or whatever it is that happens to medical men, but they'd throw in their lot with ours and take the risk. My parents were planning to be at Southampton. We'd had a wire saying so. Once having safely run the gamut of the health inspector I could go direct to a hotel where Mother would take care of me. Mother would in due course write the captain that what we'd thought was a cold had turned into measles. The main hope was that my rash wouldn't manifest itself until they'd gotten me safely on land. I spent the forenoon in a stupor, roused now and then by Emily, who would shine a painfully bright miniature flash-light (I believe they were called 'bug-lights') in my face, study its condition and say in the tone of someone trying to pep up a losing team: 'You hold that rash back!'

Later I was left comparatively alone. The day was balmy, there was a smell of land in the air and after those hours of dank fog and slate-coloured sky Emily was much too elated to bother about my measles. The misty outline of a headland lay like a cloud bank on the northern horizon. Gulls flew out to form a circling, soaring convoy, their cries like the creak of a pulley, the late afternoon sun gilding their fat snowy bellies. Fishing boats suddenly appeared and small craft began dotting the sea, making it seem a friendly lake. Occasionally someone would call out from the calm water below in a voice that rang with the unmistakable lilt of Ireland. Emily watched it all with wonder and a few tears, and then came down to our little pest-hole to see if I were still alive and to do some packing. Bottles fell over and tooth-brushes clattered about in the basin. Emily cursed and I groaned. Every now and then she'd make me down a pill or a spoonful of medicine. At other times she'd hand me a glass of something to gargle, then holding up a homely object known in some locales as a 'thunder-mug' she'd say in the dulcet tone of a night nurse: 'Come on, dear, spit for Emily.' It was a ghastly night. I was really awfully sick and Emily was really awfully scared. I tossed and moaned and Emily in helpless despair kept getting up and putting cool cloths on my brow and making me spit for Emily. Neither of us slept until towards dawn when from sheer exhaustion we dozed off and immediately afterwards our slumber was shattered by those early morning noises which all steamship personnel consider a necessary accompaniment to coming into harbour. Baggage is hurtled and banged along passageways, people scamper quite a lot, and a sleepy cabin-boy whangs a gong for some special reveille-hour breakfast which nobody dreams of going to.

My face was swollen into the shape of the harvest moon. It was the colour of Chinese lacquer and it glistened. Those spots were gathering but as yet hadn't burgeoned, which was one reason I felt so wretched. Emily told me to keep on holding them back, paralysing me with the threat that if I didn't the quarantine ward in Hamburg was yearning for me. Through it all I was dimly aware of a little boy who kept sticking his head in at our door and saying: 'Would you care to see the boots, Madam?'

'Boots?' Emily would answer. 'No.'

In a few minutes he'd be back again with the same question to which Emily would snap back the same response, each time growing more irritated. The prospect of getting me off the ship had put her nerves on edge and at his fifth or sixth appearance she lost her temper.

'*No*,' she roared at the hapless child, 'I don't want to see any boots!'

I then realised what it was all about and sick as I was laughed till I cried.

'He's the "Boots", you zany!' I managed to say. 'He's polished our shoes every day and the poor little devil wants a tip.'

Emily said 'Oh' somewhat crossly and gave it to him.

Joe Aub had left us at Cherbourg. Paul White and Emily, the only ones who knew my guilty secret, had to fix me up so I could pass the health inspector. I struggled into my clothes, and with what negligible strength I had, tried camouflaging my face with slathers of foundation cream and half the contents of a box of face powder. The effect was that of someone who had been ducking for apples in a paper-hanger's bucket. This thick coating worked for a time but then the intense heat of my face baked it into a sort of dry *papier-mâché* which, if I moved any facial muscle, cracked and revealed glimpses of that gleaming flesh. My parched lips I made up with one of those orange lip-sticks which is supposed to change colour once it's applied. It did, all right. Only instead of a delicate shade of coral, the medicine I'd been taking or something turned it into a lurid violet. With some curious notion that it would distract from the rest of my visage, I painted my mouth to look twice its normal size (and it's no sweetheart rosebud to begin with). Emily asked me gently if I wasn't being a bit spectacular and I said not at all, it was merely a case of understanding the art of the theatre, and that silenced her. The hat I selected to wear was a bright red number with a cock feather that swung down rakishly under my chin. I used to think it made me look rather like Irene Bordoni. But I didn't look like Irene Bordoni then. Emily and Paul, with saint-like tolerance, refrained from comment, not did they say anything when I topped off my startling appearance with a flowing white veil which, I pointed out, would make me less conspicuous. I guess I'd gotten a little delirious by then.

We were nearing Southampton and a second wireless arrived from Mother and Father saying they'd be at the dock and couldn't wait to see us. Catching a glimpse of myself in the mirror, I wondered how they'd feel about waiting after they did.

Emily and Paul managed somehow or other to get me upstairs and into line for health inspection. They stood me between them so that in case I collapsed they'd be there to break my fall. I flashed a ghastly smile like a ballet-dancer's at the inspector, who merely shuddered and passed me as rapidly as possible. The passport gent never even looked up. The only persons who paid any attention to me were the other passengers who stared in bewilderment at the white veil and that art of the theatre make-up which gleamed through it. The ship by now was coming up to the dock and in half an hour we'd be ashore. I was propped against some cushions in a very dark corner of a deserted card room and told not to move, which, in view of the fact I scarcely could, seemed a superfluous admonition. For what seemed to me hours I sat there swathed in my white veil and utter wretchedness. Nobody came near me except a little girl who all at once skipped into the room, spied me and came to a dead stop. For some uneasy seconds she stood before me gazing with wonder. Then in an awed whisper she said: 'Do you tell fortunes?' and without waiting for an answer turned tail and ran.

Emily had gone out on deck to locate my parents. She didn't have much trouble. They were easily distinguishable, the darlings, there in the thick of the crowd staring up at the ship – Father as if he'd been interrupted in the midst of reading and only half of him had come, and Mother like an excited little bird looking for us all over the vessel. She kept waving furiously at passengers who bore not the remotest resemblance to us. Eventually she located Emily and pointed her out to Father, who had seen her for some time and had been waving intermittently in a vague but happy manner. Mother, cupping her mouth and standing on tiptoe as if that would make her voice carry higher, called out:

'Darling! Darling!' Then she added: 'We've a surprise for you girls!'

'We've got a surprise for you too,' Emily shouted back, and Mother again nodded with the tolerant smile one bestows on a child who comes up with a present of a mud pie. Then she and Father in unison sang out: 'Where's Cornelia?'

This was the question Emily had been dreading, and having no answer for it she merely smiled and waved and pretended she hadn't heard. They halloed the question again and again but her only response was to wave and smile inanely. My parents gradually became aware that all was not as it should be. After Emily's third evasion, Father felt such nonsense had gone far enough and in a tone that made even the men on the bridge turn around, bellowed 'WHERE IS CORNELIA???'

'Oh,' Emily called back as lightly as she could and still be heard, 'she's inside. She's got a little cold.'

Mother turned pale and clutched Father's arm.

The gangplank was lowered, and down it Emily rocketed like a ball in a bowling alley, rushed straight up to Mother and Father, embraced them and said in the tense sotto-voce of a conspirator: 'Don't say a word to anybody, because if it becomes known we are lost. But Cornelia has measles.'

Whereat Father, in that voice which for fifty years thrilled the topmost occupant of the highest seat in the gallery, whooped 'MEASLES!!!' and would have whooped it again only Mother put a hand with a handkerchief in it over his mouth.

'Where is she, Emily?' she asked quietly.

Emily told them they had me cooling in a dark corner, and that the doctor was with me.

They led me on to the deck, where in the harsh light of day I looked a good deal worse. Bits of that facial calcimine had flaked off revealing the fact that those long-awaited spots were coming out. But somehow the four of them got me off the ship and on to the dock.

I put on really quite a commendable act; laughed and chatted giddily, passed the customs in a dazed but grand manner, and sprang with a spurt of super-human activity into a touring car the family had waiting there for us all. This was the surprise Mother had in store for us.

The hotel was one of those British terminal ones, part caravanserai, part ticket office, right on the tracks, the sort that gives the impression of having engines running in and out of the potted palms. In the lobby I kept up my act of laughter and carefree abandon. We were allotted rooms, although the clerk gaped at me in my white veil and formidable complexion. But I carried it off, and didn't let down until I reached the room. There, once they got me in bed, I went completely and noisily delirious. And my, but that was fun! With the porter and the chambermaid coming in and God knows who else, and me sitting up in bed with the art of the theatre sagging on my face but still lurid. My four attendants would close in around me as if I were giving them football signals, screening me as best they could, then trying to hold me down as soon as the coast was clear. At last the outsiders departed and with them the threat of being found out. I sank back on a burning pillow, and for the next few days I was awfully, awfully sick.

– From *Our Hearts Were Young and Gay.*

Miss Tennant Steps Out

MARGOT ASQUITH

The first year I came out in London I did not receive many invitations
to balls and knew but few people; what I really enjoyed was riding
in the Row. I bought a beautiful hack for myself at Tattersalls, 15.2,
bright bay with black points and so well-balanced that if I had ridden
it with my face to its tail I should hardly have known the difference.
I called it Tatts; it was bold as a lion, vain as a peacock and extremely
moody. One day, when I was mounted to ride in the Row, my papa
kept me waiting so long at the door of 40 Grosvenor Square that I
thought I would ride Tatts into the front hall and give him a call; it
meant going up one step from the pavement to the porch and another
through the double doors held open by the footmen. Unluckily,
after a somewhat cautious approach by Tatts up the last step into the
marble hall, he caught his reflection in a mirror. At this he instantly
stood erect upon his hind legs, crashing my tall hat into the crystal
chandelier. His four legs all gave way on the polished floor and down
we went with a noise like thunder, the pony on top of me, the chandelier on the top of him and my father and the footmen helpless
spectators. I was up and on Tatts' head in a moment, but not before
he had kicked a fine old English chest into a jelly. This misadventure
upset my father's temper and my pony's nerve, as well as preventing
me from dancing for several days.

My second scrape was more serious. I engaged myself to be married.
If any young Miss reads this autobiography and wants a little
advice from a very old hand, I will say to her, when a man threatens
to commit suicide after you have refused him, you may be quite sure

that he is a vain, petty fellow or a great goose; if you felt any doubt about your decision before, you need have none after this and under no circumstances must you give way. To marry a man out of pity is folly; and, if you think you are going to influence the kind of fellow who has 'never had a chance, poor devil', you are profoundly mistaken. One can only influence the strong characters in life, not the weak; and it is the height of vanity to suppose that you can make an honest man of anyone. My *fiancé* was neither petty nor a goose, but a humorist; I do not think he meant me to take him seriously, but in spite of my high spirits I was very serious and he was certainly more in love with me than anyone had ever been before. He was a fine rider and gave me a mount with the Beaufort hounds.

When I told my mother of my engagement, she sank upon a settee, put a handkerchief to her eyes, and said:

'You might as well marry your groom!'

I struggled very hard to show her how worldly she was. Who wanted money? Who wanted position? Who wanted brains? Nothing in fact was wanted, except my will!

I was much surprised, a few days later, to hear from G., whom I met riding in the Row, that he had called every day of the week but been told by the footman that I was out. The under-butler, who was devoted to me, said sadly, when I complained:

'I am afraid, miss, your young gentleman has been forbidden the house.'

Forbidden the house! I rushed to my sister Charty and found her even more upset than my mother. She pointed out with some truth that Lucy's marriage and the obstinacy with which she had pursued it had gone far towards spoiling her early life; but 'the squire', as Graham Smith was called, although a character part, was a man of perfect education and charming manners. He had beaten all the boys at Harrow, won a hundred steeplechases and loved books; whereas my young man knew little about anything but horses and, she added, would be no companion to me when I was ill or old.

I flounced about the room and said that forbidding him the house was grotesque and made me ridiculous in the eyes of the servants. I ended a passionate protest by telling her gravely that if I changed my mind he would undoubtedly commit suicide. This awful news was received with an hilarity which nettled me.

CHARTY: 'I should have thought you had too much sense of humour and Mr G. too much common sense for either of you to believe this. He must think you very vain. . . .'

I did not know at all what she meant and said with the utmost gravity:

'The terrible thing is that I believe I have given him a false impression of my feelings for him; for, though I love him very much, I would never have promised to marry him if he had not said he was going to kill himself.' Clasping my two hands together and greatly moved, I concluded: 'If I break it off now and *anything should* happen, my life is over and I shall feel as if I had murdered him.'

CHARTY (*looking at me with a tender smile*): 'I should risk it, darling.'

One night, when I was dining *tête-à-tête* with my old friend Godfrey Webb, in his flat in Victoria Street, my father sent the brougham for me with a message to ask if I would accompany him to supper at Lord and Lady Randolph Churchill's, where we had been invited to meet the Prince of Wales. I said I should be delighted if I could keep on the dress that I was wearing, but as it was late and I had to get up early next day I did not want to change my clothes; he said he supposed my dress would be quite smart enough, so we drove to the Randolph Churchill's house together . . .

I was wearing a white muslin dress with transparent chemise sleeves, a fichu and a long skirt with a Nattier blue taffeta sash, I had taken a bunch of rose carnations out of a glass and pinned them into my fichu with three diamond ducks given me by Lord Carmichael, our Peeblesshire friend and neighbour.

On my arrival at the Churchills', I observed all the fine ladies wearing ball-dresses off the shoulder and their tiaras. This made me very conspicuous and I wished profoundly that I had changed into something smarter before going out.

The Prince of Wales had not arrived and, as our hostess was giving orders to the White Hungarian Band, my father and I had to walk into the room alone.

[73]

I saw several of the ladies eyeing my toilette and, having painfully sharp ears, I heard some of their remarks:

'Do look at Miss Tennant! She is in her nightgown!'

'I suppose it is meant to be "ye olde Englishe pictury!" I wonder she has not let her hair down like the Juliets at the Oakham balls!'

Another, more charitable, said:

'I daresay no one told her that the Prince of Wales was coming . . . Poor child! What a shame!'

And finally a man said:

'There is nothing so odd as the passion some people have for self-advertisement; it only shows what it is to be intellectual!'

At that moment our hostess came up to us with a charming *accueil*.

My father and I were much relieved at her greeting; and while we were talking the Prince of Wales arrived. The ladies fell into position, ceased chattering and made subterranean curtsies. He came straight up to me and told me I was to sit on the other side of him at supper. I said, hanging my head with becoming modesty and in a loud voice:

'Oh no, Sir, I am not dressed at all for the part! I had better slip away, I had no notion this was going to be such a smart party . . . I expect some of the ladies here think I have insulted them by coming in my nightgown!'

I saw everyone straining to hear what the Prince's answer would be, but I took good care that we should move out of earshot. At that moment Lord Hartington[1] came up and told me I was to go in to supper with him. More than ever I wished I had changed my dress, for now everyone was looking at me with even greater curiosity than hostility.

The supper was gay and I had remarkable talks which laid the foundation of my friendship both with King Edward and the Duke of Devonshire. The Prince told me he had had a dull youth, as Queen Victoria could not get over the Prince Consort's death and kept up an exaggerated mourning. He said he hoped that when I met his mother I should not be afraid of her, adding, with a charming smile, that with the exception of John Brown everybody was. I assured

1 The late Duke of Devonshire.

[74]

him with perfect candour that I was afraid of no one. He was much amused when I told him that before he had arrived that evening some of the ladies had whispered that I was in my nightgown and I hoped he did not think me lacking in courtesy because I had not put on a ball-dress. He assured me that on the contrary he admired my frock very much and thought I looked like an old picture. This remark made me see uncomfortable visions of the Oakham ball and he did not dispel them by adding:

'You are so original! You must dance the cotillion with me.'

I told him that I could not possibly stay, it would bore my father stiff, as he hated sitting up late; also I was not dressed for dancing and had no idea there was going to be a ball. When supper was over, I made my best curtsy and, after presenting my father to the Prince, went home to bed.

– From *The Autobiography of Margot Asquith.*

Let me go Free!

ELIZABETH HAMILTON

At college the park was all about us. From the library windows we saw crocuses in the grass, and daffodils, and tree tops swaying against the sky. The library was a place of refuge. There was silence there. You could read or think or dream the hours away. In winter, when the world outside was grey and cold, it was warm and friendly in the library. As the day closed in, the reading lamps flung white circles of light in the surrounding shadows. That was the loveliest hour. I would be reluctant to put away my books and face the outside world and the journey home.

Sometimes, if there was a party or a dance, I would spend the night at a nearby students' hostel. We would sit up till all hours drinking cocoa and putting the world to rights.

Or maybe, as I was getting ready to go, I would see on the notice board a scrap of paper with my name scrawled across it in crimson chalk. A telephone message. Perhaps an invitation from friends at Queen's Gate. And I would change hastily into an evening dress that used to hang in my locker in case of an emergency. It was made of lilac-coloured net and decorated with velvet bows of a deeper violet shade. Or it might be from Philip. Would I meet him? No need to change then. I would hurry through the park, across the canal bridge, and find him waiting, in the lamplight, by Marylebone Church. A gaunt figure. His hands plunged deep into the pockets of his greatcoat and the collar high about his ears. He, too, was a student, with no more money than most. We would eat our supper in a café in Paddington Street. Beans or spaghetti piled high on the plate and tea in thick white cups. And he would read Baudelaire aloud and talk of his plans for a novel on Radegunde, Queen of France.

I would travel home by the last train, maybe, which shuffled its way from station to station; cold, almost empty and ill-lit. At last I would reach my destination and, flinging myself out of the carriage, toil up the station slope, stupid with sleep. It might be a night of stars; and, as I gazed into their glinting splendour, my weariness would suddenly drop from me as a garment, and I would seem, as it were, to be caught up into the infinity of the heavens. As I crossed the railway bridge at the top of the slope I would look back and down into the soft, indigo darkness lit with the yellow, red and green lights of the station.

In a moment there would be a turning. Here I would instinctively look for the light that glowed through the rose-red window curtain of my parents' bedroom. The light was as a welcoming beacon. I would quicken my steps. In a moment I would be in the gate, up the stairs, recounting the doings of the day.

And, yet not all of them. For, as I thrust my childhood behind me, a reticence unknown before constrained me from sharing fully with my parents, or indeed with anyone, except of my own choice, the ideas and ambitions and experiences that were crowding in upon me.

The light from my parents' room was a symbol. It stood for their steadfast love; for the warmth and security of my home. I hailed it and I rejoiced to see it. And sometimes I asked myself could it be that one day this light would no longer shine its welcome? I knew that the day must surely come, and yet the idea seemed so remote as to be impossible.

But much as I welcomed this light, there were moments when I almost wished I would not find it shining – when I felt relief if, as sometimes happened, my parents were already asleep when I came in – so tangled, so conflicting are the emotions, as affection and habits of childhood struggle with the adult desire to live a life of one's own; think; believe; disbelieve; love; hate; be happy or unhappy in one's own way, unbeholden and unknown to anyone. 'Let me alone, everybody,' a strange voice inside me seemed to cry. 'Let me alone. *Let* me make mistakes if need be. Only let me alone – to find my own way. Do not try to be kind! Do not help me! it puts on me a burden of obligation, a debt of gratitude which, because it cannot be repaid, becomes a burden of guilt. Let me go free! leave hold of your reins of love! I'll find my way alone. . . . and when I have found it, then maybe, I will come back.'

– From *A River Full of Stars*.

PART TWO

Happy Families

Married Daughters

JOSEPHINE BLUMENFELD

Flavia

Flavia wants to shop. Will I look after the baby? 'I'd love to.'

She arrives with Lucas – (why on earth is it called Lucas?) – and puts him in the garden in his pram.

'He'll stay like that till five o'clock,' she says. 'You don't have to worry.'

'What happens at five o'clock?' I feel suddenly a little sick.

She assures me it is nothing. A small matter of changing nappies, rose-hip syrup from a bottle, a rusk to suck, and a roll on his rug.

'He adores his rusk,' she says and she smiles a secret smile recalling many sweet rusk times.

She leaves contented and gurgling Lucas in the garden, and we watch it from the drawing-room window. It laughs, it coos, it isn't sick, its eyes focus and it doesn't look as though it were going mad. It looks nice. It is nice. I quite like it, I even feel proud to be its grandmother, and make a vow not to be intimidated by it, but to go on being proud of it. After all, it is my son's son, my own flesh and blood, and if I want to hark back, which I don't, it's my own fault, because if I hadn't given birth to my son, he never would have given birth to his son. It's a pretty pink and white. It will be fun to have it to myself for a whole afternoon.

Flavia says she will be back at six. She waves, I wave. We all wave. She is pretty too. I am lucky in the two of them.

I creep to the window and peer at Lucosade (or whatever his name is) through the side of the curtain. The curtain moves; he sees me, and waves a menacing arm in my direction. I drop to the floor like

[81]

a stone and wait, and although I have sat on a drawing-pin, nothing will get me up till I think he is asleep. It seems a long time, it is a long time, with a drawing-pin sticking into one's behind, but pain has nothing on fear. I wait.

After a while I get up and turn on the wireless and open the type-writer. If I type fast enough and turn the wireless high enough, I shan't hear anything. If one doesn't hear, one doesn't know.

Type for a bit, then look again. It has changed its position and is lying face downwards. Its red, knitted hat has slipped over its face and from the window it looks as though the cap strings, tightly twined round its neck, are eating into the flesh. It looks as though it had suffocated and hanged itself.

Should I go out? It is only ten past three, and she said it would be all right till five. Decide to leave it. If it is dead I can't bring it back to life by five, and if it isn't dead at least it's quiet.

Go back to typewriter.

North country lady on Woman's Hour giving talk on family life in the Yorkshire Dales, says: 'Yung baibies are luverly things. I've 'ad twelve of them meself, and I said to my hoosband only larst week, I wouldn't mind another twelve if we 'ad the wherewhitharl to educaete them.'

She moost be mad. Switch off.

Five o'clock comes at last. Comb hair, make up face and wash hands. This gives me courage. I need courage. I am Mother Courage. Don't laugh at own pun, but go on knees and pray by the sofa.

'Please God don't let it be dead or angry.'

How could I say to Flavia, when she comes back at six: 'Glucosade is dead. He died of red, woollen hat strings and suffocation.'

Creep into garden and look. He isn't dead. He's on his back blowing bubbles through his own spit. He frowns when he sees me, and screams. A stream of perspiration runs down the back of my neck to my waist, and seeps through small holes on my forehead. Pick him up. He is terribly heavy, terribly hot and terribly wet, like boiling seaweed. All the blankets, pillows, pram covers and mattresses come up with him. I can't separate them so carry the whole lot into the house. By now he is fighting mad, lashing out, clawing at my nose and I can't see anything. Dump the lot on the floor and rush for rose-hip syrup. Never knew roses had hips till now, but it's too late to think about that. Pick up gyrating bundle and push teat into his mouth. He ceases fire, lies back in my arms and gazes at me with the unflinching stare of a hen. Suddenly he winks. I take it as a signal that he wants to draw breath and pull teat out of his mouth. It was the wrong signal and he starts up again. Stick teat in again and he swigs whole bottle-worth of rose-hip. Flavia said only a little, but whatever she said means nothing now; we have gone too far.

Put him on his back on rug and try to get off wet nappies, but he squirms, fights, rolls himself into a tight ball and won't stay flat, In the tussle his clothes come off, he is suddenly naked, and his legs turn blue. I ram in the rusk, it goes down in one and he chokes. Now his face is as blue as his legs. I pick him up and hold him upside down. Ordinary red-coloured blood seeps back into his face and he sicks up rusk. Try again to get off nappies, but he won't co-operate. Give him celluloid rattle to hold while I fold dry nappy. He grabs big end, as round as an outsize orange, and tries to milk it. I try to make him milk the other end, which is narrow and milkable, but he knows best; clutches violently to middle bit with clenched fist and goes on milking round bit. What a maddening man he is going to be! I wouldn't marry him for anything. Suppose Flavia never came back? Suppose she had been knocked down by a bus and was lying dead in the road? I'd have to make quick arrangements. Give him to a virgin lady of forty-seven with means. Wrap him in brown paper with just the head sticking out, and leave him on a doorstep in the snow.

Go automatically to string and brown paper drawer in tallboy, but stop short on hearing Flavia in the hall.

Throw waterproof pram cover over his nakedness and leave room on pretext of getting tea.

When I get back everything has changed. The room is cool and quiet; sun streams in through the open window; blankets, rugs, rattles and nappies have converged as if by magic into neatly rolled bundles in blue raffia basket, which sports sporting white woollen rabbit nibbling green raffia grass by the handle. Glucosade has reverted to pretty pink and white and is burrowing smugly in Flavia's pink and white bosom. Rose-hips wouldn't melt in his mouth.

Well-being, peace and the understanding of things which are undeniably right pervade the air.

'Was he good? Did he have his rusk? Isn't he sweet with his rusk?'

Flavia's peach-soft face glows with pride and love as she questions me over Glucosade's nestling head.

Anna

Anna, Llewellyn, Saul and newborn baby with unpronounceable Welsh name arrive by Land-Rover in the middle of night from Wales.

They are two days before schedule. They always arrive before schedule. I should know by now, but I don't know by now. Why does one never know what one knows? Why does one never know 'by now'?

As soon as they arrive there is a feeling of disruption, chaos, caravanserai-ism; and things I have never worried about before start to creak, break and spring out.

Saul stretches out his fat arms from under the red flannel shawl, catches hold of my under lip, beams and murmurs: 'Dordoign'. He smells of Wales and hay. The baby in handwoven basket squirms and screams. Anna drops everything, flings her arms round me and Saul. Her glasses, which are held together by Elastoplast, fall off her short shiny nose and she doesn't pick them up. Huddled in airman's fur-lined jacket, Icelandic sweater, black ski-ing combinations to the ankle, embroidered blue Bulgarian slippers, long Welsh skirt made out of long Welsh shawl and Black Watch tartan scarf tied over black hair, it is difficult to tell which way up she is.

From behind all this her eyes blaze like the blue glass in police station lamps.

'Aren't we lovely?' she sings. 'Aren't you lovely? Isn't it all lovely?'

Llewellyn staggers in under bursting brown paper parcels, half-open suitcases, a bird cage, a bowl of cream oozing over the sides, a sack of books and a dead bunch of daffodils.

We set up cot and put Saul to bed. He stands on his head, his orange nightgown falling over his head like a tent, says two more 'Dordoign's', then burrows his round, tired body under the blankets and sleeps. Anna feeds the newly born on the stairs.

So swiftly that I have hardly had time to notice, my neat little house has become an intellectual rummage stall. There is Strindberg and orange juice in the lavatory, Dostoevsky on the stairs, Ibsen on the gas stove, Freud in the grate, exercise books under the beds, unsharpened pencils in the tea-cups, tins of baby powder on the sofa, nappies on the window sills, Gerard Manley Hopkins on the landing and Leonardo's *Notebooks* in the linen cupboard.

Milk boils over saucepans, gas jets blaze with nothing to blaze under, ovens are left on all night, taps run. We are a 'lived-in house' and get to bed at three.

Can't sleep, and do all the things people do who can't sleep. Punch and pinch up pillows, heave up sheets, stick feet out at end of bed. Feet freeze, body burns, mouth dries. Get up for drink of water, water cold and sets teeth aching, stumble back yawning and fall over Fanny who thinks it is morning, is wagging tail and wants biscuit out of biscuit tin. Biscuit tin empty. Get back to bed and try to read *The Bible Designed to be Read as Literature.* 'The first shall be last and the last shall be first.' This applies to Anna, my first-born, last up in the morning, last to bed at night, last for meals and first in leaving undone that which she should have done.

They are to stay for a week. '*The Bible Designed to be Read as Literature*' says: 'There is a time for everything.'

Awake all night herding and counting sheep. They breed as I count, get their legs stuck in swamps and their heads between wire fencing.

In the morning Anna goes off to British Museum directly after breakfast leaving me with broken biscuits, an uncollapsible collapsible pram, a play-pen with nails sticking out in the wrong direction, Saul, who has found an axe in the garden, and a month-old baby which has to be fed every four hours.

Llewellyn goes to the Tate Gallery.

'We'll be back,' they say and then wave. People think that by waving everything is going to be all right.

[85]

By lunch-time the newly born is yelling to be fed. Llewellyn arrives. 'You see,' he says. 'I said I would be back for lunch.' School friend of Anna's arrives. Having passed through the stages of Communism, Existentialism, Roman Catholicism, Buddhism and Deep Breathing, she is now a moderately clean 'do it yourself' trained hospital nurse with only pale toe-nails peeping through leather sandals to show that she was ever anything but a nice person with square teeth and a happy smile.

We sit and wait for Anna. We daren't have lunch in the middle of the screams. But what can we do? I can't feed it, my milking days being over. Llewellyn can't feed it, and Anna's school friend can't feed it because one imagines, or vainly hopes, that she is still a virgin, and Fanny, even though she has had sixteen puppies in her day can't feed it either, there is nothing for it but to wait.

Anna arrives an hour late. Horrified that we should have worried or waited, she feeds the baby, handing out pictures of Egyptian mummies she has seen in British Museum with spare hand. 'British Museum so peaceful,' she says.

After lunch Llewellyn says he has to buy books in Charing Cross Road and order hay lifts in Seven Dials. Anna and school friend take Saul to the Park. The newly born one is left in its basket.

Anna and school friend arrive back in time for tea.

'We don't want tea,' Anna says, 'we've only brought Saul back. We are going to see the Persian Miniature Paintings. Wanda should see the Persian Miniatures.'

'Where are the Persian Miniatures?' I ask with sinking heart. They don't know. We look up Persian Miniature Paintings. They are showing at the Arts Council in St James's Square. It shuts at five. It is now half-past four. It will take them half an hour to get there.

I am suddenly firm. 'You can't see the Persian Miniatures, they are too far. The baby will be screaming again and anyway who really wants to see Persian Miniature Paintings? We all know what they are like.'

'Wanda doesn't.' Anna looks suddenly sad and much smaller, as though someone had hit her on the head. She has always looked sad and small when she hasn't had her own way.

I say: 'I will tell Wanda about Persian Miniatures instead.'

Wanda sits beside me meekly and I tell her about Persian Miniature Paintings.

She listens intently as though she were a little deaf.

'Have you been to see them?' she asks at length. I tell her I don't have to see them. I say I am half Persian on my grandmother's side and the feeling for Persian Miniatures is strong within me.

She thanks me politely and follows Anna to the studio. Later as I am pulling up weeds near the studio window I hear them muttering to each other. It is a kind of cheated mutter. In it there is a plan to go early next morning to see the Persian Miniature Paintings.

– From *Pin a Rose on Me*.

Mother and Son

WILLIAM PLOMER

Toby, who was obviously feeling some nervous strain . . . said
he would seek relief . . . in painting. He would paint some still-
lifes.

'None of your crumpled dinner-napkins for me,' he said, 'with a
newspaper, a coffee-pot, and a pound of sour apples. No. Opulence
is what I'm after.'

The trouble was that he now elected to paint in his mother's
drawing-room. He could have used that upper room from which I
had once fled, or he could have hired a studio, but he liked painting
at home, and he liked the light in the drawing-room, so a round
Empire table, inlaid with lapis lazuli, was heaped up with a fantastically
lavish display of things, many of which in former years not long
past the d'Arfeys or the Mountfaucons would have produced on
their own estates, but which now, so times had changed, had to be
ordered at much expense from the florist's, the poulterer's, and the
fishmonger's. In the middle of the table, an immense urn held a sheaf
of arum lilies and kniphofias, with huge roses and the big scabious
whose flowers look like dark red pincushions stuck with white pins,
with branches of magnolia and white buddleia, heads of crown
imperial, sprays of love-lies-bleeding, and specimens of a new white
iris with petals like very fine silk handkerchiefs, or like delicate
membranes scribbled over with a fine puce network – all these inter-
mingled with trails of a showy creeper with tubular crimson flowers.
Heaped up round the urn were melons with figured rinds, bunches of
monstrously big black and white grapes, a pineapple, clusters of
lychees, some peaches, nectarines, and avocado pears, together with

a fresh and tasselled ear or two of maize, the husks partly open and revealing what looked like perfect rows of grinning pearly teeth. A seventeenth-century clock of crystal and silver (now in the British Museum) was slightly flushed with the ripeness and efflorescence that overhung it, and just touching it were the relaxed-looking claws of one of a brace of guinea-fowl that lay prone, with lolling heads, like two neatly dressed but flighty matrons who had 'passed out' as a result of drinking too much. The head and forequarters of a hare dangled over the edge of the table, and beneath it, on the carpet, a Meissen sauceboat – part of a dinner service which the King of Saxony had given to Morven Mountfaucon's father – had been care-carefully placed by Toby to catch any blood that might drip from the hare's nose. In the foreground of the whole composition, in itself a work of talent, were a heavyweight lobster and a bouquet of gar-denias tied with a bow of crimson velvet ribbon.

Round this tremendous spectacle hovered Mrs Mountfaucon, a tremendous spectacle herself in a gauzy and expensive summer frock which Butterball Evans had encouraged her to buy from a famous new dressmaker. She was a prey to conflicting emotions which made her prance about restlessly, like a colossal butterfly uncertain where to settle.

'For God's sake, Mother, keep still!' cried Toby, tapping his foot irritably on the carpet.

Poor Mrs Mountfaucon clasped her hands together as if trying an exercise in self-control. She knew that, whatever she said, her 'head would be bitten off', but putting on a sweet and childlike look she said with a sigh: 'Oh, what a marvellous arrangement!' She was right, and it would have been difficult not to admire the skill and boldness and prevailing red and white of the arrangement, especially if one's own child had made it.

'Now for God's sake, Mother, do tell that crackpot maid not to come near this table, or I'll tear the pants off her.'

'My dear Toby,' Mrs Mountfaucon unclasped her hands and spread them out in a large and confident gesture full of warmth and humanity, 'if you mean our poor "Countess", I'm afraid there's nothing she'd like better.'

'. . . Well, then, tell her simply that if I catch her in here with a duster I'll ram it down her throat.'

'Toby dear,' his mother became suddenly grave, 'you'll have to be very quick with your painting. In this weather, I mean.'

'I know, Mother, I know,' he said petulantly; and then, rolling a naughty eye, 'But after all it won't matter if the drawing-room smells a bit *faisandé*. We're a bit *faisandé* as a family, aren't we? Our whole civilization is a bit *faisandé* – so another little aroma won't do us any harm.'

'Oh, Toby!' She ducked her head and smilingly looked up at me as if to say: 'Isn't he a caution?' Then she turned to him and said solemnly: 'You might get diphtheria.'

'Why diphtheria?' Toby was adjusting his easel. 'What an extraordinary idea! Why not typhus, leprosy, bilharzia, botulism, psittacosis, or yaws? And now,' he propped a large clean canvas on the easel and began to fix it in place, 'you'd better leave me, or I shall never get this thing started.'

'Very well, dear . . . Oh, it's going to be a *wonderful* picture!'

'That'll *do*, Mother.'

With her gauzes flying and her head down, Mrs Mountfaucon almost ran out of the room, and I followed less precipitately.

The next day the sky was overcast and the light in the drawing-room was 'all wrong', so Toby said, but he worked undisturbed all the morning. I came down a little before luncheon and tactfully paid no attention to what he was doing. I may have fancied it, but the air seemed to me already slightly gamy. Presently Mrs Mountfaucon came in.

'Can't you do something about this damned thing, Mother?' said Toby, without looking up from his palette. 'It won't keep still.'

'What thing, dear?'

'This abominable lobster, of course. It can't possibly be dead. How can I paint a thing that keeps waving its antennæ at me? It's no more a still-life than you are. Can't you kill it, or do *something*?'

'Very well, dear, I'll see. But it will have to be moved.'

'Oh, all right then, let it – so long as nothing else is touched.'

'You're going out to luncheon, you said?'

'Yes, but I shall come back later and go straight on painting.'

I was remaining to eat with Mrs Mountfaucon. As soon as Toby had gone out she came back to deal with the lobster. She had put on a large pale-grey hat trimmed with a spray of realistic artificial ivy, and was carrying a very small basket and a handkerchief embroidered with forget-me-nots. I asked if I could help, and she said she would be delighted if I came with her, though 'it' would only take a minute or two. I went to put on my hat, and when I came back she had got the lobster on to the basket rather than into it and had spread the handkerchief over its back; the creature protruded a good way beyond the edge of the basket at both ends. She slipped the handle of the basket over her arm, in the style of Little Red Riding Hood, and then she tripped along the hall and I followed her out into the street. I supposed we were going to the fishmonger's.

Two women were gossiping on the pavement. One of them, as soon as she caught sight of Mrs Mountfaucon's hat, nudged the other. When she saw the little basket and the lobster sticking out of it, she gave her a second and more violent nudge. Serenely unconscious and full of maternal solicitude, Mrs Mountfaucon pranced round the corner, but not in the direction of the fishmonger's. She made straight for the chemist's, a somewhat imposing shop, old-established and with an air of luxury. As I followed her in, a severe-looking, very clean, youngish man, rather like a solicitor, materialised behind the counter. Mrs Mountfaucon paused in the middle of the shop.

'Good afternoon,' she said, with her sweetest smile, the midday sunshine glinting in her very golden curls as she waved a white-gloved hand towards the little basket. 'I have a lobster here.'

The chemist could hardly believe his ears or eyes.

'Pardon?' he said.

'A *lobster*,' said Mrs Mountfaucon in her most winsome manner. She withdrew the forget-me-not handkerchief as if she were unveiling a memorial. The lobster waved a deprecatory feeler.

'You see,' she explained, 'my son is painting it. A still-life, you know.' She smiled sweetly. 'But unfortunately it simply *won't* keep still.'

The chemist shrank behind his glassy barricade of bath salts and laxatives, and Mrs Mountfaucon glanced at me with a look of puzzled inquiry. 'Perhaps I'd better buy something,' she murmured to me. Then aloud to him she said: 'Oh, and I want some scent. Have you got a bottle of *Mon Béguin*? If not, I'll take *Folie Lunaire*.'

As the man hesitated, apparently hypnotised by the lobster, she said ingratiatingly: 'I was wondering if you couldn't do something to it – some drug, perhaps, just a mere whiff of something, something *humane*, like veronal perhaps? To make it keep still, poor thing, and gently put it out of its misery.'

The chemist recovered himself.

'I'm sorry, madam,' he said coldly. 'I couldn't undertake to do that. You'd better take it back to the fishmonger.'

'Oh, how right you are! Now why didn't I think of that at first? *Good* afternoon!' she said, restored the handkerchief to its place, and turned to go. As the door was about to close behind us, the snooty expression which the man had assumed instantly faded. 'Blimey!' I heard him say, as he hurried to the back of the shop, no doubt to tell the dispenser what he had just heard and seen.

Before Toby returned, the lobster was back in its place: it had been given its quietus by the fishmonger. But that generously planned still-life was never finished. Petals and pollen fell from the flowers on to the clock, the fruit, and the game. The ripest of the fruit grew soft, discoloured, and then rotten. The two guinea-fowls and the hare began to assail the nose. And at last the 'Countess', wearing an expression of distaste, was allowed to clear away the whole arrangement.

– From *Museum Pieces*.

Fun with the Gilbreths

FRANK B. GILBRETH, JR.

AND

ERNESTINE GILBRETH CAREY

We spent our summers at Nantucket, Massachusetts, where Dad bought two lighthouses, which had been abandoned by the government, and a ramshackle cottage, which looked as if it had been abandoned by Coxey's Army. Dad had the lighthouses moved so that they flanked the cottage. He and Mother used one of them as an office and den. The other served as a bedroom for three of the children.

He named the cottage *The Shoe*, in honour of Mother, who, he said, reminded him of the old woman who lived in one.

Customarily, en route from Montclair to Nantucket, we spent the night in an hotel in New London, Connecticut. Dad knew the hotel manager and all of the men at the desk, and they used to exchange loud and good-natured insults for the benefit of the crowds that followed us in from the street.

'Oh, Lord, look what's coming,' the manager called when we entered the door. And then to an assistant: 'Alert the fire department and the house detective. It's the Gilbreths. And take that cigar-cutter off the counter and lock it in the safe.'

'Do you still have that dangerous guillotine?' Dad grinned. 'I know you'll be disappointed to hear that the finger grew in just as good as new. Show the man your finger, Ernestine.'

Ernestine held up the little finger of her right hand. On a previous visit she had pushed it inquisitively into the cigar-cutter, and had lost about an eighth of an inch of it. She had bled considerably on

[93]

a rug, while Dad tried to fashion a tourniquet and roared inquiries about whether there was a doctor in the house.

'Tell me,' Dad remarked, as he picked up a pen to register in the big book, 'do my Irishmen come cheaper by the dozen?'

'Irishmen! If you were wearing a sheet, you'd call them Arabs. How many of them are there, anyway? Last year, when I went to make out your bill, you claimed there were only seven. I can count at least a dozen of them now.'

'It's quite possible there might have been some additions since then,' Dad conceded.

'Front, boy. Front, boy. Front, boy, Front, boy. You four boys show Mr and Mrs Gilbreth and their seven – or so – Irishmen to 503, 504, 505, and 506. And mind you take good care of them, too.'

When we first started going to Nantucket, which is off the tip of Cape Cod, automobiles weren't allowed on the island, and we'd leave the Pierce Arrow in a garage at New Bedford, Massachusetts. Later, when the automobile ban was lifted, we'd take the car with us on the *Gay Head* or the *Sankaty*, the steamers which plied between the mainland and the island. Dad had a frightening time backing the automobile up the gang-plank. Mother insisted that we get out of the car and stand clear. Then she'd beg Dad to put on a lifebuoy.

'I know you and it are going into the water one of these days,' she warned.

'Doesn't anybody, even my wife, have confidence in my driving?' he would moan. Then on a more practical note: 'Besides, I can swim.'

The biggest problem, on the boat and in the car, was Martha's two canaries, which she had won for making the best recitation in Sunday School. All of us, except Dad, were fond of them. Tom Grieves, the handyman, who had to clean up the cage, named the birds Peter Soil and Maggie Mess. Mother wouldn't let us use those full names; she said they were 'Eskimo.' (Eskimo was Mother's description of anything that was off-colour, revolting, or evil-minded.) We called the birds simply Peter and Maggie.

On one trip, Fred was holding the cage on the stern of the ship while Dad backed the car aboard. Somehow, the wire door popped open and the birds escaped. They flew to a piling on the dock, and then to a roof of a warehouse. When Dad, with the car finally stowed away, appeared on deck, three of the younger children were sobbing. They made so much noise that the captain heard them and came off the bridge.

'What's the trouble now, Mr Gilbreth?' he asked.

'Nothing,' said Dad, who saw a chance to put thirty miles between himself and the canaries. 'You can shove off at any time, Captain.'

'No one tells me when to shove off until I'm ready to shove off,' the captain announced stubbornly. He leaned over Fred. 'What's the matter, son?'

'Peter and Maggie,' bawled Fred. 'They've gone over the rail.'

'My God,' the captain blanched. 'I've been afraid this would happen ever since you Gilbreths started coming to Nantucket.'

'Peter and Maggie aren't Gilbreths,' Dad said irritatedly. 'Why don't you just forget about the whole thing and shove off?'

The captain leaned over Fred again. 'Peter and Maggie who? Speak up, boy!'

Fred stopped crying. 'I'm not allowed to tell you their last names,' he said. 'Mother says they're Eskimo.'

The captain was bewildered. 'I wish someone would make sense,' he complained. 'You say Peter and Maggie, the Eskimos, have disappeared over the rail?'

Fred nodded. Dad pointed to the empty cage. 'Two canaries,' Dad shouted, 'known as Peter and Maggie and by other aliases, have flown the coop. No matter. We wouldn't think of delaying you further.'

'Where did they fly to, sonny?'

Fred pointed to the roof of the warehouse. The captain sighed.

'I can't stand to see children cry,' he said. He walked back to the bridge and started giving orders.

Four crew members, armed with crab-nets, climbed to the roof of the warehouse. While passengers shouted encouragement from the rail, the men chased the birds across the roof, back to the dock, on to the rigging of the ship, and back to the warehouse again. Finally

[95]

Peter and Maggie disappeared altogether, and the captain had to give up.

'I'm sorry, Mr Gilbreth,' he said. 'I guess we'll have to shove off without your canaries.'

'You've been too kind already,' Dad beamed.

Dad felt good for the rest of the trip, and even managed to convince Martha of the wisdom of throwing the empty, but still smelly, bird-cage over the side of the ship.

The next day, after we settled in our cottage, a cardboard box arrived from the captain. It was addressed to Fred, and it had holes punched in the top.

'You don't have to tell *me* what's in it,' Dad said glumly. 'I've got a nose.' He reached in his wallet and handed Martha a note. 'Take this and go down to the village and buy another cage. And after this, I hope you'll be more careful of your belongings.'

Our cottage had one small lavatory, but no hot water, shower, or bath-tub. Dad thought that living a primitive life in the summer was healthful. He also believed that cleanliness was next to godliness, and as a result all of us had to go swimming at least once a day. The rule was never waived, even when the temperature dropped to the fifties, and a cold, grey rain was falling. Dad would lead the way from the house to the beach, dog-trotting, holding a bar of soap in one hand, and beating his chest with the other.

'Look out, ocean, here comes a tidal wave.'

Then he'd take a running dive and disappear in a geyser of spray. He'd swim under water a way, allow his feet to emerge, wiggle his toes, swim under water some more, and then come up head first, grinning and spitting a thin stream of water through his teeth.

'Come on,' he'd call. 'It's wonderful once you get in.' And he'd start lathering himself with soap.

Mother was the only non-swimmer, except the babies. She hated cold water, she hated salt water, and she hated bathing-suits. Bathing-suits itched her, and although she wore the most conservative models, with long sleeves and black stockings, she never felt modest in them. Dad used to say Mother put on more clothes than she took off when she went swimming.

Mother's swim consisted of testing the water with the tip of a black bathing-shoe, wading cautiously out to her knees, making some tentative dabs in the water with her hands, splashing a few drops on her shoulders, and, finally, in a moment of supreme courage, pinching her nose and squatting down until the water reached her chest.

Then, with teeth chattering, she'd hurry back to the house, where she'd take a cold-water sponge bath, to get rid of the salt.

As in every other phase of teaching, Dad knew his business as a swimming instructor. Some of us learned to swim when we were as young as three years old, and all of us had learned by the time we were five. It was a sore point with Dad that Mother was the only pupil he ever had encountered with whom he had no success.

Once they had gone down to the beach, Dad would take her hand and lead her. Mother would start out bravely enough, but would begin holding back about the time the water got to her knees. We'd form a ring around her and offer her what encouragement we could.

'Don't be scared, now. Come on. This time it will be different. You'll see.'

Dad towed her out until the water was just above her waist. 'Now the first thing you have to do,' he said, 'is to learn the dead man's float. If a dead man can do it, so can you.'

'I don't even like its name. It sounds ominous.'

'Like this, Mother. Look at me.'

'You kids clear out,' said Dad. 'But, Lillie, if the children can do it, you, a grown woman, should be able to. Come on now. You can't help but float, because the human body, when inflated with air, is lighter than water.'

'You know I always sink.'

'That was last year. Try it now. Be a sport. I won't let anything happen to you.'

'I don't want to.'

'You don't want to show the white feather in front of all the kids.'

'I don't care if I show the whole albatross,' Mother said. 'But I don't suppose I'll have another minute's peace until I try it. So here goes.'

Mother took a deep breath, stretched herself out on the surface, and sank like a stone. Dad waited a while, still convinced that under the laws of physics she must ultimately rise. When she didn't, he finally reached down in disgust and fished her up. Mother was gagging, choking up water, and furious.

Coughing and blowing her nose, she started for the beach.

'I still don't understand it,' Dad muttered. 'She's right. It completely refutes Archimedes.'

When Anne came home from school one afternoon and announced that she had been invited to her first dance, she seemed so happy that both Dad and Mother were happy for her. 'Joe Scales has asked me to go with him to the prom next Friday night.'

'That's lovely, dear,' Mother said.

'That's just fine,' Dad smiled. 'Is he a nice boy?'

'Nice? Gee, I'll say. He's a cheer-leader and he has a car.'

'Two mighty fine recommendations,' Dad said. 'If only he had a raccoon coat I suppose he'd be listed in the year-book as the one most likely to succeed.'

The sarcasm was lost on Anne. 'He's going to get his raccoon coat next year when he goes to Yale,' she hastened to assure Dad. 'His father's promised it to him if he passes his work.'

'That takes a load off my mind,' said Dad. 'It used to be that a father promised his son a gold watch if he didn't smoke until he was twenty-one. Now the kids get a raccoon coat as a matter of routine if they manage to stumble through high-school.'

He shook his head and sighed. 'Honestly, I don't know what the world's coming to,' he said. 'I really don't. Friday night, you say?' He pulled a notebook out of his pocket and consulted it. 'It's all right. I can make it.'

'You can make what?' Anne asked him suspiciously.

'I can make the dance,' said Dad. 'You didn't think for a minute I was going to let you go out by yourself, at night, with that – that cheer-leader, did you?'

'Oh, Daddy!' Anne moaned. 'You wouldn't spoil everything by doing something like that, would you? What's he going to think of me?'

'He'll think you're a sensible, well-brought-up child, with sensible parents,' Mother put in. 'I'm sure that if I called up his mother right now, she'd be glad to hear that your father was going along as a chaperon.'

'Don't you trust your own flesh and blood?'

'Of course we trust you,' Dad said. 'I know you've been brought up right. I trust all my daughters. It's that cheer-leader I don't trust. Now you might as well make up your mind to it. Either I go, or you don't.'

Anne had become philosophic about breaking Dad down a little at a time, and she had suspected all along that there was going to be a third person on her first date.

'I guess I'll have to tell him. I don't know what he's going to say, though.'

'He'll probably be tickled to death to have someone along to pay for the sodas,' Dad told her.

'Shall I tell him we'll go in his car, or ours?' Anne asked.

'His car? I haven't seen it, but I can imagine it. No doors, no fenders, no top, and a lot of writing about "in case of fire throw this in". I wouldn't be seen dead in it . . .'

As Dad predicted, Anne's friend drove up to the house in an ancient Model T, with writing on it. We could hear the car several blocks before it actually hove into sight, because it was equipped with an exhaust whistle that was allowed to function as a matter of routine. When the car proceeded at a moderate speed, which was hardly ever, the whistle sounded no worse than a hellish roar. But when young Mister Scales stepped on the gas, the roar became high-pitched, deafening, and insane.

As the Model T bumped down Eagle Rock Way, heads popped out of the windows of neighbouring houses, dogs raced into the woods with their tails between their legs, and babies started to scream.

The exhaust whistle, coupled with the natural engine noises, precluded the necessity of Mister Scales giving any further notice about the car's arrival at its destination. But etiquette of the day was rigid, and he followed it to the letter. First he turned off the engine, which automatically and mercifully silenced the whistle. Then, while lounging in the driver's seat, he tooted and re-tooted the horn until Anne finally came to the front door.

'Come on in, Joe,' Anne called.

'Okey, baby. Is your pop ready?'

Dad was peeking at the arrival from behind a curtain in his office. 'If he "pops" me, I'll pop him,' Dad whispered to Mother, 'My God. Lillie. I mean, Great Cæsar's ghost. Come here and look at him. It's Joe College in the flesh. And he just about comes up to Anne's shoulder.'

Anne's sheik was wearing a black-and-orange-striped blazer, grey Oxford bags, a bow tie on an elastic band, and a brown triangular porkpie hat, pinched into a bowsprit at the front.

'You and I are going to the dance,' Joe shouted to Anne. 'And so's your Old Man. Get it? So's your Old Man.'

'Of course she gets it, wise guy,' Dad grumbled for Mother's benefit. 'What do you think she is, a moron? And let me hear you refer to me tonight as the "Old Man" and you'll get it, too. I promise you.'

'Hush,' Mother warned him, coming over to peek out the curtain. 'He'll hear you. Actually, he's kind of cute, in a vest-pocket way.'

'Cute?' said Dad. 'He looks like what might happen if a pigmy married a barber pole. And look at that car. What's that written on the side? "Jump in, sardine, here's your tin".'

'Well, don't worry about the car,' Mother told him. 'You'll be riding in yours, not that contraption.'

'Thank the Lord for small favours. You stall him and Anne off until I can get the side curtains up. I'm not going to drive through town with that blazer showing. Someone might think he was one of our kids.'

Dad disappeared in the direction of the barn, and Mother went into the living-room to meet the caller. As she entered, Joe was demonstrating to Frank and Bill how the bow tie worked.

'It's a William Tell tie,' he said, holding the bow away from his neck and allowing it to pop back into position. 'You pull the bow and it hits the apple.'

Both Frank and Bill were impressed.

'You're the first cheer-leader we ever saw up close,' Frank said. 'Gee!'

Joe was sitting down when he was introduced to Mother. Remembering his manners, he tipped his hat, unveiling for just a moment a patent-leather hair-do, parted in the middle.

'Will you lead some cheers for us?' Bill begged. 'We know them all. Anne and Ernestine taught them to us.'

Joe leaped to his feet. 'Sure thing,' he said. He cupped his hands over his mouth and shouted in an adolescent baritone that cracked and made Mother shudder:

'Let's have a hoo, rah, ray and a tiger for Montclair High. A hoo, rah, ray and a tiger. I want to hear you holler now. Readddy?'

He turned sideways to us, dropped on one knee and made his fists go in a circle, like a squirrel on a treadmill.

'Hoo,' he screamed, at the top of his voice. 'Rah, ray . . .'

It was at this point that Dad entered the room. He stood viewing the proceedings with disgust, lips pursed and hands on hips. At the end of the cheer, he sidled over towards Mother.

'The car won't start,' he whispered, 'and I can't say that I blame it. What shall I do?'

'You could go in his car.'

'With that insane calliope and those signs?' Dad hissed. 'Do I look like a sardine looking for a tin to leap into?'

'Not exactly,' Mother conceded. 'Why don't you call a cab, then?'

'Look at him,' Dad whispered. 'He doesn't come up to her shoulder. He wouldn't dare get funny with her – she'd knock him cold.'

Dad walked over to where Joe and Anne were sitting.

'I hope you youngsters won't mind,' he said, 'but I won't be able to go to the dance with you.'

'We don't mind at all, Daddy,' said Anne. 'Do we, Joe?'

'A hoo, rah, ray and a tiger for me, is that it?' Dad asked.

Joe made no attempt to hide his elation. 'That's it,' he said. 'Come on, baby. Let's shake that thing. We're running late.'

– From *Cheaper by the Dozen*.

The Opened Door

JAMES KIRKUP

When I began to remember my early childhood, the only things I could bring to mind were the door and the shining doorknob of the house where I was born. These humble memories were also symbolic ones. I gazed, as I did when an infant boy, into the reflections my hands could not reach. My looking turned to finding, and the door slowly opened on the sea that lay beyond the house, waiting to be explored.

I

Bad Language

I was an only child, but not a lonely one. My parents probably thought that the little ragamuffins in our neighbourhood were not suitable companions for me, and I know I was often on my own, but I didn't mind that at all. I would be perfectly happy lying back in my pram, looking up at the silk-fringed canopy it had on hot, sunny days. Or I would crawl contentedly round the pavement in front of our step, digging up the thick black dirt between the flagstones. Or I would lie beside the boot-scraper, looking out over the vast, steeply-cambered stretch of cobblestones to the other side of the street. From my pavement-level viewpoint, it was like looking out over a high sea of stone, and discovering an unknown land where I might never be allowed to go, where strange children played and people who were not a bit like those on our side of the street went about their business in queer ways. Such washings and scrubbings of front steps and pavements I remember from those times! Every self-respecting housewife would 'stone' her front step with a yellow stone each morning – was it called a 'Bath' stone? – then she would wash a semi-circular piece of pavement in front of it with a 'wesh-rag' or 'wesh-cloot', the lowliest of kitchen accessories. Some fanatics would wash large areas of pavement in front of their houses, but my mother very properly thought this was carrying things too far, and I admired her for her common sense.

Though I was always silent with strangers, I learned to talk very soon in a rapid and fluent manner with my parents, and they may have warned me not to repeat certain bad words which I heard in the street. Occasionally, I remember, I would go to my mother and whisper in her ear that I had just heard someone say something bad.

'What was it?' she would ask, smiling.

'I don't like to say it,' I would reply. 'It was bugger.'

What a chill of horror used to run through me as I said the awful word! My mother would pretend to be terribly shocked.

'He shouldn't have said that, should he?' she would say gravely.

'No, he shouldn't have said bugger,' I would reply, with pious relish.

Then we would laugh together over the man's wicked stupidity, and I would promise never to use 'that word' myself. It was a happy and sane way of sending the Devil packing.

About this time, too, some little girls teased me by saying that they would tell my mother I had been using bad language to them. I was overwhelmed by the monstrousness of the lie; I was too simple to see that it was all just a rather nasty piece of bluff. Miserably frightened, I felt I could never face my mother and father again, and decided to 'run away'. I did not get much farther than the corner of our back lane, where I hung about in the gathering darkness for what seemed to me to be hours. I watched the lamp-lighter with the spark burning at the end of his long pole light all the gas-lamps in Robertson Street. The men came tramping home from work, and I kept out of my father's sight when I saw him coming. I was sick at heart, and cold, and hungry. It was autumn, the long nights were coming on, and the ships moving down the river to the open sea blew lingering, melancholy blasts on their sirens, and the fog-horn began to hoot.

Eventually I went home shaking with cold and misery, and was met on our front doorstep by my bewildered mother, to whom I told my tearful tale, passionately protesting my innocence. I still remember the pang of joy I felt when I realised that the girls had *not* told her lies about me, and the wonderful feeling of security and self-confidence I had when she said:

'We knew you wouldn't say *that* sort of thing, hinney!'

How my heart ached with love for her, who loved me so much, so perfectly, and who understood my innocence! My father, too, helped to drive away my awful fear with a great burst of laughter. I was hoisted on to the kitchen table, where the bobbled table-cloth had been drawn back, and my hands and face and finally my knees were washed in warm, soap-clouded, carbolic-scented water. It was grand to see one knee washed clean and rosy, and the other beside it, still black with grime. Then supper, and nursery rhymes on my father's lap, and several performances of *This little piggy went to market*, played on my firelit toes; then off to bed in the 'front room' which was also my parents' bedroom. There the gas lamp in the street outside would be casting its pale, lemon-yellow moonlight through the stiff white lace window-curtains on to the plaster-decorated ceiling. And as I lay there, warm and happy, watching the slightly stirring shadows of the flowery lace, and listening to the far-off moaning of the ships, I would drift off into long, deep sleep, a sleep without fear, without care, lulled by the gentle breathing of the sea beyond the pitheads and the houses.

II

At Granny Kirkup's

Granny Kirkup's house had a small, privet-bordered garden with ornamental iron railings in front and a squeaky iron gate. From the outside it looked like a child's drawing of a house. A big frosted-glass porch stood in the centre, with a coloured-glass door behind, and on each side of the porch there was a bay window. On the first floor there were three windows partnering those below. The walls were of dingy red brick, the roof was slated, and at each end of the roof there were chimneys. Near the house, across a little, narrow cobbled back lane, was a small police station, which was a great comfort to my nervous paternal grandmother. The policemen were great friends of hers, and one of them had given her an old-fashioned, painted truncheon, which she kept hanging at the foot of the stairs, in case of burglars.

I can still remember the cold, metal feel of the door handle as I opened the door of the porch. The outer door was often swollen by damp, and had to be slammed hard before it would shut; this caused the whole porch to shake and rattle like a kaleidoscope. There were several white-painted shelves inside, on which stood pots of ferns and mosses and geraniums and other plants. This little conservatory was a great delight to me. It smelt always of autumn and the sea, and on autumn and winter nights it would be full of mist. There was always an odour of damp earth and dead geranium leaves and moist ferns and other growing things. One of the plants was a creeper, which grew from a hanging basket and was called 'Wandering Sailor'. To me, it was a fine, exotic place, because we had nothing like it at our house.

Inside, there was a good smell of spicy cooking, jam-making, chintz, minced meat, musty books, coal fires, flowers – generally chrysanthemums – and mint imperials, which my Granny used to suck 'for her chest'. It was an utterly different smell to the one in our little flat in Cockburn Street, which was a compound of strong tobacco, wood shavings, boiled onions, floor polish and soot. I loved the sweet, old-maid smell of Granny's house, though I always felt that our own was the only right smell for a house to have. I was peculiarly sensitive to the smell of other people's houses. My Granny Johnson's smelt of snuff and shaving soap and boot polish and Woodbines. Mrs Battey's smelt of washing and hot girdle scones. But most of the houses in our street had the unmistakable, unforgettable smell of poverty – an airless, stuffy, rancid smell, as if the very air, like the tea leaves, had been used over and over again. It was a stale and sour smell of cold, unwashed sheets and bodies, the greasy aroma of pans of vegetable broth, the mustiness of dry crusts, the breath children exhale when they chew dry bread – the very essence of misery.

I sniffed appreciatively at the air in Granny Kirkup's house. She was a genial, plump body with a sweet, rosy, country girl's face. Her large, slightly myopic grey eyes used to twinkle delightfully behind her gold-rimmed glasses, and though she had false teeth, they were so small and white and well made that for many years I did not know they were false. She spoke with a trace of Norfolk accent that I found very agreeable after the broad 'Geordie' talk of Cockburn Street. My Granny and my Aunt Anna were strict Methodists, and went regularly to a large, ugly brick chapel called 'The Glebe' – a name that I found very perplexing. There was no snuff-taking, gambling or beer-drinking in *this* household, and only weak ginger wine at Christmas and New Year. But there was always a silver threepenny piece hidden in the very slice of cake that my Granny cut for me. 'My, my!' she would exclaim. 'You'm a lucky crittur!'

The other person I used to meet at Granny Kirkup's was my Aunt Anna. She was a busy dressmaker and was often out working if we called on a week-day evening. She, too, had short-sighted, large grey eyes, and wore a gold-rimmed pince-nez with a thin gold chain that hooked over one ear. I adored it when she took her spectacles off and wiped them with a neat little folded pocket hanky. Her eyes then appeared even larger, lustrous and vague: they seemed to be looking nowhere in particular, or to be just amiably reposing on dim, far-off things. The strangeness of their expression haunted me, though I also found it rather embarrassing when she removed her glasses: I felt as if I were looking at something I shouldn't see, as if my own sharp eyes were asserting an unfair advantage over her mild, defenceless gaze. Then I would almost tearfully beg her to put her spectacles on again, and until she had finished wiping them I would bury my face in the soft crochet-work of her home-made blouse. Another characteristic that intrigued me was the almost soundless way she blew her nose and sneezed, making no more noise than a little bird. I was so used to my father's impressive trumpetings into his enormous handkerchiefs: I found it very funny when Aunt Anna gave a very lady-like little 'cheep' into her tiny, folded hanky, but I believed her when she told me it was not polite to make too much noise when blowing one's nose. My father roared with laughter when I told him that, and said she was quite right, but I noticed that his own sneezes did not become any less earth-shaking.

My Aunt Anna's expression was a little severe, due perhaps to the 'Hapsburg' lip. But she was most wonderfully kind and gentle, and 'spoilt' me, and I adored her. We used to go through a ritual on Sunday mornings after she had come back from chapel. She would carry me through the big, Sunday-dinner-smelling kitchen, out into the long, narrow backyard, which I thought was very grand, because they did not have to share it with anyone else. There, with me sitting on her shoulder, we would look up at the telegraph pole that stood in the lane. I would cry 'Whee-ee! Whee-ee! Whee-ee!' in imitation of the wind in the wires, and my Aunt Anna, to my intense delight, would cry 'Whee-ee!' too. I had never seen anything so tall and impressive as that great giant out in the back lane, covered with struts and little black things like birds. When there were clouds behind it, blowing in from the sea, it would seem to be falling down on us, and we would rush breathlessly back into the house, slamming the door behind us. Then Aunt Anna would let me slide down the curved lid of the silk-pleated piano, and after teaching me some five-finger exercises she would play some of the tunes from 'Moody & Sankey's' hymn book. I can still recall the words of one of the hymns:

Count your blessings, count them one by one,
And it will *surprise* you what the Lord has done!

Another had a plaintive, and, after the last verse, dramatic refrain: I can't remember the exact words, but it went something like this:

Passing by! Passing by!
Jesus of Nazareth *has* passed by!

Another had a good, rollicking tune, and unfortunately the exact words again escape me:

When we meet beyond the morning of that bright and happy
day,
We shall know each other better, when the mists have rolled
away!

My irrepressible father used to sing a very sacrilegious version of
this which I found irresistible:

Wash me in the water that you washed your dirty daughter,
And I shall be whiter than the whitewash on the wall!

Then the refrain:

Whi————
ter than the whitewash on the wall,
Whi————
ter than the whitewash on the wall!
Wash me in the water that you washed your dirty daughter,
And *I* shall be whiter than the whitewash on the wall!

Then we would stand in front of a large dark engraving of
Shakespeare who was depicted sitting meditatively, dressed in black
tights, in a 'baronial' chair, with his creations all around him in a
kind of cloudy empyrean, each wreathed in its appropriate quotation.
I believe this picture was issued by the makers of Pears Soap, which
I did not like because it made my eyes sting, and who produced
a companion picture of a large fat squalling baby in a tin bath trying
to get a tablet of the soap that lay just beyond his reach: it was entitled
'He won't be happy till he gets it', a saying which was frequently
quoted whenever I wanted something I shouldn't have, and which
became almost a family motto.

The Shakespeare picture gave me quite a stock of popular quotations,
and often, for the reward of a penny, I would recite in a whisper of
intense loathing:

'Let me not hold my tongue; let me not, Hubert.
Or Hubert, if you will, cut out my tongue,
So I may keep mine eyes: O, spare mine eyes! . . .'

We would give fresh water to Dick, the canary, whose cage hung in the bay window of the sitting-room; he would then take a vigorous bath, chirruping wildly, and showering us with bird seed and bath-water.

After that, we would look at the needlework picture of the eighteenth-century boy asleep on a sheep dog; then she would very conspiratorially open the sideboard drawer and give me one of Granny's mint imperials while Granny was out in the kitchen making the dinner. Granny would pretend not to know what was going on, and when she came back from the kitchen she would exclaim: 'Lawks! Who's been at my minty sweeties?' I shall not easily forget the way those mint imperials melted in the mouth – how the hard, smooth outer casing grew rough and finally collapsed on one side, releasing the delicious softness of the filling. And I always asked for a glass of cold water afterwards, because I was a sensationalist, and the shock of cold water in my peppermint-heated mouth was one of my first sensuous discoveries.

Then came the best part of the morning, when, among the smells of roasting meat, cooking vegetables and stewing apples, my aunt would take me on her knee and read to me. There was nothing I liked better than being read to. On Saturday afternoons, my father coming home from work would bring in *Bubbles* or *Tiger Tim*, or some other brightly-coloured children's comic, and some chocolate cream whirls. My mother and I would lie down on the sofa after the midday meal, and while my father washed the dishes, we would munch the chocolate cream whirls, and my mother would read the whole of *Bubbles* for me from beginning to end. I would follow her eyes – how blue! – as they moved across the page, and I could always tell when she tried to skip anything. I would stop her then, and insist on hearing every word.

When the reading was finished, it would be time for my father and me to leave and go back to Cockburn Street, where my mother was 'on with the dinner'. And off I would go to the tram stop, with another mint imperial in my mouth, after kissing Granny and Aunt Anna – something I never liked doing, for I only liked kissing my mother and father. It was horrible to have to kiss other people. I don't think I ever stayed to dinner at Ada Street on Sundays, possibly because I always used to refuse to eat anything that had not been cooked by my mother. Other people's food used to make me sick. I always dreaded being taken out to tea or dinner, and having to eat other people's messes.

– From *The Only Child.*

The Durrells in Corfu

GERALD DURRELL

Once Spiro had taken charge he stuck to us like a burr. Within a few hours he had changed from a taxi-driver to our champion, and within a week he was our guide, philosopher and friend. He became so much a member of the family that very soon there was scarcely a thing we did, or planned to do, in which he was not involved in some way. He was always there, bull-voiced and scowling, arranging things we wanted done, telling us how much to pay for things, keeping a watchful eye on us all and reporting to Mother anything he thought she should know. Like a great, brown, ugly angel he watched over us as tenderly as though we were slightly weak-minded children. Mother he frankly adored, and he would sing her praises in a loud voice wherever we happened to be, to her acute embarrassment.

'You oughts to be carefuls whats you do,' he would tell us, screwing up his face earnestly; 'we donts wants to worrys your mothers.'

'Whatever for, Spiro?' Larry would protest in well-simulated astonishment. 'She's never done anything for us . . . why should we consider her?'

'Gollys, Master Larrys, donts *jokes* like that,' Spiro would say in anguish.

'He's quite right, Spiro,' Leslie would say very seriously; 'she's really not much good as a mother, you know.'

'Donts says that, *donts says that*,' Spiro would roar. 'Honest to Gods, if I hads a mother likes yours I'd gos down every mornings and kisses her feets.'

So we were installed in the villa, and we each settled down and adapted ourselves to our surroundings in our respective ways. Margo, merely by donning a microscopic swim-suit and sun-bathing in the olive-groves, had collected an ardent band of handsome peasant youths who appeared like magic from an apparently deserted landscape whenever a bee flew too near her or her deckchair needed moving. Mother felt forced to point out that she thought this sun-bathing was rather *unwise*.

'After all, dear, that costume doesn't cover an awful lot, does it?' she pointed out.

'Oh, Mother, don't be so old-fashioned,' Margo said impatiently. 'After all, you only die once.'

This remark was as baffling as it was true, and successfully silenced Mother.

It had taken three husky peasant boys half an hour's sweating and panting to get Larry's trunks into the villa, while Larry bustled round them, directing operations. Once they were installed, Larry spent a happy day unpacking them, and the room was so full of books that it was almost impossible to get in or out. Having constructed battlements of books round the outer perimeter, Larry would spend the whole day in there with his typewriter, only emerging dreamily for meals. On the second morning he appeared in a highly irritable frame of mind, for a peasant had tethered his donkey just over the hedge. At regular intervals the beast would throw out its head and let forth a prolonged and lugubrious bray.

'I ask you! Isn't it laughable that future generations should be deprived of my work simply because some horny-handed idiot has tied that stinking beast of burden near my window?' Larry asked.

'Yes, dear,' said Mother; 'why don't you move it if it disturbs you?'

'My dear Mother, I can't be expected to spend my time chasing donkeys about the olive-groves. I threw a pamphlet on Christian Science at it; what more do you expect me to do?'

'The poor thing's tied up. You can't expect it to untie itself,' said Margo.

'Can't one of you go and move it?'

'It's not disturbing us,' said Leslie.

'That's the trouble with this family,' said Larry bitterly: 'no give and take, no consideration for others.'

'*You* don't have much consideration for others,' said Margo.

'It's all your fault, Mother,' said Larry austerely; 'you shouldn't have brought us up to be so selfish.'

'I like that!' exclaimed Mother. 'I never did anything of the sort!'

'Well, we didn't get as selfish as this without *some* guidance,' said Larry.

In the end, Mother and I unhitched the donkey and moved it farther down the hill.

Leslie meanwhile had unpacked his revolvers and startled us all with an apparently endless series of explosions while he fired at an old tin can from his bedroom window. After a particularly deafening morning, Larry erupted from his room and said he could not be expected to work if the villa was going to be rocked to its foundations every five minutes. Leslie, aggrieved, said that he had to practise. Larry said it didn't sound like practice, but more like the Indian Mutiny.

In between keeping a watchful eye on us all, Mother was settling down in her own way. The house was redolent with the scent of herbs and the sharp tang of garlic and onions, and the kitchen was full of a bubbling selection of pots, among which she moved, spectacles askew, muttering to herself. On the table was a tottering pile of books which she consulted from time to time. When she could drag herself away from the kitchen, she would drift happily about the garden, reluctantly pruning and cutting, enthusiastically weeding and planting.

This doll's-house garden was a magic land, a forest of flowers through which roamed creatures I had never seen before. Among the thick, silky petals of each rose-bloom lived tiny, crab-like spiders that scuttled sideways when disturbed. Their small, translucent bodies were coloured to match the flowers they inhabited: pink, ivory, wine-red or buttery-yellow. On the rose-stems, encrusted with green flies, lady-birds moved like newly painted toys; lady-birds pale red with large black spots; lady-birds apple-red with brown spots; lady-birds orange with grey-and-black freckles. Rotund and amiable, they prowled and fed among the anæmic flocks of greenfly. Carpenter bees, like furry, electric-blue bears, zigzagged among the flowers, growling fatly and busily. Humming-bird hawk-moths, sleek and neat, whipped up and down the paths with a fussy efficiency, pausing occasionally on speed-misty wings to lower a long, slender proboscis into a bloom. Among the white cobbles large black ants staggered and gesticulated in groups round strange trophies: a dead caterpillar, a piece of rose-petal or a dried grass-head fat with seeds. As an accompaniment to all this activity there came from the olive-groves outside the fuchsia hedge the incessant shimmering cries of the cicadas. If the curious, blurring heat-haze produced a sound, it would be exactly the strange, chiming cries of these insects.

At first I was so bewildered by this profusion of life on our very doorstep that I could only move about the garden in a daze, watching now this creature, now that, constantly having my attention distracted by the flights of brilliant butterflies that drifted over the hedge. Gradually, as I became more used to the bustle of insect life among the flowers, I found I could concentrate more. I would spend hours squatting on my heels or lying on my stomach watching the private lives of the creatures around me, while Roger sat near by, a look of resignation on his face. In this way I learnt a lot of fascinating things.

I found that the little crab-spiders could change colour just as successfully as any chameleon. Take a spider from a wine-red rose, where he had been sitting like a bead of coral, and place him in the depths of a cool white rose. If he stayed there – and most of them did – you would see his colour gradually ebb away, as though the change had given him anæmia, until, some two days later, he would be crouching among the white petals like a pearl.

I discovered that in the dry leaves under the fuchsia hedge lived another type of spider, a fierce little huntsman with the cunning and ferocity of a tiger. He would stalk about his continent of leaves, eyes glistening in the sun, pausing now and then to raise himself up on his hairy legs to peer about. If he saw a fly settle to enjoy a sun-bath he would freeze; then, as slowly as a leaf growing, he would move forward, imperceptibly, edging nearer and nearer, pausing occasionally to fasten his life-line of silk to the surface of the leaves. Then, when close enough, the huntsman would pause, his legs shift minutely as he got a good purchase, and then he would leap, legs spread out in a hairy embrace, straight on to the dreaming fly. Never did I see one of these little spiders miss its kill, once it had manœuvred into the right position.

All these discoveries filled me with a tremendous delight, so that they had to be shared, and I would burst suddenly into the house and startle the family with the news that the strange, spiky black caterpillars on the roses were not caterpillars at all, but the young of ladybirds, or with the equally astonishing news that lacewing-flies laid eggs on stilts. This last miracle I was lucky enough to witness. I found a lacewing-fly on the roses and watched her as she climbed about the leaves, admiring her beautiful, fragile wings like green glass, and her enormous liquid golden eyes. Presently she stopped on the surface of a rose-leaf and lowered the tip of her abdomen. She remained like that for a moment and then raised her tail, and from it, to my astonishment, rose a slender thread, like a pale hair. Then, on the very tip of this stalk, appeared the egg. The female had a rest, and then repeated the performance until the surface of the rose-leaf looked as though it was covered with a forest of tiny club moss. The laying over, the female rippled her antennæ briefly and flew off in a mist of green gauze wings.

The crumbling wall that surrounded the sunken garden alongside the house was a rich hunting ground for me. It was an ancient brick wall that had been plastered over, but now this outer skin was green with moss, bulging and sagging with the damp of many winters. The whole surface was an intricate map of cracks, some several inches wide, others as fine as hairs. Here and there large pieces had dropped off and revealed the rows of rose-pink bricks lying beneath like ribs. There was a whole landscape on this wall if you peered closely enough to see it; the roofs of a hundred tiny toadstools, red, yellow and brown, showed in patches like villages on the damper portions; mountains of bottle-green moss grew in tuffets so symmetrical that they might have been planted and trimmed; forests of small ferns sprouted from cracks in the shady places, drooping languidly like little green fountains. The top of the wall was a desert land, too dry for anything except a few rust-red mosses to live in it, too hot for anything except sun-bathing by the dragon-flies. At the base of the wall grew a mass of plants, cyclamen, crocus, asphodel, thrusting their leaves among the piles of broken and chipped roof-tiles that lay there. This whole strip was guarded by a labyrinth of blackberry hung, in season, with fruit that was plump and juicy and black as ebony.

The shyest and most self-effacing of the wall community were the most dangerous; you hardly ever saw one unless you looked for it, and yet there must have been several hundred living in the cracks of the wall. Slide a knife-blade carefully under a piece of the loose plaster and lever it gently away from the brick, and there, crouching beneath it, would be a little black scorpion an inch long, looking as though he were made out of polished chocolate. They were weird-looking little things, with their flattened, oval bodies, their neat, crooked legs, the enormous crab-like claws, bulbous and neatly jointed as armour, and the tail like a string of brown beads ending in a sting like a rose-thorn. The scorpion would lie there quite quietly as you examined him, only raising his tail in an almost apologetic gesture of warning if you breathed too hard on him. If you kept him in the sun too long he would simply turn his back on you and walk away, and then slide slowly but firmly under another section of plaster.

I grew very fond of these scorpions. I found them to be pleasant, unassuming creatures with, on the whole, the most charming habits.

By crouching under the wall at night with a torch, I managed to catch some brief glimpses of the scorpions' wonderful courtship dances. I saw them standing, claws clasped, their bodies raised to the skies, their tails lovingly entwined; I saw them waltzing slowly in circles among the moss cushions, claw in claw. But my view of these performances was all too short, for almost as soon as I switched on the torch the partners would stop, pause for a moment, and then, seeing that I was not going to extinguish the light, they would turn round and walk firmly away, claw in claw, side by side. They were definitely beasts that believed in keeping themselves *to* themselves. If I could have kept a colony in captivity I would probably have been able to see the whole of the courtship, but the family had forbidden scorpions in the house, despite my arguments in favour of them.

Then one day I found a fat female scorpion in the wall, wearing what at first glance appeared to be a pale fawn fur coat. Closer inspection proved that this strange garment was made up of a mass of tiny babies clinging to the mother's back. I was enraptured by this family, and I made up my mind to smuggle them into the house and up to my bedroom so that I might keep them and watch them grow up. With infinite care I manœuvred the mother and family into a matchbox, and then hurried to the villa. It was rather unfortunate that just as I entered the door lunch should be served; however, I placed the matchbox carefully on the mantelpiece in the drawing-room, so that the scorpions should get plenty of air, and made my way to the dining-room and joined the family for the meal. Dawdling over my food, feeding Roger surreptitiously under the table and listening to the family arguing, I completely forgot about my exciting new captures. At last Larry, having finished, fetched the cigarettes from the drawing-room, and lying back in his chair he put one in his mouth and picked up the matchbox he had brought. Oblivious of my impending doom I watched him interestedly as, still talking glibly, he opened the matchbox.

Now I maintain to this day that the female scorpion meant no harm. She was agitated and a trifle annoyed at being shut up in a matchbox for so long, and so she seized the first opportunity to escape. She hoisted herself out of the box with great rapidity, her babies clinging on desperately, and scuttled on to the back of Larry's hand. There, not quite certain what to do next, she paused, her sting curved up at the ready. Larry, feeling the movement of her claws, glanced down to see what it was, and from that moment things got increasingly confused.

He uttered a roar of fright that made Lugaretzia drop a plate and brought Roger out from beneath the table, barking wildly. With a flick of his hand he sent the unfortunate scorpion flying down the table, and she landed midway between Margo and Leslie, scattering babies like confetti as she thumped on to the cloth. Thoroughly enraged at this treatment, the creature sped towards Leslie, her sting quivering with emotion, Leslie leapt to his feet, overturning his chair and flicked out desperately with his napkin, sending the scorpion rolling across the cloth towards Margo, who promptly let out a scream that any railway engine would have been proud to produce. Mother, completely bewildered by this sudden and rapid change from peace to chaos, put on her glasses and peered down the table to see what was causing the pandemonium and at that moment Margo, in a vain attempt to stop the scorpion's advance, hurled a glass of water at it. The shower missed the animal completely, but successfully drenched Mother, who, not being able to stand cold water, promptly lost her breath and sat gasping at the end of the table, unable even to protest. The scorpion had now gone to ground under Leslie's plate, while her babies swarmed wildly all over the table. Roger, mystified by the panic, but determined to do his share, ran round and round the room, barking hysterically.

'It's that bloody boy again . . .' bellowed Larry.

'Look out! Look out! They're coming!' screamed Margo.

'All we need is a book,' roared Leslie: 'don't panic, hit 'em with a book.'

'What in earth's the *matter* with you all?' Mother kept imploring, mopping her glasses.

'Look at the table . . . knee-deep in scorpions . . .'

'Quick . . . quick . . . do something . . .'

'You're worse than the dog . . . Shut *up*, Roger . . .'

'By the Grace of God I wasn't bitten . . .'

'But *how* did the scorpions get on the table, dear?'

'That bloody boy. . . . . Every matchbox in the house is a death-trap . . .'

Eventually, after impassioned pleas on my part, backed up by Mother, Leslie's suggestion that the whole lot be slaughtered was quashed. While the family, still simmering with rage and fright, retired to the drawing-room, I spent half an hour rounding up the babies, picking them up in a teaspoon and returning them to their mother's back. Then I carried them outside on a saucer and, with the utmost reluctance, released them on the garden wall.

With March came the spring, and the island was flower-filled, scented and a-flutter with new leaves. The cypress-trees that had tossed and hissed during the winds of winter now stood straight and sleek against the sky, covered with a misty coat of greenish-white cones. Waxy yellow crocuses appeared in great clusters, bubbling out among the tree-roots and tumbling down the banks. Under the myrtles, the grape-hyacinths lifted buds like magenta sugar-drops, and the gloom of the oak-thickets was filled with the dim smoke of a thousand blue day-irises. Anemones, delicate and easily wind-bruised, lifted ivory flowers the petals of which seemed to have been dipped in wine. Vetch, marigold, asphodel and a hundred others flooded the fields and woods. Even the ancient olives, bent and hollowed by a thousand springs, decked themselves in clusters of minute creamy flowers, modest and yet decorative, as became their great age. It was no half-hearted spring, this: the whole island vibrated with it as though a great, ringing chord had been struck. Everyone and everything heard it and responded. It was apparent in the gleam of flower-petals, the flash of bird wings and the sparkle in the dark, liquid eyes of the peasant girls. In the water-filled ditches the frogs that looked newly enamelled snored a rapturous chorus in the lush weeds. In the village coffee-shops the wine seemed redder and, somehow, more potent. Blunt, work-calloused fingers plucked at guitar strings with strange gentleness, and rich voices rose in lilting, haunting song.

Margo was always badly affected by the spring. Her personal appearance, always of absorbing interest to her, now became almost an obsession. Piles of freshly laundered clothes filled her bedroom, while the washing-line sagged under the weight of clothes newly washed. Singing shrilly and untunefully she would drift about the villa, carrying piles of flimsy underwear or bottles of scent. She would seize every opportunity to dive into the bathroom, in a swirl of white towels, and once in there she was as hard to dislodge as a limpet from a rock. The family in turn would bellow and batter on the door, getting no more satisfaction than an assurance that she was nearly finished, an assurance which we had learnt by bitter experience not to have any faith in. Eventually she would emerge, glowing and immaculate, and drift from the house, humming, to sun-bathe in the olive-groves or go down to the sea and swim. It was during one of these excursions to the sea that she met an over-good-looking young

Turk. With unusual modesty she did not inform anyone of her frequent bathing assignations with this paragon, feeling, as she told us later, that we would not be interested. It was, of course, Spiro who discovered it. He watched over Margo's welfare with the earnest concern of a St Bernard, and there was precious little she could do without Spiro knowing about it. He cornered Mother in the kitchen one morning, glanced surreptitiously round to make sure they were not overheard, sighed deeply and broke the news to her.

'I'm very sorrys to haves to tells you this, Mrs Durrells,' he rumbled, 'buts I thinks you oughts to knows.'

Mother had by now become quite used to Spiro's conspiratorial air when he came to deliver some item of information about the family, and it no longer worried her.

'What's the matter now, Spiro?' she asked.

'It's Missy Margo,' said Spiro sorrowfully.

'What about her?'

Spiro glanced round uneasily.

'Dos you knows shes meetings a *mans*?' he inquired in a vibrant whisper.

'A man? Oh . . . er . . . yes, I did know,' said Mother, lying valiantly.

Spiro hitched up his trousers over his belly and leant forward.

'But dids you knows he's a *Turk*?' he questioned in tones of blood-curdling ferocity.

'A Turk?' said Mother vaguely. 'No, I didn't know he was a Turk. What's wrong with that?'

Spiro looked horrified.

'Gollys, Mrs Durrells, whats wrongs with it? He's a *Turk*. I wouldn'ts trust a sonofabitch Turk with any girls. He'll cuts her throats, thats what he'll do. Honest to Gods, Mrs Durrells, it's not safe, Missy Margo swimmings with hims.'

'All right, Spiro,' said Mother soothingly, 'I'll speak to Margo about it.'

'I just thoughts you oughts to knows, thats all. Buts don'ts you worrys . . . if he dids anythings to Missy Margo, I'd fix the bastard,' Spiro assured her earnestly.

Acting on the information received, Mother mentioned the matter to Margo, in a slightly less bloodcurdling manner than Spiro's, and suggested that the young Turk be brought up to tea. Delighted, Margo went off to fetch him, while Mother hastily made a cake and some scones, and warned the rest of us to be on our best behaviour. The Turk, when he arrived, turned out to be a tall young man, with meticulously waved hair and a flashy smile that managed to convey the minimum of humour with the maximum of condescension. He had all the sleek, smug self-possession of a cat in season. He pressed Mother's hand to his lips as though he was conferring an honour on her, and scattered the largesse of his smile for the rest of us. Mother, feeling the hackles of the family rising, threw herself desperately into the breach.

'Lovely having you . . . wanted so often . . . never seems time, you know . . . days simply *fly* past . . . Margo's told us so much about you . . . do have a scone . . .' she said breathlessly, smiling with dazzling charm and handing him a piece of cake.

'So kind,' murmured the Turk, leaving us in some doubt as to whether he was referring to us or himself. There was a pause.

'He's on holiday here,' announced Margo suddenly, as though it was something quite unique.

'Really?' said Larry waspishly. 'On holiday? Amazing!'

'I had a holiday once,' said Leslie indistinctly through a mouthful of cake; 'remember it clearly.'

Mother rattled the tea-things nervously, and glared at them.

'Sugar?' she inquired fruitily. 'Sugar in your tea?'

'Thank you, yes.'

There was another short silence, during which we all sat and watched Mother pouring out the tea and searching her mind desperately for a topic of conversation. At length the Turk turned to Larry.

'You write, I believe?' he said with complete lack of interest.

Larry's eyes glittered. Mother, seeing the danger signs, rushed in quickly before he could reply.

'Yes, yes,' she smiled, 'he writes away, day after day. Always tapping at the typewriter.'

[121]

'I always feel that I could write superbly if I tried,' remarked the Turk.

'Really?' said Mother. 'Yes, well, it's a gift, I suppose, like so many things.'

'He swims well,' remarked Margo, 'and he goes out terribly far.'

'I have no fear. When I ride the horse, I have no fear, for I ride superbly. I can sail the boat magnificently in the typhoon without fear.'

He sipped his tea delicately, regarding our awestruck faces with approval.

'You see,' he went on, in case we had missed the point, 'you see, I am not a fearful man.'

The result of the tea-party was that the next day Margo received a note from the Turk asking her if she would accompany him to the cinema that evening.

'Do you think I ought to go?' she asked Mother.

'If you want to, dear,' Mother answered, adding firmly, 'but tell him I'm coming too.'

'That should be a jolly evening for you,' remarked Larry.

So that evening Mother and Margo, dressed becomingly, made their way down the hill to meet the Turk. The only cinema was an open-air one in the town, and we calculated that the show should be over by ten at the latest. Larry, Leslie and I waited eagerly for their return. At half-past one in the morning Margo and Mother, in the last stages of exhaustion, crept into the villa and sank into chairs.

'Oh, so you've come back?' said Larry; 'we thought you'd flown with him. We imagined you galloping about Constantinople on camels, your yashmaks rippling seductively in the breeze.'

'We've had the most awful evening,' said Mother, easing her shoes off, 'really awful.'

'What happened?' asked Leslie.

'Well, to begin with he stank of the most frightful perfume,' said Margo, 'and that put me off straight away.'

'We went in the cheapest seats, so close to the screen that I got a headache,' said Mother, 'and simply crammed together like sardines. It was *so* oppressive I couldn't breathe. And then, to crown it all, I got a flea. I couldn't very well scratch. I had to keep pressing myself against the seat. Then in the interval he went out and came back with some of that horrible, sickly Turkish Delight, and before long we were all covered with white sugar, and I had a dreadful thirst. In the second interval he went out and came back with flowers. I ask you, dear, flowers in the middle of the cinema. That's Margo's bouquet, on the table.'

Mother pointed to a massive bunch of spring flowers, tied up in a tangle of coloured ribbons. She delved into her bag and produced a minute bunch of violets that looked as though they had been trodden on by an exceptionally hefty horse.

'This,' she said, 'was for me. . . . I'm afraid you'll just *have* to choose your boy friends more carefully in future, Margo. I thought we'd *never* get away.'

'You didn't make yourself fearful enough,' said Larry.

– From *My Family and Other Animals.*

Eventide à la Française

ROSE C. FELD

All during my stay in France, I spent several days each month with Aunt Lucienne. With the coming of the cold weather, however, I moved down to the Cap d'Antibes on the Riviera to share a house with some American friends. Before I left, I paid a final visit to Aunt Lucienne. Although she said she would miss me, she approved highly of my plans to spend the winter months in the warm sunshine. Not only was it sensible, she declared, but very *chic*.

My concern over her own comfort, she swept aside. In the hallway of her apartment, against one wall, she had neatly stacked a supply of firewood.

'It is not very elegant,' she commented, 'but it saves me steps going down the cellar. The kitchen stove keeps me warm during the day, and evenings I light a little fire in the *salon*. You must not worry about me. I am accustomed to this way of living. I am not as soft as you Americans. Even in Paris, we did not have central heating in our apartment. I do not know if I quite approve of it. Pierre has it but there are times when they shiver with cold. The *concierge* has overslept or has had too much to drink or is annoyed because somebody has failed to give him a *pourboire* for some service. No, I much prefer a few sticks of wood that I can light myself.'

Later, she told me that she would spend the month of February with Pierre and his family.

'I have accepted their invitation but frankly I do not look forward to it. Their place is very luxurious compared to this but I miss my own four corners. I shall be glad when the month is over.'

But she did not stay the month with her son's family. The latter part of February I received a letter from her telling me she had returned to her home.

'I am back again in my own apartment,' she wrote. 'I stayed two weeks with Pierre and it was enough. It is not that Suzanne was unkind but it is I who am difficult. To put it briefly, I am a mother-in-law. How can I explain what that means? When Suzanne had guests for dinner and I joined them at table, I was lost for they talked of things that are now foreign to my way of life – fashions, theatres, night clubs. So I sat silent, like an old fool, smiling or nodding my head when they remembered to address me. And if Suzanne, out of consideration to me, to be sure, suggested that I eat with the children, I was offended although I realised it was better that way.

'I regret it very much but I am a failure as a grandmother as well as a mother-in-law. There are women, I know, who are happy to devote themselves to their grandchildren but I am not one of them. One hour with them and I have had enough. It is something which I do not confess with pride. Although Suzanne says nothing, I am sure she is critical of me and with reason. There is a traditional picture of a grandmother, the gentle old soul who listens to the prattle of little ones, who tells them stories, who remains at home with them when papa and mama go out for an evening's pleasure, who knits their stockings and mends their clothes. And what do I turn out to be? A selfish old woman who has a weakness for exciting stories of mystery and murder and who smokes continuously. Truly, I am ashamed that I cannot please her but I cannot pretend to be what I am not.

'We had no words, you understand, but I told her it would be better if I returned home. Pierre was very much distressed. He worries about my living alone which is very foolish. All I can say is that the day may come when he will be offered a chair at the fireside of his son-in-law and find that the flames give no warmth.'

A few weeks later, I received another letter from Aunt Lucienne, telling me she had been very ill with the grippe, as had most of her friends, but that she was now well again and looking forward to the blessed warmth of the spring and to my return. Shortly after, I myself was caught in an epidemic of influenza that was sweeping the south of France and was seriously ill for several weeks. It was while I was in bed that the postman brought a special delivery letter from Aunt Lucienne asking how soon I was coming north again.

'*Chére petite*,' she wrote, 'I am in the midst of a grave *crise* and I need your help and advice. I cannot bring myself to write of it but I will tell you all when you come here. In the meantime, I am praying to *le bon Dieu* to guide me. But come soon, I pray you.'

My concern over this mysterious communication was increased when a telegram from Pierre was delivered to my sick room. 'Please come back as soon as possible,' he wired. 'Need your help and influence. *Maman* is planning to get married.'

I wired to each of them explaining that I was bedridden and that I would get on a train as soon as I was well enough to move. Whether it was because of the news that Pierre sent me which made me run into a new bout of fever or the natural course of the disease, it was two weeks before I was able to make the overnight trip.

A smiling Aunt Lucienne met me at the bus. There was no sign of a *crise* in her face or manner, no mention of it in her words. Her main concern was over my pallor which she said would soon disappear under her care and cooking. Deliberately, it seemed to me, she was withholding the information that set a stamp of triumph on her features. As always, it was an *apéritif* and a cigarette which opened the door of her confidences.

'The *crise* is over, *ma petite*. I have won.'

'Won what?' I asked. 'I know nothing except what Pierre wrote me. Are you getting married?'

Her eyes crinkled in wry amusement.

'Don't be foolish, my dear. But it served.'

'You are talking in riddles,' I complained. 'Exactly what happened?'

Her face grew very grim.

'I smile now but it was no matter for laughter, I assure you. I will begin from the beginning. I wrote you that I stayed with Pierre and Suzanne for two weeks in February and that later I was ill with the grippe. I remind you of that for one thing led to another, that is to say they are important in the chain of events that followed.

Neither Pierre nor Suzanne visited me when I was ill. I wrote them that it was unnecessary. After all, I have had the grippe every year and I have always managed without them.'

One bright Sunday, after she had recovered, she continued, Pierre and Suzanne called on her in their car to take her for a drive. She thought it was very *aimable* on their part for she dearly loved a ride and the day was 'smiling with sunshine'.

'We rode for over an hour,' she said, 'and then we came to a large stone house surrounded by a brick wall. We stopped and they invited me to come in with them. I thought it strange for they had said nothing about making any visits but I asked no questions. Perhaps, I thought, they have planned a pleasant surprise for me.

'It was a surprise, I assure you, but not a pleasant one,' she went on, her eyes dark in anger. 'The minute I entered the house I knew what it was. I could tell by the smell. Your Uncle Paul,' she said by way of explanation, 'used to joke about it. He used to say that, with eyes closed, he could tell whether a young woman, an old woman or a nun were in the same room with him. He was quite right. My nose is not as keen as his was but when a house is filled with old women and nuns, there is no mistaking it. I knew what this place was, a religious *maison de retraite*. You understand? A home for homeless old women.'

She covered my hand with hers when she saw the shock in my face.

'Do not let yourself be too disturbed,' she comforted me. 'It is over, but let me continue. Yes, a home for old women. The visit had all been arranged beforehand. The Mother Superior, a very fine woman, no doubt, greeted me with a warm welcome. You can believe me I was deeply agitated although I shook hands with her with great composure. She showed us all over the house – the *salon*, the dining-room, the bedrooms, the chapel, the *cabinets de toilette*. It was all very clean and very orderly and very impressive. There was, I should add, not an ashtray in the place. I particularly noticed that.'

'After we left, Pierre suggested we go to a café for an *apéritif*. I assure you, I needed it.'

' "*Eh bien?*" ' he said.

' "*Non*, my son," ' I replied, trembling with rage and, I might as well be honest with you, with fear as well. *"Absolument, non!"*

' "You would live like a princess in this house," Suzanne said to me. "You will have no cooking to do, no cleaning; you will have your own room and they will wait on you hand and foot."

' "Thank you," I said, "but I am too old to learn to live like a princess. And I have my own room, I like to cook and I clean when I feel like it. Please take me home."

' "But we thought you would be pleased," Suzanne went on. "This is no ordinary *maison de retraite*. It was the Countess who told us about it. She herself would adore to come here some day but it is too expensive for her. She would envy you, be assured."

' "I will give the Countess no cause for envy, my friend," I responded. "And do not seek to impress me with something that will please the Countess. She may have a taste for an expensive entombment but I do not. It still remains an entombment. I prefer to be alive and that means staying where I am. I beg of you, have the grace to take me home." '

They drove her home, she related, but for days following she received long letters from them urging her, for her own sake and for the peace of their minds, to enter the house.

'They spoke of my illness as though it were a thing that happened only to old people. They said they could not let me stay alone another winter, to die without attention or care. Frankly, I do not like this emphasis on death. It makes you feel that this is all young people have in mind when they look at you. "It would be easier for you, no doubt," I answered, "if I die *with* attention and care. But I cannot offer you this consolation. It brings none to me. I wish to die in my own bed." '

'Do not think I did not consider their peace of mind,' Aunt Lucienne continued after a pause in which she refilled our wine glasses. 'I realise that they worry about me. But I questioned myself in all honesty, what was more important to me, their peace of mind or mine? I decided it was mine. I am very content here; I have my friends, I have my four walls. Although I miss your Uncle Paul greatly, I have learned there is some pleasure in living alone. You live by your own tastes; you make and break your own rules.

'I was firm,' she went on, 'but I was also very frightened inside. My affairs, as you know, are in the hands of Pierre. Suppose, in anger, in stubbornness, he stopped sending me my monthly cheque.'

'He wouldn't do that,' I assured her.

'No, he wouldn't. You are right,' she agreed. 'But he could threaten to do it. And when one is in torment, one thinks of the worst. I tried to think of myself in that *maison* but I could not face it. To be surrounded all day long by women who were preparing their souls for death; to be waited on by the Sisters of Mercy. I am religious, you understand, but not as religious as all that.'

She lit a cigarette and exhaled the smoke with deep satisfaction. 'I told you there were no ashtrays in the place. No cigarettes, and the only reading, prayer books and the lives of the saints. The life of a princess indeed! The life of a princess waiting for the kiss of death.'

'Well, anyway, you managed to persuade them to let you stay here,' I said, anxious to hear the rest of the story.

'Yes, I persuaded them,' she replied with an ironic smile. 'I wrote them I would get married.'

So shocked had I been by her recountal of the visit to the *maison de retraite* that I had almost forgotten about the contemplated marriage.

'Whom were you going to marry?' I asked her.

'You remember,' she said, 'when we visited Suzanne last year, the Countess was talking about her admirers and I mentioned a retired *fonctionnaire* with liver trouble who used to work in the office of the *préfet*. You thought I was making it up to show that I, too, had some-body who looked upon me with favour. To be sure, I made up many stories during that holiday but this one was true. Well, partly true. There is a Monsieur – his name is Aristide Vidère – he has liver trouble, he is attentive to me but he is not a retired *fonctionnaire*. He used to keep books for a wine merchant in Tours. He is a gentle old man with no income whatsoever and he lives with his married daughter, which is to say with his son-in-law. Naturally, he does not enjoy it and that I can understand for I realise what it means to be the fifth wheel on a family wagon. He knows I have this apartment which is really too large for one person; he knows Pierre is a man of means; he finds in me a companion much to his taste. I would be obliged to have my

head examined if I believed that it is my charm or beauty that draws
him. All the same I believe him when he tells me he would end his
years happily if I would share them with him. It would assuredly be
a marriage of convenience – for him, that is to say.'

She chuckled.

'The situation was also very convenient for me. It was, one might
say, a card up my sleeve. I wrote to Pierre and Suzanne and told them
that I had received an offer of marriage and that this would solve all
their problems. I would not be living alone and I would not die
without attention or care. Naturally, I did not tell them that Monsieur
Vidère has liver trouble and that it would be I who would have to
give him attention and care. But I did make it clear that he had no
sou in his sock and it would mean I would have to draw more money
from my estate for our living expenses. With their approval, I said,
I would accept Monsieur Vidère. Thus they would have their peace
of mind and I should have mine. It was very logical, no?'

'No question about it,' I agreed.

She reponded with a smoke-laden laugh.

'This time it was they who had the *crise*. They came to see me post
haste. They pleaded with me to do nothing rash. An old man needed
waiting on, cooking, washing, and a thousand irksome services. I
agreed but I said it was better than living with a lot of old women.
Eh bien, the shoe was on the other foot. They did everything to persuade me to renounce this project and to remain as I am, where I
am. *Alors*, I let myself be persuaded. Their *crise* is over and so, *grâce
à Dieu*, is mine. Here I am and here I stay.' She sighed. 'When you
see Pierre and Suzanne in Paris,' she said, 'they will tell you I am a
foolish old woman in my second childhood and you must agree.'

She flicked the ash off her cigarette and her eyes grew misty.

'All the same, they are very kind and generous to me, Pierre and
Suzanne. It is they who had a card up their sleeve but they didn't
use it, and for that I shall never cease to be grateful. I must be honest
with you, my dear; I do not wish you to think too badly of them.
I know very well that your Uncle Paul left nothing; that it is a pretence
when Pierre says he is taking care of my estate. To save my pride,
I let the pretence stand. It is for that reason I live so economically.

When Pierre asked me what I needed to live on, I gave him the lowest figures I could so that I would not be too great a burden on him.'

'But, Aunt Lucienne,' I said, after voicing my approval of her son's silence, 'suppose they had agreed to this plan of your marrying Monsieur Vidère. What would you have done?'

The sadness which had shadowed her face dissolved in a wide smile.

'Don't be ridiculous, my dear,' she responded. 'I know my Pierre and I know my Suzanne. Apart from the money involved in taking care of another person, a total stranger, they have their social pride It is one thing to speak of your father or your father-in-law as a celebrated painter; it is another to introduce a man at your table whose life has been spent adding up figures in a wine shop. I am not a snob, you must know, but that I can understand. To be the widow of your Uncle Paul is something but to be the wife of Monsieur Vidère . . .' Words failed her and she did not complete the sentence. 'All the same,' she added after a thoughtful pause, 'I am grateful to this man for he has done me a service I can never repay. I think,' she said, reaching for the bottle of wine, 'that we must drink to his health.'

– From *My Aunt Lucienne.*

Bicycles Built for Two

RICHARD CHURCH

. . . Father thought so much better of my promising intelligence that he began to talk openly of his long-laid plan, the ordering of two tandems to be built of Chater-Lea parts, so that he and Mother on one machine, and Jack and I on the other, might be equipped to take the roads of England as our province, gypsies for the rest of our lives, free to say, with George Borrow, 'to the right, or to the left' whenever we should come to a parting of the highway.

This plan involved a serious economic reorganisation. The joint income at that time, made by my father as a sorter in the Post Office and my mother as a teacher employed by the School Board for London (a body taken over by the London County Council in 1902), was not more than £240 a year, though Father made a few pounds extra for a week or two before Christmas, in compulsory overtime. During those weeks of strained excitement he was on duty night and day, and we saw nothing of him until Christmas morning, which he spent in bed, cosseted and petted after his heroic labours.

Out of this income, modest even in those days of low prices, when Britain was on top of the world, Mother was contriving to buy the house, through a building society. The owner, who formerly lived in it, was a rubicund character who worked on the *News of the World* and smoked cigars on weekdays as well as Sundays; a sign of prosperity. I remember the day he came over to see my parents, to clinch the bargain, and how he led a procession, consisting of himself, his wife, and a daughter of my age at whom I looked incredulously, and our family. He took us round our own home, pointing out its virtues from the builder's point of view. He had a reiterative phrase which

I have never forgotten, for he drilled it into our minds as though he were hammering red-hot rivets into armour plate. Smacking a door-post or stamping on a concrete surround to a drain-pipe, he shouted: 'Take a load o' dynamite to move that, old boy!'

'Old boy' was my father, though the landlord ought rather to have addressed himself to 'old girl', for Mother was the really interested party. Father would willingly have lived in his cycle-house, content to be near the steed and unhampered by static possessions.

The machines were the latest thing in the cycle trade, especially the smaller one specially built for two boys aged twelve and eight. The handlebars were so designed that they could be adjusted through an infinity of positions, and the saddle-pins were elongated for a like purpose.

It was impossible not to share Father's triumph and excitement. His pleasure might even be called delirium, except that the idea of fever within so perfect and healthy a body was inconceivable.

Although he was still sleepy on Christmas Day, after so many eighteen-hour stretches of work during the postal rush over several weeks, he got up early that morning, as soon as Jack and I had unpacked our stockings, and was out of doors before breakfast. While Mother cooked the Christmas dinner, he was busy with spanners and rags, tightening nuts and polishing spokes, summoning one or other of us in turn to see if our respective saddles were at the right height and pitch.

Mother had to summon him in several times, with some sharpness, so that he should be ready for the ceremony of Christmas dinner; but there he was, in his wooden armchair at the head of the kitchen table, skilfully sharpening the old carving-knife on the steel, the stag-horn handles of both clasped in his square fists. Before him lay the aitch-bone, a mountain of meat shaped like the Rock of Gibraltar, still sizzling and spitting beads of fat and oozing blood-gravy into the little well at one end of the willow-pattern dish.

'Ah!' cried Father: and his teeth gleamed under his black moustache as he smiled at us, his small family seated with him at the table on that first Christmas Day of a new century, with all the roads of the world open before it. His grey eyes reflected those limitless vistas, and I could see his mind busy with the prospect of pleasures ahead to which he would introduce us now that we were equipped to accompany him.

Mother, flushed and tired after the hard morning's work in the hot kitchen, sat opposite him, and the steam from the joint and the mounds of potatoes, sprouts, and mashed swedes clouded her spectacles; or maybe they were dimmed by the heat from her face. She took them off and wiped them on the edge of the tablecloth, while Father carved the beef, filling our plates with thin slices, wielding his weapons with a flourish, while maintaining a gay discourse on his wife's genius as a cook, and how lucky we boys were to have such parents who could feed us like this and show us the glories of nature and the far cities of the earth.

Mother's brown eyes, without the disguise of her spectacles, looked at Father where he sat enthroned in his enthusiasm, like a god in a nimbus of light. I saw her worshipping him and I wondered which of his family round that table admired him most, Mother, Jack or I.

What a meal it was; the plates covered with a layer of roast beef, batter pudding and vegetables piled on that British base: the Christmas pudding that followed, black in its ripeness, and flaming with brandy: then the crackers, the almonds and raisins, and a glass of port for each of us.

When the feast was finished, and Jack and I had rolled like young Roman patricians from the table, Father over-rode Mother's protestations and ordered her upstairs for a rest, while he and the boys would wash up.

Then the last saucepan was scrubbed with Monkey Brand soap, the bowl and sink flushed down with hot water and soda, and the job was done.

'Now, boys,' cried Father. 'We'll have a lesson on mounting!'

By this time my distended stomach was beginning to rebel, but I dared not say so. We went out to the yard and the cold air struck through my super-heated skin, waking me from my lethargy, so that I realised, with a shock, the ordeal confronting me.

Father brought forward the smaller tandem, as proud of it as a cavalry officer of his horse. I stood shivering on the concrete, my swollen belly fluttering as though I had swallowed a live bird instead of a plate of beef. I was frightened as well as cold. This lesson was my initiation as a cyclist. I looked helplessly at Jack, who took the occasion calmly because he was already experienced, having possessed a small machine of his own for the past year or two.

'Come along,' he said quietly, 'you'd better try now. It'll make things easier when we have to go out on the road.'

So I took my position beside the rear saddle of the tandem, while Jack held the front handlebars, Father seized my right foot and my posterior, hoisted me into the saddle, explaining at the same time how I must push off on the right pedal, in time with Jack. After several repetitions of this exercise, we tried the process together, and to my terror I found myself in the saddle and the tandem rushing up the yard. Jack, not used to the length and weight behind him, wobbled and applied the brake. Whereupon I fell off and barked my shin on the rat-trap pedal. But again I dared not give in, and for the rest of the afternoon we went through the movements of mounting and dismounting, until by tea-time the ritual was mastered and I felt some confidence, though by now Jack was bored and grumpy. Father, however, was jubilant. He patted us on our strained and aching backs, and promised us a real ride next day, and a lesson in correct pedalling, with the ankle dropped and heel at the correct angle to get the most power in every push.

Darkness saved us from further drill. Silent, exhausted, we crept into the house, leaving Father to bed the tandem down in its stable and to follow us indoors, as cheerful as ever, where he greeted Mother with a kiss and drank half a dozen cups of tea, while describing the route which we were to follow next day on our first family ride . . .

That Christmas evening our gloom was deepened by foreboding, as Father sat tuning his fiddle and giving us our marching orders, or rather pedalling orders, for the morrow. He proposed to take us for our first family excursion to Virginia Water and back. That was his idea of a gentle ride, without strain for Mother, and bearing in mind that this would be my introduction, as a cyclist, to the 'rolling English road'. Only Father knew the mileage and the weight of the tandems.

'Are you sure it's all right?' asked Mother.

He pooh-poohed the misgiving and reminded her that he and Jack would be at the head of the tandems, bearing the brunt . . .

Boxing Day dawned bleakly with thick fog and frost. Mother refused to set off, as had been proposed, after breakfast. Father was annoyed and took himself into the back room, where he played his flute in solitude until dinner-time.

We all sat in silence round the table, consuming cold beef, bubble-and-squeak, and cold Christmas pudding. 'Tom!' said Mother, suddenly, at the end of the meal. Both Jack and I detected the note of warning in her voice, and we looked at each other apprehensively. It made us shy and miserable to see Father rolled over and bounced in the flood, as though he were no older than ourselves, though we knew that in the end, as the clouds rolled away, Mother would contrive to restore his dignity and set him up again as the head of the house who could do no wrong and whose word was law.

But this time the heavens were on Father's side, for the fog broke and a gleam of sunlight, like a dusty yellow handkerchief, flicked across the bay window of the kitchen and almost brought the aquarium and its inmates to life.

It also flicked the sulkiness and disappointment out of Father's grey eyes. He looked up, squinted at the sky, and said:

'You were quite right, my girl. We've done better to wait. But it'll have to be a short ride round the houses today. After all, there's a lifetime before us.'

Mother could not deny him a second time, and we got ourselves ready for a local expedition. Father wore a short covert coat of fawn, a cap, knickerbockers, stockings and spats. Mother veiled her straw hat as though she were a bee-keeper, fastened the edges of her skirt with clips and yards of elastic to the insteps of her shoes, and carried a little fox-fur tippet round her neck. Jack and I both wore buckled knickerbockers, black stockings, marine jerseys, and cloth caps. I was also wound into a long scarf made of squares of red and black knitting (like the quilt on our bed), and I wore a pair of woollen gloves.

The front door was locked, the cat put out, and we all emerged into the backyard.

'Now then,' said Father, 'we're off, my dears! I'll lead the way, Jack; and we'll make for the park, ride round once or twice, then come out by the Queen's Road and beat the boundaries of the parish. There will be no traffic about on Boxing afternoon.'

He was right, as he always was, in outdoor affairs. The streets of Battersea, after the revels of Christmas Day and the morning of fog, were deserted. We had no need for self-consciousness as we wheeled the long tandems round to the street, accompanied by the cat, who sat on the coping mewing with dismay at being turned out of her armchair on a cold and frosty afternoon.

Mother and Father mounted and left the mooring of the kerbstone. 'Come on,' said Jack, 'or we shall lose sight of them.'

I shivered, gulped, and obeyed. Jack was already in his saddle, grasping the handlebars and balancing the machine beside the kerb, with the offside pedal raised and his foot on it ready for the push-off.

I put my foot over the low centre bar and took my seat.

'Now push!' cried Jack.

We were afloat. We glided on, and the pedals carried my feet round with them. Gradually feeling the regularity of this movement, I began to take my share in keeping it going, leaning forward convulsively and pushing on the downstroke. But I forgot the other pedal rising on an unaccented syllable, and the foot on it was lost, was waggling in mid-air, and the ankle was angrily bitten by the rat-trap pedal.

The pain was sharp and unexpected. Tears streamed down my face, and the cold air chilled them to pellets of steel. But Jack was desperate, and wholly concerned to keep the machine on an even keel. He was fighting against the weight and length of the monster and the useless lump of mortality seated behind him.

I could do nothing but hang on, my hands convulsive on the brown felt grips. Jack urged me to push, for he could not propel the tandem alone. I did my best, and slowly the numbed foot came to life again, though by now my fingers were frozen to the bars.

We rounded the corner safely at the top of the street, and this gave us confidence. After all, the tandem was a handsome specimen, and unique. Our parents were sailing on ahead and I heard Father call aloud:

'Come along, boys, keep close.'

His voice floated merrily over the ghostly parish, and I saw a window curtain drawn aside and a face peering out at us.

On we pedalled, and by the time we reached the park gates near Prince of Wales's Mansions, I had caught the knack of free-wheeling at the same time as Jack, though this meant a slight lag in my rhythm, the difference between pushing with him and being on the alert for pushing with him. This gave him the burden, though neither of us knew that I was not taking my share.

I could see little ahead; only the faded blue of Jack's jersey and the nape of his neck. But to my right and left I had a prospect of Battersea that commanded my attention by its stillness. I have never forgotten that quiet scene, so negatively emphasised. Even the fashionable bicycle track round the park was empty. We circled it twice, Father and Mother slowing down and riding abreast of us, so that Father could give us a taste of his vitality as an open-air guide. Nothing quelled his high spirits. I watched his shapely calves working as steadily as the pistons of a locomotive, his ankles and heels dropping on the turn, regular, exact. The pressure needed no exertion and he still had all his breath to feed that flood of conversation, buoyed upon outbursts of song, usually a stave or two from his favourite ballad:

> *'Oh merry goes the day*
> *When the heart is young'*

His heart was congenitally young, and appeared to be totally unaffected by the hardship and humiliations of his early life. Like Hardy's 'Darkling Thrush', he poured abroad his triple repeated ecstasies:

> *'When Frost was spectre-gray,*
> *And Winter's dregs made desolate*
> *The weakening eye of day.'*

These words from Hardy's poem, written that week, on the 31st of December, aptly describe the afternoon of Boxing Day and the boskage of Battersea Park, where the morning's fog still lingered under the bare trees, though their higher branches 'scored the sky' with some faint suggestion of colour and form, brown against pink, but all of it dusted with the gathering consolidation of frost.

That frost deadened my feet, which moved round, each in its cold circle, like corpses in a whirlpool. Even Father's animal warmth could not thaw them, though he rode beside us and from time to time put an encouraging hand on my back, a giant's gesture that caused our tandem to leap forward as though the road were suddenly declined beneath it.

Battersea is never a sun-drenched district. It lies in what used to be marsh and mudflats, a stretch of land succumbed to the lazy embrace of a wide curve of the Thames. In primeval times the mists must have lingered there winter and summer. In the Victorian Age of smoke and iron they lingered there still, but deepened with an over-head obscuration never wholly dispelled. That may be why, in those days, few birds inhabited there; only a desolate colony of sparrows, their feathers monotoned and as drab as their feeble twitterings.

Leaving the park, by an eastern gate, we followed the parental tandem over Chelsea Bridge. Father had evidently changed his mind. I was to discover that once on the road he threw all consecutive plans to the winds. Often, on a tour, he would start off in the morning by wetting his finger, holding it up to feel which way the wind blew, and choosing our course by deciding to run before the wind 'to help the boys along', but also, I suspected, to enjoy a greater sense of freedom and to spread the wings of his panic heart in a justified irresponsibility.

Over the bridge, we turned westward along the Chelsea Embankment. Here we passed one or two broughams carrying rich children to the parties of other rich children; fabulous creatures wholly outside our ken. The sooty gardens in front of Cheyne Row lay dead. How sombre, how ominous was Victorian London in winter, especially to a child susceptible to colour and clean line, and to whom cold and damp were specially abhorrent because they increased the periodical bouts of pain in his stomach.

Father pointed out the place where he had thrown the pickled onions at Thomas Carlyle, but the story meant little to me, for the name was unknown, and I was beginning to flag. Our tandem was built not of light alloys, but of the steel that was the chief foundation of the British Empire, permitting it to pile superstructure upon superstructure of wealth. I felt as though I were propelling the whole of the steel industry at each rise of the pedals. But Jack did not think so. He grumbled at me for being a mere passenger, and he was probably right, for he had to lean over his handlebars and groan as he pushed.

'Drop your ankle! Drop your ankle!' cried Father, disapproving of this uncontrolled exertion. Jack only muttered to himself, and I could see from the pose of the back of his head that he too was at the point of exhaustion. I began to feel miserable, and I looked at Mother, but she was still veiled and she sat behind Father like Patience upon the monument, though I was certain she was not smiling. . . .

Father now proposed that we should plunge past the house where the painter J. M. W. Turner once lived in squalor, into the district so aptly named the World's End, and that we should continue westward along King's Road, Chelsea, to Walham Green, ultimately to cross the river by Wandsworth Bridge and so home by the York Road past the malodorous candle factory.

But the veiled figure of Patience riding behind Father suddenly came to life, and an angry life. She insisted on dismounting. Accordingly we drew into the side by the river-pavement. Jack's strength, however, was not enough to support the tandem while I jumped off. Nor was I capable of jumping, my inadequate body being by now rigid with cold. We both collapsed and lay on the pavement with the tandem on top of us. The situation was not graceful, and it offended Jack's overmature dignity. After we had struggled up, unhurt, he stood white with anger, and not daring to vent it on Father he picked upon me as the scapegoat. I was past caring. I stood in a coma of general discomfort, every part of my anatomy aching, except those parts too numbed by cold even to ache.

There followed, upon the pavement of Chelsea Embankment, still happily deserted, one of those scenes when Mother broke through her usual policy of government by seeming acquiescence, and staged an open revolt.

Without a word, she brushed us both down, leaving Father to pick up the shining tandem and rest it against the trunk of a plane tree. Then, snatching off my gloves, and feeling my hands, then Jack's, in search of evidence, she opened her attack. She cursed the tandems, their weight, their length, their manœuvrability. She referred to the disabilities of the female body and particularly of mothers of children, she pointed out the singular delicacy of her own children and enumerated several reasons for it, all connected with Father's heredity, personal stupidity and callousness. She called upon God to witness the universal unfairness between the sexes, with woman as the eternal victim and slave.

Jack, during this oration, retreated to the balustrade, and looked at the ebbing tide and the seagulls lamenting over the mudbanks of Chelsea Reach.

Still Mother had not finished. She was flushed, as I could see because she had unfastened her veil. The smoky sunset clouded the lenses of her spectacles, otherwise the fire of her eyes would have annihilated poor Father, who stood quietly waiting as though being photographed beside the new machine.

Mother's vehemence terrified me by its extravagant range. I wanted to implore her to stop, to leave the rest unsaid, so that the whole universe of nature and man should not be made to depend upon my father's innocent impulses, his premature opening of the summer campaign for the conquest of the English roads.

At last Mother's breath gave out. She stopped, and drew me to her as though we were now to face the spears of a hostile tribe, or the rifles of a firing party.

'That's all right, old girl,' said Father. 'We'll take a short cut home over Battersea Bridge.'

– From *Over the Bridge*.

Lord Fortinbras and the English Aristocracy

NANCY MITFORD

The purpose of the aristocrat is most emphatically not to work for money. His ancestors may have worked in order to amass the fortune which he enjoys, though on the whole the vast riches of the English lords come from sources unconnected with honest toil; but he will seldom do the same. His mind is not occupied with money, it turns upon other matters. When money is there he spends it on maintaining himself in his station. When it is no longer there he ceases to spend, he draws in his horns.

All this should not be taken as a sign that our lords are lazy or unenterprising. The point is that, in their view, effort is unrelated to money. Now this view has, to a large extent, communicated itself to the English race and nation with the result that our outlook is totally different from that of our American cousins, who had never had an aristocracy. Americans relate all effort, all work, and all of life itself to the dollar. Their talk is of nothing but dollars. The English seldom sit happily chatting for hours on end about pounds. In England, public business is its own reward, nobody would go into Parliament in order to become rich, neither do riches bring public appointments. Our ambassadors to foreign states are experienced diplomatists, not socially ambitious millionairesses.

This idiosyncratic view of money has its good side and its bad. Let us glance at the case history of Lord Fortinbras. Fortinbras is ruined – we are now in the 1930's. (All English noblemen, according to themselves, are ruined, but Fortinbras really is). He is not ruined because of death duties, since his father died when he was a child, before they became so heavy, but because he and his forebears have always regarded their estates with the eyes of sportsmen rather than of cultivators. It is useless for him to plead that the policy of cheap corn has been his downfall; an intelligent landowner has always been able to make money with prize cattle, racehorses, market gardens, timber, and so on. But Fortinbras's woods have been looked after by gamekeepers and not by woodmen, his farms have been let to tenants chosen for their tenderness towards foxes and partridges rather than for their agricultural efficiency. His land is undercapitalised, his cottagers live in conditions no better than those of their Saxon forebears, water and electric light are laid on in his stables but not in the dwellings of his tenantry. He has made various unwise speculations and lost a 'packet' on the Turf. In short, he deserves to be ruined and he is ruined.

Now what does he do? He is young, healthy, and not stupid; his wife, the daughter of another peer, is handsome, bossy, and energetic. She is the kind of woman who, in America, would be running something with enormous efficiency and earning thousands. They have two babies. Dominick and Caroline, and a Nanny. Does it occur to either Lord or Lady Fortinbras to get a job and retrieve the family fortunes? It does not. First of all they sell everything that is not entailed, thus staving off actual want. They shut up most of the rooms in their house, send away the servants (except, of course, Nanny), and get the Dowager Lady Fortinbras and her sister to come and cook, clean, dust, and take trays upstairs to the nursery. Old Lady Fortinbras is quite useful, and Lady Enid is a treasure. The Fortinbrases realise that they are very lucky, and if at heart they wish there were a mother's hall for the two ladies to sit in of an evening, they never say so, even to each other. Fortinbras chops the wood, stokes the boiler, brings in the coal, washes the Morris Cowley, and drives off in it to attend the County Council and sit on the Bench. Lady Fortinbras helps in the house, digs in the border, exercises the Border terriers, and also does a great deal of committee work. They are both on the go from morning to night, but it is a go that does not bring in one penny.

Their friends and neighbours all say: 'Aren't the Fortinbrases wonderful?'

Comes the war. They clear the decks by sending Nanny and the children to an American couple, the Karamazovs, whom they once met at St Moritz and who have sent them Christmas cards ever since. Fortinbras goes off with his territorials and Lady Fortinbras joins the A.T.S. Their war records are brilliant in the extreme, their energy, courage, and instinct for leadership have at last found an outlet, and in no time at all they both become generals. After the war they are not surprised to find themselves more ruined than ever. The Karamazovs, whose lives for several years have been made purgatory by Dominick, Caroline and Nanny, especially Nanny, send in a modest bill for the schooling of the young people which Fortinbras has no intention of settling. It would seem unreasonable to pay for one's children to be taught to murder the English language and taught, apparently, nothing else whatever. Dominick, failing to get into Eton, has had to be sent to some dreadful school in Scotland. Besides, what did the Karamazovs do in the war? Nothing, according to Nanny, but flop in and out of a swimming pool. The Karamazovs come to England expecting to be thanked, fêted, and paid, only to find that their friends have left for the Northern Capitals.

Now the Fortinbrases are getting on, over fifty. Dominick having come of age, they have broken the entail and sold everything, very badly, as the house is full of dry rot and the farms are let to tenants who cannot be dislodged. However, a little money does result from the sale. They arrange a mews flat behind Harrods where, generals once again, they will continue to cook and wash up for the rest of their days. They both still sit on endless committees, Fortinbras goes to the House of Lords, they kill themselves with overwork, and have never, except for their Army pay, earned one single penny. 'Aren't the Fortinbrases wonderful?' Well yes, in a way they are.

Now, while the Fortinbrases have the typical aristocratic outlook on money, the state of their finances is by no means typical. Most people, nowadays, take it for granted that the aristocracy is utterly impoverished, a view carefully fostered by the lords themselves. It takes a shooting affray, letting police and reporters into a country house, to remind the ordinary citizen that establishments exist where several menservants wait on one young woman at dinner. There are still many enormous fortunes in the English aristocracy, into which income tax and death duties have made no appreciable inroads. Arundel, Petworth, Hatfield, Woburn, Hardwicke, Blenheim, Haddon, Drumlanrig, Alnwick, Stratfield Saye, Harewood, Knole, Knowsley, Wilton, Holkham, Glamis, Cullen, Cliveden, Highclere, Althorp, Mentmore – all vast houses – are still inhabited by lords who have inherited them, or by members of their families. This little list is a mere fraction of the whole. The treasures such houses contain are stupendous. When the Duke of Buccleuch came to visit the Louvre, the curator, who had been to England and seen the Duke's collection of French furniture, greeted him with the words: 'I apologise for the furniture of the Louvre, M. le Duc.'

The English, so censorious of those foreigners (the French peasantry for instance) who do not pay their taxes as they should, have themselves brought tax evasion within legal limits to a fine art. Death duties can be avoided altogether if the owner of an estate gives it to his heir and then lives another five years. One agreeable result of this rule is that old lords are cherished as never before. Their heirs, so far from longing to step into their shoes, will do anything to keep them alive. Doctors and blood donors hover near them, they are not allowed to make the smallest effort, or to be worried or upset, and are encouraged to live in soft climates and salubrious spots.

The crippling effects of supertax also can be overcome in various ways by those who own large capital sums. The aristocrat can augment his fortune in many a curious manner, since he is impervious to a sense of shame (all aristocrats are: shame is a bourgeois notion). The lowest peasant of the Danube would stick at letting strangers into his house for 2s. 6d., but our dukes, marquesses, earls, viscounts, and barons not only do this almost incredible thing, they glory in it, they throw themselves into the sad commerce with rapture, and compete as to who among them can draw the greatest crowds. It is the first topic of conversation in noble circles today, the tourists being referred to in terms of sport rather than of cash – a sweepstake on the day's run, or the bag counted after the shoot.

'I get twice as many as Reggie, but Bert does better than me.'

The baiting of the trap is lovingly considered.

'Mummy dresses up in her Coronation robes, they can't resist it.'

'I say, old boy, look out – you don't want to pay entertainment tax.'

'No, no – I've taken counsel's opinion.'

'We've started a pet's cemetery – a quid for a grave, three quid for a stone, and a fiver if Daphne writes a poem for it.'

Of course the fellow countrymen of people who will descend to such methods of raising cash imagine that they must be driven to it by direst need. The fact is they thoroughly enjoy it. Also it has become a matter of policy to appear very poor. The lords are retrenching visibly, and are especially careful to avoid any form of ostentation: for instance, only five of them saw fit to attend the last coronation in their family coaches. Coronets on luggage, motor-cars, and so on are much less used than formerly. Aristocrats no longer keep up any state in London, where family houses hardly exist now...

Divest, divest, is the order of the day. The nobleman used to study a map of his estate to see how it could be enlarged, filling out a corner here, extending a horizon there. Nowadays he has no such ambitions; he would much rather sell than buy. The family is not considered as it used to be; the ancestors are no longer revered, indeed they are wilfully forgotten, partly perhaps from a feeling of guilt when all that they so carefully amassed is being so carelessly scattered. The dead are hardly mourned. 'Far the best for him,' the children say, cheerfully (so long, of course, as he has lived the requisite five years). Nobody wears black any more. The younger generation is no longer planned for, and there is a general feeling of *'après nous le déluge'*.

The instinct of the lords to divest themselves of age-long influence and rights extends to their influence and rights in the Church. Most of them are members of the Church of England; though there are forty-seven Roman Catholics with seats in the House of Lords. On the whole, the lords, in common with most of their fellow country-men, have always regarded religious observance as a sort of patriotic duty. The Church is the Church of England and must be supported to show that we are not as foreigners are. A friend of mine voiced this attitude during the war: 'Well, you know, I don't do fire-watching or Home Guard and I feel one must do something to help the war, so I always go to Church on Sunday.' I am sure he did not imagine that his prayers would drive back the German hordes; he went as a gesture of social solidarity. Hitherto, the livings of our Church have been the gift of landowners, who have generally chosen downright, muscular Christians of low Church leanings. 'Don't want lace and smells in my Church.' Zeal has always been frowned upon. As it is impossible to remove a parson once he is installed in his living, some of the most ringing rows of all time have been between the Manor and the Vicarage. Now, however, faithful to the spirit of divest, divest, the temporal lords are busily putting their livings at the disposal of their spiritual colleagues, the Bishops.

Does this apparent abdication of the lords in so many different directions mean that the English aristocracy is in full decadence and will soon exist only like the appendix in the human body, a useless and sometimes harmful relic of the past? It would not be safe to assume so. The English lord has been nurtured on the land and is conversant with the cunning ways of the animal kingdom. He has often seen the grouse settle into the heather to rise and be shot at no more. He has noticed that enormous riches are not well looked on in the modern world and that in most countries his genus is extinct. It may be that he who for a thousand years has weathered so many a storm, religious, dynastic, and political, is taking cover in order to weather yet one more. It may be that he will succeed. He must, of course, be careful not to overdo the protective colouring. An aristocracy cannot exist as a secret society. Nor must he overdo an appearance of destitution.

– From 'The English Aristocracy' in *Noblesse Oblige*.

F

PART THREE

Below Stairs

The Edwardian Kitchen

URSULA BLOOM

Wot price me and you in Bel–gra–vi–a?
Both hon our best behavi–ar;
Walk, talk, dress ourselves too,
Jus' like the Dukies and Dukesses do !

How did the elegant Edwardians superintend the running of those
homes in which they never did a stroke of work? If the fire required
poking, one rang for a maid to fulfil this duty. No lady made any
effort.

In every kitchen a comfortably robust cook reigned over a glittering
range which it was beneath her to clean. The tweeny did that.
Parlourmaids still coquetted to the front doors, and admitted guests
in the correct manner. Linen aprons were the right thing on print
frocks 'of a morning', but in the afternoon the embroidered apron
with cross-over shoulder-straps at the back, and the cap. Caps were
changing. There had been attractive Norwegian-type caps in 1906,
now there had come in a couple of muslin rosettes with a connecting
band, intended to lie flat on the head, and to show hardly at all. Maids
had never liked caps which they felt to be a sign of bondage, and some
mistresses refused to allow them to wear the new rosette caps, because
they looked absurd.

Every maidservant entering service had a tin box varnished a ginger
shade of brown, and in it two print dresses for mornings, one black
dress for afternoons, shoes for both occasions, and a jumble of under-
clothing which you could hardly have called lingerie. No maid
dressed the same morning and afternoon. It was a routine that she

changed at midday into her post-midday apparel, after which time she was ready to go to the door to admit visitors.

Visitors were frequent, for the high standard of friendship was important. No one was warned of an approaching visit, and it was quite correct to 'call in' when in the village. I have always felt it was the better method.

Shopping, as we know it today, was non-existent. Today it takes pride of place in every woman's morning, for she sits down to breakfast saying wearily: 'I simply *must* get around to the shops.' Then no woman went to the shops save on rare occasions, and I myself had scarcely seen the inside of a grocer's shop in years, and most certainly never inside a butcher's.

Once a month Mr Frederick Ballance arrived in his gig to take orders. He was Stratford's leading grocer. He looked rather like a small Father Christmas, and would sit in the drawing-room with my mother, and take down notes from her previously prepared list, for the goods which would be delivered by van on the following Friday. This order never included flour, which came from Talton Mill. There was no such item as 'self-raising' flour, for this was made at home by the simple method of adding baking powder. Margarine was not seen, and everyone acquired their own cooking-fat from the roasts.

Cooking eggs, too, were non-existent. Only the new-laid kind appeared, and these were used for all purposes. It was an eye-opener to me years later, when I went into a grocer's shop in St Albans, and saw different labels on baskets of eggs. Breakfast eggs. Cooking eggs. Farm eggs. New-laid eggs. Pickled eggs. And just *eggs*!

Sugar was bought by the stone at about a penny a pound, which would have been much too expensive for preserving, so for jam a special sugar was procured costing three farthings a pound. It would have been thriftless to order cakes or biscuits, and everything on the tea table had to be made at home.

Even as late as 1908 furniture polish was made in the rectory with beeswax and turpentine. Monkey soap, arriving in a solid cake, was labelled *Won't Wash Clothes*, and filled the place of today's scouring powder. Hearthstone was used in great quantities, for maids took a pride in a magnificent snowy doorstep, and the flagged halls were worked out in suitable patterns with this hearthstone, which were supposed to be 'the thing'.

Tinned goods had to be treated with the utmost caution because one did hear such things! There were the most excellent sardines, usually served for Sunday tea when my father had had a hard day, and passed as being safe because they were tinned in oil, which minimised the chance of poisoning. Corned beef was sold. Tins of salmon which we adored and which had lovely little round bones like dolls' serviette rings in them, were immensely popular. Potted meat was most dangerous, and there were frequent cases of poisoning with this.

Mr Ballance ponderously wrote down his order, was given a glass of his own cooking sherry, or some sloe gin, and faithfully on the Friday his van turned in at the stable yard, and everything was delivered on to the kitchen table.

The goods were then put into store, and my mother had a special pantry for this, which was kept permanently locked. So much was given out on a Monday, and if more was used it had to be accounted for, which to any thriftless servant added to the complications.

Meat also was bought in a weekly order. The Sunday joint came out by carrier's cart, with the kidneys for the special patties always made at home, and sausages arrived with them. If the carrier did not bring them, there were occasions when the butcher's tall light cart appeared in the stable yard, with the high-stepping horse, said to move so rapidly because it was spurred on by the smell of blood! The carts had to have yellow wheels, and most of the young butchers who brought out the meat were a good deal faster than the village young men, which gave the tweenies heart-throbs, and made old Cook sour because she was too old for 'that sort of thing'.

All country people kept pigs and cured their own bacon, whilst hams hung in calico bags between the kitchen rafters. We usually kept six to eight pigs, and had a henyard also, so we did not look like starving. Vegetables were grown in a very large kitchen garden, but about these there was an infinite sameness, and we were never able to eat out the too frequent apples, and the tiresome rhubarb which we detested.

Fish was an infrequent luxury, so little known in the centre of England that one year when May Aldington came on a visit with a gift of a lobster and a crab in a rush basket, the cook who opened it promptly fainted, because she had never seen anything like it before. But the river provided coarse fish, perch which were delicious, pike for stuffing, chub and eels for a pie, one of my father's favourites.

No lady ever lifted a duster. She merely put a finger on the bell handle, twirled it round, and instantly at the opposite end of the house one of the dangling bells on great wire hoops jingled derisively. She then showed the maid that the piano was dusty, and the maid dealt with the matter. She never cooked. She did 'do' the flowers, but her day was otherwise entirely unhomely. . . . She read, it is true. She did delightful needlework, and of course there were far more parties, taking tea out, and paying calls.

But soon the first difficulties with maidservants had begun to be encountered. Not only were the girls less anxious to work, but the wicked thing was that wages were going up to the most fanciful heights. A parlourmaid asked as much as twenty pounds a year; cooks were twenty-two pounds; tweenies, fifteen!

'Whatever is happening to the world?' asked indignant mistresses.

But whatever else there was, as yet no enforced day off was established. No holidays were expected or given. If one of their relations was ill, then they were sent home, otherwise they stayed in their 'place'.

– From *The Elegant Edwardian.*

Father Hires a Cook

CLARENCE DAY

One late afternoon when Father came up from down town, he found his home much upset. Our cook had walked out and left us. I was a child of four, George was two, and there was a new baby besides. Mother was ill. She hadn't been able to leave us to go to an agency. And as she was no hand at cooking herself, the outlook for dinner was poor.

This state of affairs was unprecedented in all Father's experience. In his father's home, they never changed their servants suddenly; they seldom changed them at all; and as his mother was a past mistress of cooking, he had always been doubly protected. Since his marriage, he had had to live a much bumpier life. But this was the worst yet.

He asked Mother, who was lying in bed, what she was going to do about it. There were no telephones then, and she couldn't do anything at all, at the moment; but she said she would try to go to an agency in the morning and see what she could find. 'In the morning? Good God!' Father said. 'Where is the place, anyhow?' And he clapped on his hat and strode out again, over towards Sixth Avenue.

As I heard the story years afterwards, it was late when he got there, and he bounded up the front stoop two or three steps at a time and went quickly into the little office, where the gaslights were burning. He had never been in such a place before, and to his surprise it was empty, except for a severe-looking woman who sat at a desk at one side. 'Where do you keep 'em?' he urgently demanded, his mind on the question of dinner.

She looked at him, got out her pen, and opened a large book deliberately. 'I will take your name and address,' she informed him, 'and then, if you please, you may give me the details as to what kind of person you require and when you would wish her to call.'

But Father had no time, he told her, for any damned fol-de-rol. 'Where do you keep 'em?' he said again. She was standing in the way of his dinner. I can imagine how his face must have reddened and how his eyes must have blazed at her. 'I am asking you where you keep them!' he roared.

'Why, the girls are in there,' the lady explained, to calm him, 'but clients are not allowed in that room. If you will tell me the kind of position you wish me to fill for you, I will have one come out.'

Before she'd half-finished, Father had thrown open the door and gone in. There sat a crowd of the girls, young and old, sickly and brawny, of all shapes and sizes; some ugly, some pretty and trim and stylish, some awkward; nurses, ladies' maids, waitresses, washerwomen, and cooks.

The manager was by now at Father's elbow, trying to make him get out, and insisting that he tell her the position he wished to fill. But Father was swiftly glancing around at the crowd, and he paid no attention. He noticed a little woman in the corner, with honest grey eyes, who sat there, shrewd-looking and quiet. He pointed his cane over at her and said: 'I'll take that one.'

The manager was flustered, but still she kept trying to enforce her authority. She protested she didn't yet know the position. . . .

'Cook,' Father said, 'cook.'

'But Margaret doesn't wish to be a cook, she wants . . .'

'You can cook, can't you?' Father demanded.

Margaret's plain little face was still pink with excitement and pleasure at being chosen above all that roomful by such a masterful gentleman. Father had probably smiled at her, too, for they liked each other at once. Well, she said, she had cooked for one family.

'Of course she can cook,' Father said.

He said afterwards, when describing the incident: 'I knew at once she could cook.'

The manager didn't like this at all. The discipline of the office was spoiled. 'If you are going to take her anyhow,' she said acidly, 'what day would you wish her to come, and will you please give me your name?'

'Yes, yes,' Father said, without giving it. 'Come on, Margaret.' And he planked down the fee and walked out.

Margaret followed him through the door and trotted over to our home at his heels. He sent her down to the kitchen immediately, while he went upstairs to dress.

'I don't know why you make such a fuss about engaging new servants. It's simple enough,' he said comfortably to Mother that evening, after Margaret's first dinner.

It was the first of a long series, for she stayed with us twenty-six years.

– From *Life with Father*.

Mrs Wrench

BEVERLEY NICHOLS

Of these five little rooms which Mrs Wrench had to look after, four were, at the time of her domination, furnished so simply that they could hardly be described as 'furnished' at all. The Garden Room, it is true, was gradually taking shape, but my study held little more than a table, a chair, and a piano, while the bedrooms contained only a steel bed, a cupboard, a rug, and a washstand, on which reposed a pitcher filled with amber-coloured rain-water. They could all be 'done out', by an energetic housemaid, in the course of an hour.

Therefore, the idea that Mrs Wrench could possibly be over-worked never for one moment presented itself. And it was not till after a long series of incidents, small in themselves, but all pointing in the same direction, that I realised what was the matter.

It began with a curious phrase which constantly came to Mrs Wrench's lips. This phrase was: 'I was having five minutes.' She would say, for example, that the vicar had called during the week. 'I was having five minutes, after dinner, so he took me by surprise.' Or perhaps there had been a telegram which she had not known whether to open or not. 'But I was having five minutes when it came,' she would say, 'so I was able to deal with it all right.'

At first this singular phrase went in at one ear and came out at the other. It meant nothing at all to me. It did not suggest, as it ought to have suggested, the first rumblings of approaching thunder. No – it was merely an odd note, like some constantly recurring refrain in a long poem. Like, for example, the extraordinary couplet which echoes through the work of Blake:

The caterpillar on the leaf
Reminds thee of thy mother's grief.

A wild couplet, that, to which, in all solemnity, we may apply the tragic adjective *insane*. Such was Mrs Wrench's constant assertion: 'I was having five minutes.'

A very minor incident gave to this phrase, for the first time, its full significance . . . I arrived, with a friend an hour earlier than usual at the cottage.

I was feeling very happy that afternoon. The country was a paradise. The fields were dancing with buttercups, the hedges aflame with the sweet white fires of may. Over the wall the lilac leant its tipsy plumes, giving itself in lazy wantonness to the breeze. Every thrush was a nightingale, that day, and every starling a lark. And many were the thrushes and starlings and sparrows who fluttered into the air as I opened the gate of the secret garden, took a deep breath and, said: 'I am home.'

And then framed in the window, a black figure appeared. Mrs Wrench. Black not only in vesture but in countenance – a countenance made all the blacker by flaming red hair above it. She advanced heavily.

'You're early,' she said.

'Why yes . . .'

Was it imagination, or did a cloud pass over the sun?

'*I was having five minutes*,' said Mrs Wrench.

She stared at me reproachfully. I stared back.

She turned and went.

Five minutes *what?* Was she, perhaps, engaged in some illicit enterprise? Coining? Or even worse, taking in other people's washing? Was she drinking? But no – she was a teetotaler.

I could no longer ignore the obvious. Mrs Wrench meant that she was having five minutes respite from the toils of slaving for *me*.

And yet . . . it seemed impossible. I had not been at the cottage, during the last six weeks, for more than three nights. Last week-end I was up for Sunday night only. It was now Saturday. She could *not* mean what she seemed to mean. Impatiently I jumped to my feet.

She must be sought out, and this dreadful problem must be solved.

She was in the kitchen, washing a salad. As I opened the door, I suddenly remembered that I had no particular cause to see her. So I said, on the spur of the moment: 'Oh, Mrs Wrench, *have* you seen the bluebells in the orchard? They're too lovely.'

Mrs Wrench inclined her head. 'Yes,' she said, 'I took five minutes off to go and have a look at them.' And then, with the face of gloom which she always reserved for the delivery of an aphorism, she added: 'All work and no play makes Jack a dull boy. That's what I always say.'

So it was true! I had been blind not to notice it before. And as I walked round the garden a whole flock of little memories pursued me, all revealing themselves, for the first time, in their full significance.

One of these phrases was 'it gives me a chance'. Every Monday morning, when leaving I would say good-bye to Mrs Wrench and tell her that I would be up again on Saturday, to which the invariable reply was: 'Oh: yes . . . that'll give me a chance.'

Again there was the phrase: 'I've got round.' Constantly, this was the first remark she made to me. 'I've just got round!' she would say – and I, poor innocent, concluded vaguely that she had been out for a walk, or had been in the kitchen garden when she heard the car. But no, she meant that during the week she had just been able to make the exhausting tour of my bedroom.

Now, a woman would, presumably, have seen these things long before, would have detected the delicate echoes of discontent, and opened immediate hostilities. However, my sex being of the gentler variety, I did not wish for hostilities. I wanted everything to go on quietly and peacefully. I wanted 'a good time to be had by all'.

There seemed to be no real reason for battle. It was surely only a matter for a little tact . . . a little adjustment? For, in all truth, Mrs Wrench's position was *not* one of slavery. She was, to begin with, as strong as a horse. She ate enormously. She slept perfectly. For at least four days of the week she could stay in bed, if she so desired.

I decided to go and ask John what he thought about it. I found him in his bedroom, surrounded by piles of silk shirts, bottles, and tissue paper.

'Mrs Wrench is complaining.'

'What about?'

'The work. She thinks there's too much to do.'

'There probably is a great deal.'

'But my dear John, I'm hardly ever here.'

'She's a woman,' said John loftily. 'She isn't a machine.'

It would be tedious to narrate our many efforts to relieve Mrs Wrench. How we carried out the tea-things, manfully declined to have coffee after dinner, fetched wood for the fire.

The preparations we made, before finally retiring for the night, were exhaustive. We carefully scooped out the ash-trays, tiptoed with them up to the bathroom, washed and dried them, and tiptoed downstairs again, to place them on their appointed tables, retreating a few steps to see how clean and sparkling they looked. We shook out the cushions and dug our fingers into the chintz seats of the sofa to smooth out the creases. We both made a vow not to sit on the sofa again in case we should disturb its marble serenity. We put every chair in its appointed place, and I swept the mud off the staircase carpet, using John's clothes-brush for the purpose. We polished the tumblers from which we had drunk our whiskies and sodas, and carefully deposited a saucer under the syphon, whose nose was dribbling. Finally, we drew back the curtains, in order that Mrs Wrench might come down in the morning to a room of sunshine.

The moonlight flooded into a room as clean as a Dutch interior.

'We can't possibly do any more,' whispered John.

'Unless we go up and undress Mrs Wrench.'

'I'm quite tired, aren't you?'

'Exhausted.'

'I think I'll have a final whisky.'

'You can't. It'll spoil the tumbler.'

In the morning I was the first to rise.

Mrs Wrench was in the hall, putting two glasses of orange juice on the table. When she saw me her face fell.

'Oh!' she exclaimed, 'will it be earlier than usual?'

'It' meant a pot of coffee and four pieces of toast, which was all the breakfast we ever had.

'Oh, no, Mrs Wrench.' I was bitterly disappointed that she had not made any reference to our beautiful clean room.

She breathed a sigh of relief. Then she pointed to the orange juice. 'I've got the orange juice done.' She spoke as though she had picked and pressed the entire contents of a large orange grove. 'I did it as soon as I got down. And then . . . Well, I mustn't waste any more time talking.' And she bustled out.

The one benefit of all this was that Mrs Wrench formed an inexhaustible topic of conversation. In those days I was moving about in a great many varieties of social circles, high, low, stupid, and intelligent, and I always found that if Mrs Wrench were mentioned, she held the stage. The eyes of Cabinet Ministers lit up at the catalogue of her vices, and large, important women hung eagerly upon every detail.

'Of course, you should sack her *at once*,' they said in trembling voices.

'I suppose I should.'

'But *at once*. Too ridiculous . . . she ought to consider herself an extremely lucky woman. How many bedrooms did you say?'

'Three.'

'And only two occupied . . . for week-ends?'

The large important women knew the answer to this, only too well, because we had it all out at dinner the night before. But they longed to be told it all again. They usually were . . . . Which made me think that Mrs Wrench must be a universal figure.

However, in spite of her value as a topic of conversation, she was rapidly becoming so impossible that a crisis could not be far off.

I had arranged to go up to the cottage on Saturday as usual, with John. However, Friday morning dawned so exquisitely, so gaily, that even the roofs of Westminster looked as though they had been laid with gold-leaf overnight. 'It is a sin to stay in London on a day like this,' I said to myself, and I got on the telephone to John. Could he come up to-day instead of to-morrow? Yes – he would be delighted.

I sighed with relief and arranged to call for him immediately after lunch.

When we arrived at the cottage, the little country gate that leads into the garage was closed. Normally, it was always open, so that one could drive straight in. But to-day, the strain of opening the gate would obviously have been too much for Mrs Wrench, who had only had three hours in which to open it.

The next portent was when I walked along the path towards the kitchen, opened the kitchen door, and called out: 'Mrs Wrench.'

There was no answer.

'Mrs Wrench!' Still no answer.

Leaving John to look after himself, I went through to the front of the house. She was nowhere to be found. I ran up the stairs. And there she was, in my bedroom, surrounded by sheets, pillows, and blankets.

'Good afternoon, Mrs Wrench.'

'Good afternoon, sir.'

She lifted a pillow as though it weighed a ton, and heavily put it on the bed.

'It's a lovely afternoon.'

She turned round and looked out of the window. 'Is it, sir?'

'But haven't you been out, Mrs Wrench?'

'No, sir, I have not.' She looked at me as a tortured mulatto might look at a particularly sadistic slave-driver. 'I *was* going to take five minutes, and go up the lane, but then your telegram came . . .'

Something began to boil in me. In a voice that cannot have been quite steady, I said:

'But why don't you take a whole day off, Mrs Wrench, if you want to? Or two or three days?'

She continued to stare.

'I'd take from Tuesday to Friday, if I were you,' I went on, madly. 'And just go out, or stay in bed, whichever you prefer. I think that'd be a good idea.' With a frantic effort I smiled at her. 'We'll have dinner at seven-thirty, I think.'

I then went down, tense with rage, knocked my head against several beams, and poured out my troubles to John.

By the time that dinner arrived I was in a state bordering on hysteria. Mrs Wrench had informed us that we should have to dine off cold tongue – a depressing prospect in any case, rendered even more depressing by the acid remarks which had accompanied this information . . . such as 'the country isn't London, sir, you can't just run out round the corner.' Lord – if only Mrs Wrench *would* just run out round the corner, whatever that meant, and never come back!

When Mrs Wrench dumped the cold tongue in front of me, and lumbered to the sideboard to fetch the wine, I turned to John, and in trembling but crystalline tones observed:

'I think it so wonderful how your mother, with only one servant, manages to give all those marvellous dinners.'

John gulped. He had not been quite prepared for this. 'Er . . . yes,' was all he could manage.

'She bakes the bread too, doesn't she?'

'Who?'

'Your servant . . . Ada, isn't that her name?'

'Ada?' Another kick. Then he pulled himself together. Mrs Wrench was now just behind me, pouring out the wine, and I was able to give him a wink.

'Oh *Ada*! 'He nodded gravely. 'Yes . . . of course, she bakes deliciously.'

'And helps in the garden?'

'A great deal. And then, of course, the massage takes up a good deal of time.'

'The massage?' This was a stroke of genius. I cast a furtive look at Mrs Wrench's face. It was as black as the blackest thundercloud that ever loured over the Black Mountains.

'From ten to eleven,' said John, warming to his task, 'my mother is always massaged by Ada. From eleven to twelve she bakes. From twelve to one . . .'

A raven-like croak interrupted us. It was Mrs Wrench. She said:

'Will there be anything else, sir?'

'Anything else?' With hideous brightness I smiled at Mrs Wrench. 'Well, have you made anything, Mrs Wrench?'

I waited for the reply as one waits who has cast a stone into a deep well. And after a pause, *de profundis*, the reply came:

'No sir, I have *not*.'

The hideous brightness continued. 'In that case, we'll just have coffee.'

She turned to go. She was half-way through the door when I called out:

'And Mrs Wrench – as it's such a lovely night, I think we'll have coffee in the garden.'

There was no reply. All I remember is that the black cloud in the doorway swelled, deepened, prepared to burst, thought better of it, and vanished. The echoes of the slamming door rang through the house.

'Well,' said John, 'that's done it.'

My first feeling on opening the telegram was one of the utmost relief. It read:

Mrs Wrench left this morning shall I sleep in – Parsons.

It was only gradually that I was able to piece together the full story of her departure. But the main facts are as follows:

On the morning when the odd-job man sent me the telegram Mrs Wrench suddenly appeared in the kitchen door, dressed, as the odd man described it: 'Like nobody.' She wore a fur coat, silk stockings, shoes with very high heels, and she carried a silver-mesh bag. In a a hoarse and lofty voice, without a trace of Scottish accent, she commanded Parsons to take her suit-case to the village Ford, which at that moment arrived outside the door. He was so thunderstruck that he obeyed, gazing at his late companion in awe. As they walked down the path Mrs Wrench briefly informed him that she was leaving for good, as she had come into money, that she did not propose to give any address, as she was going to Canada, and was sick of the sight of England, and that she would 'waive' the question of any wages I might owe her. As she had been paid in advance, 'waive' seems the right word.

That was absolutely all. She was off, in the Ford, before any more could be said. And from that instant, a darkness as deep as the grave descends on Mrs Wrench. There is one brief flash of light, at the station where, for a moment, the astonished porters saw her entering a first-class carriage. But after that . . . there is darkness. Let her rest in it.

– From *A Thatched Roof.*

A Sequence of Servants

JAMES THURBER

When I look back on the long line of servants my mother hired during the years I lived at home, I remember clearly ten or twelve of them (we had about a hundred and sixty-two, all told, but few of them were memorable). There was, among the immortals, Dora Gedd, a quiet, mousy girl of thirty-two who one night shot at a man in her room, throwing our household into an uproar that was equalled perhaps only by the goings-on the night the ghost got in. Nobody knew how her lover, a morose garage man, got into the house, but everybody for two blocks knew how he got out. Dora had dressed up in a lavender evening gown for the occasion and she wore a mass of jewellery, some of which was my mother's. She kept shouting something from Shakespeare after the shooting – I forget just what – and pursued the gentleman downstairs from her attic room. When he got to the second floor he rushed into my father's room. It was this entrance, and not the shot or the shouting, that aroused father, a deep sleeper always. 'Get me out of here!' shouted the victim. The situation rapidly developed, from then on, into one of those bewildering involvements for which my family had, I am afraid, a kind of unhappy genius. When the cops arrived Dora was shooting out the Welsbach gas mantles in the living-room, and her gentleman friend had fled. By dawn everything was quiet once more.

There were others. Gertie Straub: big, genial, and ruddy, a collector of pints of rye (we learned after she was gone), who came in after two o'clock one night from a dancing party at Buckeye Lake and awakened us by bumping into and knocking over furniture. 'Who's down there?' called Mother from upstairs. 'It's me, dearie,' said Gertie,

'Gertie Straub.' 'What are you *doing*?' demanded Mother. 'Dusting,' said Gertie.

Juanemma Kramer was one of my favourites. Her mother loved the name Juanita so dearly that she had worked the first part of it into the names of all her daughters – they were (in addition to a Juanita) Juanemma, Juanhelen, and Juangrace. Juanemma was a thin, nervous maid who lived in constant dread of being hypnotised. Nor were her fears unfounded, for she was so extremely susceptible to hypnotic suggestion that one evening at B. F. Keith's theatre when a man on the stage was hypnotised, Juanemma, in the audience, was hypnotised too and floundered out into the aisle making the same cheeping sound that the subject on the stage, who had been told he was a chicken, was making. The act was abandoned and some xylophone players were brought on to restore order. One night, when our house was deep in quiet slumber, Juanemma became hypnotised in her sleep. She dreamed that a man 'put her under' and then disappeared without 'bringing her out'. This was explained when, at last, a police surgeon whom we called in – he was the only doctor we could persuade to come out at three in the morning – slapped her into consciousness. It got so finally that any buzzing or whirling sound or any flashing object would put Juanemma under, and we had to let her go. I was reminded of her recently when, at a performance of the movie 'Rasputin and the Empress', there came the scene in which Lionel Barrymore as the unholy priest hypnotises the Czarevitch by spinning before his eyes a glittering watch. If Juanemma sat in any theatre and witnessed that scene she must, I am sure, have gone under instantly. Happily, she seems to have missed the picture, for otherwise Mr Barrymore might have had to dress up again as Rasputin (which God forbid) and journey across the country to get her out of it – excellent publicity but a great bother.

Before I go on to Vashti, whose last name I forget, I will look in passing at another of our white maids (Vashti was coloured). Belle Giddin distinguished herself by one gesture which fortunately did not result in the bedlam occasioned by Juanemma's hypnotic states or Dora Gedd's shooting spree. Bella burned her finger grievously, and purposely, one afternoon in the steam of a boiling kettle so that she could find out whether the pain-killer she had bought one night at a tent-show for fifty cents was any good. It was only fair.

Vashti turned out, in the end, to be partly legendary. She was a comely and sombre negress who was always able to find things my mother lost. 'I don't know what's become of my garnet brooch,' my mother said one day. 'Yassum,' said Vashti. In half an hour she had found it. 'Where in the world was it?' asked Mother. 'In de yahd,' said Vashti. 'De dog mussa drug it out.'

Vashti was in love with a young coloured chauffeur named Charley, but she was also desired by her stepfather, whom none of us had ever seen but who was, she said, a handsome but messin' round gentleman from Georgia who had come north and married Vashti's mother just so he could be near Vashti. Charley, her fiancé, was for killing the stepfather but we counselled flight to another city. Vashti, however, would burst into tears and hymns and vow she'd never leave us; she got a certain pleasure out of bearing her cross. Thus we all lived in jeopardy, for the possibility that Vashti, Charley, and her stepfather might fight it out some night in our kitchen did not, at times, seem remote. Once I went into the kitchen at midnight to make some coffee. Charley was standing at a window looking out into the backyard; Vashti was rolling her eyes. 'Heah he come! Heah he come!' she moaned. The stepfather didn't show up, however.

Charley finally saved up twenty-seven dollars towards taking Vashti away but one day he impulsively bought a ·22 revolver with a mother-of-pearl handle and demanded that Vashti tell him where her mother and stepfather lived. 'Doan go up dere, doan go *up* dere!' said Vashti. 'Mah mothah is just as rarin' as he is!' Charley, however, insisted. It came out then that Vashti didn't have any stepfather; there was no such person. Charley threw her over for a yellow gal named Nancy: he never forgave Vashti for the vanishing from his life of a menace that had come to mean more to him than Vashti herself. Afterwards, if you asked Vashti about her stepfather or about Charley she would say, proudly, and with a woman-of-the-world air: 'Neither one ob em is messin' round *me* any mo'.'

Mrs Doody, a huge, middle-aged woman with a religious taint, came into and went out of our house like a comet. The second night she was there she went berserk while doing the dishes and, under the impression that Father was the Antichrist, pursued him several times up the backstairs and down the front. He had been sitting quietly over his coffee in the living-room when she burst in from the kitchen waving a bread knife. My brother Herman finally felled her with a piece of Libby's cut-glass that had been a wedding present of Mother's. Mother, I remember, was in the attic at the time, trying to find some old things, and, appearing on the scene in the midst of it all, got the quick and mistaken impression that Father was chasing Mrs Doody.

Mrs Robertson, a fat and mumbly old coloured woman, who might have been sixty and who might have been a hundred, gave us more than one turn during the many years that she did our washing. She had been a slave down South and she remembered 'having seen the troops marching – a mess o' blue, den a mess o' grey.' 'What,' my mother asked her once, 'were they fighting about?' 'Dat,' said Mrs Robertson, 'Ah don't know.' She had a feeling, at all times, that something was going to happen. I can see her now, staggering up from the basement with a basketful of clothes and coming abruptly to a halt in the middle of the kitchen. 'Hahk!' she would say, in a deep, guttural voice. We would all hark; there was never anything to be heard. Neither, when she shouted 'Look yondah!' and pointed a trembling hand at a window, was there ever anything to be seen. Father protested time and again that he couldn't stand Mrs Robertson around, but mother always refused to let her go. It seems that she was a jewel. Once she walked unbidden, a dishpan full of wrung-out clothes under her arm, into Father's study, where he was engrossed in some figures. Father looked up. She regarded him for a moment in silence. Then – 'Look out!' she said, and withdrew. Another time, a murky winter afternoon, she came flubbering up the cellar stairs and bounced, out of breath, into the kitchen. Father was in the kitchen sipping some black coffee; he was in a jittery state of nerves from the effects of having had a tooth out, and had been in bed most of the day. 'Dey is a death watch downstairs!' rumbled the old coloured lady. It developed that she had heard a strange 'chipping' noise back of the furnace. 'That was a cricket,' said Father. 'Um-*hm*,' said Mrs

Robertson. 'Dat was uh death watch!' With that she put on her hat and went home, poising just long enough at the back door to observe darkly to Father. '*Dey ain't no way!*' It upset him for days.

Mrs Robertson had only one great hour that I can think of – Jack Johnson's victory over Mistah Jeffries on the Fourth of July, 1910. She took a prominent part in the coloured parade through the South End that night, playing a Spanish fandango on a banjo. The procession was led by the pastor of her church who, Mrs Robertson later told us, had 'splained that the victory of Jack over Mistah Jeffries proved 'de ' 'speriority ob de race'. 'What,' asked my mother, 'did he mean by that?' 'Dat,' said Mrs Robertson, 'Ah don't know.'

Our other servants I don't remember so clearly, except the one who set the house on fire (her name eludes me), and Edda Millmoss. Edda was always slightly morose but she had gone along for months, all the time she was with us, quietly and efficiently attending to her work, until the night we had Carson Blair and F. R. Gardiner to dinner – both men of importance to my father's ambitions. Then suddenly, while serving the entrée, Edda dropped everything and, pointing a quivering finger at father, accused him in a long rigmarole of having done her out of her rights to the land on which Trinity Church in New York stands. Mr Gardiner had one of his 'attacks' and the whole evening turned out miserably.

– From *My Life and Hard Times.*

Period Piece

SID CHAPLIN

Life at the big house was ups and downs. When my Auntie Katie worked for Mrs Ramshaw it was all downs. The housekeeper was a slave-driver.

But sometimes she assisted the Head Butler, and that was interesting and exciting. Mr Sangster was round-shouldered with a curiously flat face which was always placid.

He had served in great houses all his life and could reel off the names of the aristocracy as a miner will recite the names of famous footballers. And, as a miner can trace the pedigree of his whippet, so could he track down the forebears of Lords and Ladies. And he knew their secrets as well as he knew the dark places of their halls. Mention some Duke and he would go into a rapturous trance, mumbling the complicated story of relations and inter-relations. And pride! A miner may rise to the Cabinet; a mill-lad may become a millionaire; but that was nothing compared to his rise from boot-boy to head butler, Lord of the Pantry and High Priest of the Silver!

Katie took him in hand. One day they went up to Leeds to see a football match. Mr Sangster escaped from his pantry for one wild hour and yelled with the crowd. But he never went to Leeds again. He was slightly ashamed of himself and implored Katie not to tell.

She didn't greatly care for the life. Only one thing kept her working: the memory of clay and pit-boots. She loved the good food and the splendour; but her soul rebelled against the servility, and if the servants had one thing in common it was this.

Madam floated through the rooms like a vision; Sir Robert came in for his meals, then slouched back to his horses or the kennels.

Then Madam began to get up late; the whisper went around the servants' hall that an heir was expected.

Katie was in the wine-cellar one day when Sir Robert wandered down to select some bottles to be sent to a friend. The wine-cellar was his department. 'Hello, lassie,' he said. 'How d'you like working for the swanks, now?'

'Oh, it's not so bad,' said Katie.

'Well,' he said, 'I'm pleased to hear that.'

'And Ah was pleased to hear about the baby coming,' said Katie. 'I hope it's a lovely little boy.'

'Good Lord!' he cried. 'How on earth did you get to know?'

Now Katie had heard first about it from Cook, but she didn't want to split. 'Oh, I've got eyes,' she said carelessly, remembering a favourite phrase of her mother.

'Well, I'll be damn'd,' he said. 'How old are you?' 'Sixteen and a half, sir.' He raised his eyebrows. 'Here's half-a-crown, and keep your mouth shut.' She refused the half-crown. 'I can keep a secret,' she said, 'but Ah don't want paying for it, sir.' 'Don't be such a little fool, lassie,' he said. 'You take it and buy some chocs.'

So she took it and went up the flight of steps. When she got to the door she turned round and looked down. She smiled. 'Ah hope it's a boy.

He stared back for a moment, then smiled back. It takes a good man to stand up to Auntie Katie's smile. 'So do I,' he said.

It was the dinner party that finished Katie's career. She might have been housekeeper there now, if it hadn't been for that dinner party.

Madam decided to have this dinner party before her temporary retirement. It was to be a great affair, designed to keep her reputation as a great hostess alive during her absence. There was a flurry of excitement and preparation; long conferences with Mrs Ramshaw and Mr Sangster. The silver was polished until it was like glass, then polished again until every piece seemed a rare, unreal thing. Then, three days before the great event, half the staff went down with 'flu. In a moment of madness it was arranged that Katie should help to serve. Madness, because he or she who serves at the meals of the aristocracy must be a silently efficient machine.

The fatal evening arrived, and with it the guests. Generals and admirals came; there were a lord and his lady; and last, but not least, a notable bishop, whose love of good food and wine exceeded his love for matters spiritual.

The table was a splendid sight, said my Aunt Katie, all a-glitter with silver and the flame of splendid candles. After all those years she still remembered the food and the wines, though she confessed that she might have them in the wrong order.

There was hors-d'œuvre first, then turtle soup. There was a noble saddle of mutton or, for those who did not care for this solid fare, there was duck. There was a luscious sweet of rich strawberry cream, or, if this palled, the more enlivening brandy-snap. For savoury there were devils on horseback, and these delightful devils the bishop devoured with amazing speed. Then came dessert with an abundance of almonds, peaches, nectarines, and grapes, with fondants and Turkish Delight . . .

The food was perfect, the wines superb, and all might have gone well had it not been that Katie was serving. The first rift occurred during the serving of the main course, when, confronted with a choice of two sauces, the undecided Bishop was advised that the one was better than the other. With true Christian humility, the Bishop accepted the advice, the nearer guests stared in absolute astonishment, Madam went crimson, Mr Sangster pale. Sir Robert smiled.

Hastily reprimanded behind the dining-room doors, Katie was sent back to do better. This she did. During dessert, the conversation turned to investments. An admiral confessed that he was considering an investment with a mining concern. Katie was at once all afire with interest and excitement, she knew the firm's name all too well. The bishop, having disposed of a mouthful of nectarine, gave his advice. 'Keep clear of these mining concerns, my dear Edward,' he said, 'a most uncertain industry; and I hear that that one is having a rather difficult time.'

'Oh, no!' cried Katie, 'they're a very big firm, and they've got the best pits in the country. I should know. My Da and all my brothers work for them.'

There was a deep silence, broken only by the eventual coughing of Sir Robert, a choking cough which, in some measure, succeeded in distracting attention from the awful spectacle of a talking menial . . .

But the worst was yet to come. Dessert was finished, the ladies departed for coffee, leaving the admirals and all in unrestrained freedom. It was unfortunate that the ladies should choose a most controversial subject and one which raised Katie's ire. Her short-comings before had been a mixture of naïvety and a certain chummi-ness, which comes easily to those born and bred in pit villages, but the new subject aroused her temper and led to the final scene of that unusual evening.

Encouraged by the retreat of the great lady to some private place where she could regain her composure, the female guests had embarked on a general discussion of the events of the evening. This had led to the subject of the mining community, since the country was at that time being held to ransom by a nation-wide strike of these dissatisfied plutocrats. The conversation touched upon the fat wage-packets earned; Katie remained silent. There were fleeting references to miners' wives who flaunted their fur coats; and Katie had a vision of her hard-working mother, tied to an eternal cycle of scrubbing, washing and cooking. . . . The conversation touched upon the luxury in which the miner's whippet was kept – rich steaks and chops and diced liver, while the children went barefooted. But when one young thing spoke with contempt of the gambling habits of the mining people, all restraint went by the wind.

'Cats,' Katie cried, 'sneaking, overfed, slinking cats, the lot of you. Why, the meal you've just eaten would keep my family in luxury for a year. And as for you,' she cried, pointing at the startled débutante, whose foolish mouth now hung aslew at this attack, 'the fruit you ate for dessert would pay all my Dad's bets for a twelvemonth.'

They sat petrified like images, the fat and the thin, with their dazzling gowns and flashing jewellery, with their rigid faces; twisted lips forming distorted 'O's.'

Katie surveyed them with contempt. 'Well,' she concluded, 'if your brains were as big as your mouths you'd be really brilliant people.'

.   .   .   .

[175]

The next day she packed. But first she said goodbye to Mr Sangster and the stable-boy and Cook. Mr Sangster was sorry, yet pleased. No one could fail to love Katie, least of all Mr Sangster; but she had upset his world; and she knew about the football match; she was the one person in the world who had seen Mr Sangster shout, 'Goal!' I think the stable-boy was in love with Katie; anyway, he promised to write, so he must have been. Cook was a genius in her own way, an aristocrat. She was so good a cook that she could hold her own anywhere. She was not afraid of Mrs Ramshaw, she had a great contempt for almost everyone at the great house. She was a free-born democrat who shook with laughter when Katie told her what she had done and said.

Then Katie went to the wine-cellar and got half-a-dozen bottles of Chianti to take home for her Dad. She put them in her bag underneath her clothes and was just pressing the clasp down to lock it when there came a knock at the door. 'Come in,' she said. Sir Robert wandered in. 'Thought I'd drop in to say goodbye,' he said. 'Goodbye,' said Katie. 'Not so fast as that,' he said with a smile. 'Can I help you to pack?' So she sat on the bag. 'I'm finished packing,' she said. 'Oh, no,' he answered, and pulled a box of cigars out of his pocket. 'Find room for these,' he said. 'Give them to your Dad, with my regards.'

She took the box. He walked to the window and looked out, then came over to the bed and held out his hand. 'Well, thanks for last night . . . It was great.' She had to stand up then and shake hands.

Then he said: 'I'll have to go now.' He went to the door, opened it, then turned again. 'Have a bottle of that Chianti with your Dad when you get home. It's good stuff. Keep it for special occasions, and drink it slowly. And don't forget to toast your old friend.'

And when they opened the first bottle in the pigeon-cree, with the pictures of racers pinned up all around them, with the pigeons cooing and fluttering and stepping delicately in the loft, you can bet your boots my Auntie Katie didn't forget.

– From 'What Katie Did' in *The Leaping Lad*.

The Virtuoso?

MAX BEERBOHM

. . . I am well aware that the survival of domestic service, in its old
form, depends more and more on our agreement not to mention it.

Assuredly, a most uncomfortable state of things. Is it, after all,
worth saving? – a form so depleted of right human substance, an
anomaly so ticklish. . . . I have seen, from time to time, butlers who
had shed all semblance of grace, butlers whose whole demeanour
was a manifesto of contempt for their calling and of devotion to the
Spirit of the Age. I have seen a butler in a well-established household
strolling around the diners without the slightest droop, and pouring
out wine in an off-hand and quite obviously hostile manner. I have seen
him, towards the end of the meal, yawning. I remember another
whom, positively, I heard humming – a faint sound indeed, but
menacing as the toll of tumbrils.

These were exceptional cases, I grant. For the most part, the butlers
observed by me have had a manner as correctly smooth and colourless
as their very shirt-fronts. Aye, and in two or three of them, modern
though they were in date and aspect, I could have sworn there was
'a flame of old-world fealty all bright'. Were these but the finer
comedians? There was one (I will call him Brett) who had an almost
dog-like way of watching his master. Was this but a calculated touch
in a merely æsthetic whole? Brett was tall and slender, and his movements were those of a greyhound under perfect self-control. Baldness
at the temples enhanced the solemnity of his thin smooth face. It is
more than twenty years since first I saw him; and for a long period
I saw him often, both in town and in country. Against the background
of either house he was impeccable. Many butlers might be that

but Brett's supremacy was in the sense he gave one that he was, after all, human – that he had a heart, in which he had taken the liberty to reserve a corner for any true friend of his master and mistress. I remember well the first time he overstepped sheer formality in relation to myself. It was one morning in the country, when my entertainers and my fellow guests had gone out in pursuit of some sport at which I was no good. I was in the smoking-room, reading a book. Suddenly – no, Brett never appeared anywhere suddenly – Brett appeared, paused at precisely the right speaking distance, and said in a low voice: 'I thought it might interest you to know, sir, that there's a white-tailed magpie out on the lawn. Very rare, as you know, sir. If you look out of the window you will see the little fellow hopping about on the lawn.' I thanked him effusively as I darted to the window, and simulated an intense interest in 'the little fellow'. I greatly overdid my part. Exit Brett, having done his to perfection.

What worries me is not that I showed so little self-command and so much insincerity, but the doubt whether Brett's flawless technique was the vehicle for an act of true good feeling or was used simply for the pleasure of using it. Similar doubts abide in all my special memories of him. There was an evening when he seemed to lose control over himself – but did he *really* lose it? There were only four people at dinner: my host, his wife, their nephew (a young man famous for drollery), and myself. Towards the end of dinner the conversation had turned on early marriages. 'I,' said the young man presently, 'shall not marry till I am seventy. I shall then marry some charming girl of seventeen.' His aunt threw up her hands, exclaiming: 'Oh, Tom, what a perfectly horrible idea! Why, she isn't *born* yet!' 'No,' said the young man, 'but I have my eye on her mother.' At this, Brett, who was holding a light for his master's cigarette, turned away convulsively, with a sudden dip of the head, and vanished from the room. His breakdown touched and pleased all four beholders. But – was it a genuine lapse? Or merely a feint to thrill us? – the feint of an equilibrist so secure that he can pretend to lose his balance?

If I knew why Brett ceased to be butler in that household, I might be in less doubt as to the true inwardness of him. I knew only that he was gone. That was fully ten years ago. Since then I have had one glimpse of him. This was on a summer night in London. I had gone out late to visit some relatives and assure myself that they were safe and sound; for Zeppelins had just passed over London for the first time. Not so much horror as a very deep disgust was the atmosphere in the populous quiet streets and squares. One square was less quiet than others, because somebody was steadily whistling for a taxi. Anon I saw the whistler silhouetted in the light cast out on a wide doorstep from an open door, and I saw that he was Brett. His attitude, as he bent out into the dark night, was perfect in grace, but eloquent of a great tensity – even of agony. Behind him stood a lady in an elaborate evening cloak. Brett's back must have conveyed to her in every curve his surprise, his shame, that she should be kept waiting. His chivalry in her behalf was such as Burke's for Marie Antoinette – little had he dreamed that he should have lived to see such disasters fallen upon her in a nation of gallant men, in a nation of men of honour, and of cavaliers. He had thought ten thousand taxis must have leaped from their stands, etc. The whistle that at first sounded merely mechanical and ear-piercing had become heartrending and human when I saw from whom it proceeded – a very heart-cry that still haunts me. But *was* it a heart-cry? Was Brett, is Brett more than a mere virtuoso?

He is in any case what employers call a treasure, and to anyone who wishes to go forth and hunt for him I will supply a chart showing the way to that doorstep on which last I saw him. But I myself, were I ever so able to pay his wages, should never covet him – no, nor anything like him. Perhaps we are not afraid of menservants if we look out at them from the cradle. None was visible from mine. Only in later years and under external auspices did I come across any of them. And I am as afraid of them as ever. Maidservants frighten me less, but they also . . . have always struck some degree of terror to my soul. The whole notion of domestic service has never not seemed to me unnatural. I take no credit for enlightenment. . . . Loth to obey, loth to command. Convention (for she too frightens me) has made me accept what servants would do for me by rote. But I would liefer have it ill-done than ask even the least mettlesome of them to do it better, and far liefer, if they would only be off and not do it at all, do it for myself. In Italy – dear Italy, where I have lived much – servants do still regard service somewhat in the old way, as a sort of privilege; so that with Italian servants I am comparatively at my ease. But oh, the delight when on the afternoon of some local *festa* there is no servant at all in the little house! Oh, the reaction, the impulse to sing and dance, and the positive quick obedience to that impulse! Convention alone has forced me to be anywhere a master. Ariel and Caliban, had I been Prospero on that island, would have had nothing to do and nothing to complain of; and Man Friday on that other island would have bored me, had I been Crusoe. When I was king in Babylon and you were a Christian slave, I promptly freed you.

– From 'Servants' in *And Even Now*.

PART FOUR

Success Stories for Mother

Elsa Maxwell Throws a Party

ELSA MAXWELL

No one has to tell me that few people have the facilities, much less the money, to entertain lavishly. Lord knows I wasn't able to do it. In the decade following the First World War, I lived in tiny, two-room apartments and the only servant I had was a cleaning woman who came in twice a week. I barely had enough money to meet normal expenses. Yet it was during that period that I made my reputation as a hostess. How? I threw convention out of the window.

You say you haven't adequate space or servants for a proper sit-down dinner? So what? A buffet dinner is much more fun anyway. Guests are free to circulate and mingle with everyone instead of being anchored at a table with the partners on either side of them. Any informal touch tends to break down reserve and make for conviviality in a group. A buffet is cheaper, too. A hostess can get by nicely with one main course, salad and dessert. The food must be simple, of necessity, since guests serve themselves and eat under makeshift conditions. There is another advantage in a buffet that solves a ticklish problem for the hostess who does not have complete sets of china, glasses and silverware. In the pleasant milling around, critical guests are less apt to notice that the table appointments do not match perfectly. It's a triviality, perhaps, but it disturbs the overly sensitive hostess.

What about the preparation of the dinner? That headache can be turned into the high-light of the evening by adopting a suggestion which, at first shock, appears to be a brainstorm. Have the men cook the dinner. Men always brag that cooking is a cinch they can master any time they put their hands to it. Call their bluff by turning them loose on an easy recipe that can be salvaged no matter how badly it is manhandled – something like spaghetti and meat sauce, shrimps creole or Welsh rarebit. I won't vouch for results, but I can promise a hilarious hour while the men are making messes of themselves and the kitchen.

No one will mind that dinner is late. Half the guests will declare, to a man, that they never had a better dinner. If wives are as smart as I know they are, they will play along with the gag on the off-chance that their husbands will get delusions of grandeur and relieve them occasionally of kitchen duty. That's beside the point. Even if the dinner is a culinary catastrophe, it will be fun at the moment, and that's the main purpose in giving a party.

Food doesn't make or break a party. A chef with the *Cordon Bleu* can prepare dinner and the evening still can fall as flat as a cold soufflé. The critical turning point of a party comes after dinner. That's when the ordinary hostess sees her party slough off into one of two ruts. Guests sit around and made desultory conversation or they play cards. In either case, it is a dull, static routine and the hostess pays heavily for it in the liquor lapped up. Most people drink to escape boredom. They don't need bottled stimulation if they are shown how to draw upon their own resources for amusement.

Excessive drinking turned only one of my parties into a rowdy affair. That was the Come As You Were party I gave in Paris in 1927. The big idea was that the sixty guests were pledged to appear dressed exactly as they were when the invitations were received. To make sure of a wide variety of get-ups, I had the invitations delivered by messengers at odd hours of the day and night.

Knowing my customers as well as I did, I chartered two buses and personally picked them up at their homes. Parisians are accustomed to strange sights but, after all, there are limits to their tolerance. Hiring the private buses proved to be a necessary precaution. The Marquis de Polignac was attired in full evening dress save for one conspicuous omission. He wasn't wearing his trousers. Daisy Fellowes carried her lace panties in her hand. A half-dozen women who are respectable grandmothers today came in slips that definitely were not shadow-proof. Bébé Bérard wore a dressing-gown, a telephone attached to his ear and had white make-up on his face to simulate shaving cream. Several men who rated honour above vanity came in hair-nets. Jay O'Brien was a fashion-plate in tails except for one minor detail. He wasn't wearing a white tie and somehow he looked more disreputable than anyone.

I made two mistakes in my otherwise careful planning. I installed a bar in each bus and I neglected to account for Paris's monumental traffic jams in my time-table. The buses began to pick up people at seven o'clock in the evening, but it was nine o'clock before they arrived at Meraud Guevara's apartment in Montparnasse, which I had borrowed for the occasion. By that time everyone was flying so high that there were drastic changes in some of the costumes. Countess Gabriella Robilant, an Italian, lost her skirt during manœuvres in one of the landgoing hangars. Gabriella was unconcerned, but Countess Elisabeth de Bretueil, a Frenchwoman, was outraged.

'I refuse to be seen in my own country with anyone in that scandalous condition,' she said indignantly.

'To the Bastille!' Gabriella cried, yanking off Elisabeth's skirt. 'Now a French and an Italian countess are equals.'

I gave up trying to bring the situation under control after a plea for a little restraint was answered by a volley of hard rolls fired at me by my guests. The neighbours cheered my hasty retreat. They didn't want spoil-sports, including the police, throwing a wet blanket over the free floor show in the garden. It looked like the rehearsal of a French bedroom farce.

There are safer gambits for getting guests to throw off their inhibitions at a party. My favourite device for giving a dull gathering a shot in the arm is a game, the sillier the better. The best games are those in which failure is comical rather than embarrassing.

For example, to demonstrate how the sense of smell is governed by visual association, have blindfolded players identify a series of familiar articles without touching them. The ludicrous answers will give everyone a laugh. Bananas will be tagged as violets and a sprig of parsley as expensive perfume. A hostess can save enough on liquor bills to buy herself a new hat by putting up an eighty-nine-cent bottle of domestic wine as the prize in an absurd contest such as button-sewing or draping a live model with a few yards of cheap material for the most stylish effect. The Mayfair set once rooted more frantically for their entries in a race I put on than it ever did at Epsom Downs. The entries were mechanical wind-up toys I borrowed from friends with children.

What if you're stuck with stuffed shirts who refuse to play along with your amiable stunts? I'm tempted to suggest that you cross them off your list, but I realise it may be necessary to entertain them for business or social reasons. Every hostess I know tries to make the best of a sticky situation by balancing bores with bright, amusing people at the same party. It never works. One group cramps the style of the other and, as always, mediocrity pulls talent down to its level. If you *must* have bores, always put them together or at the same table . . . They invariably have a marvellous time trading banalities in the absence of competition. Clichés roll trippingly off the tongue like sparkling epigrams, and trite observations acquire depth sinking into receptive minds. Don't ask me why. I only know it is an unfailing phenomenon.

The cocktail party easily is the worst invention since castor oil. I've never given a cocktail party.

You know what usually happens. The condemned couple greet you at the door with a clammy hand and a despairing eye. They know better than anyone the torture about to be inflicted on you. They can't accommodate all the people who have been invited and each new arrival means so many more decibels of noise and so many more gallons of noxious cigarette smoke. Everyone is screaming and smoking in self-defence. The limp anchovies on soggy biscuits are an offence to your stomach and it is compounded by lukewarm, prefabricated drinks. The hostess anxiously wonders how many diehards will hang on to the bitter end in the delusion that dinner is to be served. The host wonders how long his liquor and ice will hold out and decides to make deep inroads into both in the hope that everyone will go home when nothing is left to drink. Eventually, and not a moment too soon, the condemned couple are reprieved by the fatigue that drives their guests into the night in search of a place to sit down.

More than one woman since Lot's wife has betrayed herself by looking back, but I can't help shedding a nostalgic tear for the decline of my favourite entertainment – the costume party. I've given so many dress-up soirées that Janet Flanner once described my party activities under the generic title of Come As Somebody Else. I suppose the ham in me partly accounts for my fondness for costume balls. I always had the uncanny knack, even when I was much younger, of getting tricked up to look like any elder statesman I chose to impersonate. Among my roles were Herbert Hoover, Ben Franklin, Édouard Herriot and Aristide Briand.

On one occasion my make-up fooled entirely too many people. During the Peace Conference in 1919, Prince Murat picked me up in his car on the way to a costume ball in Paris. The Prince was masquerading as Clemenceau and I as Lloyd George, the respective leaders of the French and English delegations to the Conference. Passers-by caught a glimpse of us as we rode down the Champs-Élysées and thought we were the diplomats in the flesh. In three minutes traffic was blocked by the dense, cheering crowd that surrounded the car. I explained to the frantic gendarme trying to clear the jam that we were impersonating the heroes.

'You *are* Lloyd George and Clemenceau,' he whispered furiously. 'Bow to the crowd and tip your hats. There will be a riot if it is discovered that you are impostors. I will do nothing to protect you from the physical violence you deserve.'

I remember at this party being particularly struck by an attractive, sleek, rather slinky young woman in a kilt. She turned out to be half-American and half-European, a mixture that, like the whisky of the New World and the vermouth of the Old, can produce a subtle blend. She was the Hon. Mrs Reginald Fellowes. . . .

Daisy Fellowes was often hailed by the fashion writers as the best-dressed woman in the world, she refused to follow the crowd, she had always to strike out on a line of her own. While it was the fashion for everyone to go to Molyneux or Patou or Chanel, Daisy would forage off the byways of the boulevards to discover some dressmaker who could carry out her ideas. Invited to some elaborate party where she knew everyone would be gorgeously attired, Daisy would have recourse to one of her dressmakers, buy a simple black dress as worn by a midinette, alter it in some way, add some original accessory – and have all the women green with envy for creating a new fashion, which, of course, they quickly copied.

I remember them tearing their hair when she borrowed the idea of wearing something like a man's dinner-jacket covered in sequins. There was the night, too, when I gave a *diner des bijoux*. Everyone had to pile on every jewel they could lay hands on. And, naturally, they all arrived looking like something out of the Arabian Nights. But not Daisy. All she wore was a perfectly plain black dress, but with a belt of diamonds round her waist almost a foot deep! She certainly had the art of being provokingly unpredictable on every occasion.

Into the Daisy chain of her wide circle of friends there drifted at this time an amusing fellow, Hugo Rumbold, brother of the former Ambassador to Germany, Sir Horace Rumbold. Now Hugo was a great mimic with an unappeasable appetite for dressing up as somebody else. Even though people knew he was going to do it, knew he was going to be present, they could not recognise him. He once fooled an entire house-party while staying with Lord Lathom and pretending to be his maiden aunt. He stuttered badly, but when singing, reciting or pretending to be someone else it disappeared. The horrors we once suffered one night at a party when he rose to recite, 'The Czar is no more, he lies in his gore . . .' and suddenly realised that the Grand Duchess Marie, cousin of the Czar, was present!

I'll never forget the night when Daisy invited an imposing array of guests to meet the new Portuguese Ambassador to Paris, the Marquis di San Pedro Porto – or some such name. No one saw through his French and English laced with a heavy Portuguese accent, or suspected him in any way, till he took off his moustache and we found it was Hugo after all.

Another time Daisy and myself and Dickie Gordon were invited by Lady Diana Cooper and her husband to dine with them, and Daisy asked if she might bring a Spanish woman who, she said, was a very well-known but rather eccentric authoress. The woman, however, turned out to be the success of the party. Duff Cooper was quite taken by her charm and witty conversation, so much so that when we went on to a night club he was the first to ask her to dance. But I noticed that hardly had he placed his arm about her and embarked on the steps of a tango than he quickly led her back to the table and sat as far away from her as possible.

'What's the matter, Duff?' Dickie Gordon asked.

'I don't know,' Duff replied. Then he whispered to Daisy: 'I don't think I like that friend of yours as much as I thought.'

At which Daisy and Dickie burst out laughing. It was Hugo Rumbold again. Dickie had spent all day fitting him into her clothes, taking him to the hairdresser to arrange his wig, even lacing him into his corsets before the party.

Once Daisy and I gave a ball in her house in the Rue St James, at Neuilly. Again it was fancy dress, everybody being asked to come as some famous personality. After my success as Lloyd George I thought I would go as another Prime Minister, Monsieur Briand, because it gave me the chance of wearing a bushy soup-strainer moustache, which I always think adds such distinction to my looks. The Baroness Lo Monaco, who always loved to dress up, went as the Aga Khan, and Daisy's aunt, Princess Edmond de Polignac by marriage and a Singer heiress by birth, as a famous French author. All went well until people began asking me: 'Where's Daisy?'

I couldn't tell them, for I didn't know. I hadn't seen or recognised her and I presumed she just hadn't turned up for her own party. I could only think she had decided at the last moment to do something else. It would be quite like her. The only thing that puzzled me was the presence of that almost national French character outside the ladies' cloakroom, a *dame des lavabos*. Hardly usual in a private house, of course, but I could only imagine that Daisy had obtained her services for the evening to help the servants. Anyway, there she sat in sepulchral black and with the inevitable shawl over her head knitting away in front of a table or assisting the ladies as they entered and emerged, appropriately armed with a serviette in her hand and on the table a conspicuously placed plate to receive *pourboires*. I must say it shook all of us to the core when somebody in the small hours of the morning unmasked that *dame des lavabos* as no less than Daisy herself!

There is a sound psychological basis for the fact that every costume party in my experience has been a rousing success. By identifying themselves with another character or historical period people assume new personalities and the change usually is a distinct improvement. There is a touch of the Walter Mitty in all of us. We love to romanticise ourselves and imagine we are fascinating or dashing creatures, and a costume party is an ideal springboard for fanciful flights.

It is said that costume affairs are expensive. Ridiculous. It is cheaper to hire a costume than it is to go out and buy a new dress – and what's the matter with a home-made outfit that shows a spark of ingenuity?

Actually, a costume affair is the easiest party to run. You merely select a theme and the guests will take it from there, making their own fun. What theme? A party pegged to outmoded fashions in clothes always is a howl. (Remember the shapeless floursacks of the 1920s and the Princess Eugénie hats of the 1930s?) The outfits can be found in closets and attics people have been meaning to clean out for years. One of the most hilarious – and revealing – affairs I ever gave was a Come As Your Opposite party. Had it been cricket to do so, I could have met my expenses selling tickets to psychiatrists.

There is a certain satisfaction in being the best in any field, even if it is as superficial as painting Easter eggs, hitting a golf ball into a tin cup or giving parties. After all, not every hostess has had the distinction of being denounced in the House of Commons as a menace.

It happened after my famous – or should it be infamous? – scavenger hunt in Paris in 1927. A gallon jar of Patou's Joy perfume was offered as a prize to the player who brought back in one hour the most items, or the most unusual specimen, on a list. The objectives were a slipper taken from Mistinguett on the stage of the Casino de Paris; a black swan from the lake in the Bois de Boulogne; a *pot de chambre;* three hairs plucked from a red-headed woman (the Duchesse of D'yen, a flaming red-head, locked herself in a room to protect herself); a pom-pom off the cap of a French sailor; a work animal; and a handkerchief from the Baron Maurice de Rothschild's house.

The players took off, and a series of disturbances promptly broke out all over Paris. The manager of the Casino de Paris put in a riot call for the police when two hoodlums barged on the stage and grabbed Mistinguett's slippers, then ransacked the shoes in her dressing-room, forcing her to finish the performance in bare feet. The black swan in the Bois, a vile-tempered beast, put up such a fight that two bird fanciers went to the hospital for repairs. My landlady had hysterics when a donkey, borrowed from a pedlar, started to kick out the walls of my apartment. The Grand Duchess Marie of Russia played a lone hand and came back with the trophy that won first prize. It was a most unaristocratic exhibit – a *pot de chambre* with two big, blue inquisitive eyes painted on the inside.

– From *I Married the World.*

Noël Coward Produces 'The Vortex'

NOËL COWARD

The Everyman Theatre, Hampstead, was, in its infancy, a Drill Hall, but by the time I knew it all military flavour had departed, and it was firmly and almost defiantly a theatre. Under the management of Norman Macdermott it had achieved an excellent reputation, and several plays had been successfully launched there, later to slide down the hill into the West End.

The theatre itself was small, intimate and draughty. Its auditorium, foyer and corridors were carpeted austerely with coconut matting, and there was a subtle but determined aroma of artistic endeavour pervading the whole place.

Norman Macdermott was a short, affable man with nice eyes and a faintly unreliable expression. He invited me to go to see him after he had read *Hay Fever* and *The Vortex*, and announced, to my joy, that he would produce one of them, but that he had not quite decided which would stand the greater chance of success. He had a slight bias towards *Hay Fever*, but as there was no good part for me in that, I managed to steer him over to *The Vortex*.

Casting was even more difficult than usual owing to the rule of the Everyman Theatre that all actors appearing there must agree to do so, regardless of their position, at a fixed salary of five pounds a week. Naturally if the play was successful enough to be transferred to a West-End Theatre, they reverted to their normal London salaries. This was actually an admirable arrangement, but it limited our choice to actors who were sporting enough to take a chance. We finally collected a cast headed by Kate Cutler and myself, which included Helen Spencer, Mary Robson, Millie Sim, Bromley Davenport, Kinsey Peile, George Merritt, and Alan Hollis.

Macdermott, after a little argument, agreed that Gladys Calthrop should design the scenery and dresses, and it wasn't until all the contracts were signed and we were about to start rehearsals that he called me to his office and told me that he was sorry to say that he couldn't do the play at all, as he hadn't enough money, and that unless two hundred pounds were procured immediately the whole thing would have to be abandoned.

This was the first of the many horrible setbacks attending that production. I was in despair, and spent a black twenty-four hours racking my brains to think of someone whom I could ask for the money. Ned Lathom was out of the question, as I felt that I had already sponged on him enough. I scurried miserably through my address-book, marking with crosses the names of my richer acquaintances and later discarding them all on the fairly accurate assumption that, being rich, they wouldn't be good for more than a fiver, if that. Suddenly, on turning back to the beginning of the book again I lighted on the name Michael Arlen. I had not seen him for a year or so, and during that time *The Green Hat* had been published and was a triumphant Best Seller. I remembered our casual meetings during the last few years. I remembered our occasional heart-to-heart talks sometimes in corners at parties, sometimes in his little flat in Shepherd Market. He knew all about being poor. He knew all the make-shifts of a struggling author. He also must have known, many times, the predicament I was in at the moment, that dismal resentment at being forced by circumstances into the position of being under obligation to people. He was the one to approach all right. Success was still new to him, and the odour of recent shabbiness must still be lingering in his nostrils. I telephoned to him straight away and he asked me to dine with him that night at the Embassy.

It was a smart evening at the beginning of the winter season. We had cocktails in the newly-decorated bar and smiled with affable contempt upon the newly-decorated clientele. Half-way through dinner I blurted out my troubles, and without even questioning me about the play or making any cautious stipulations about repayment, he called for a cheque form and wrote out a cheque for two hundred pounds immediately. After that the evening seemed even more charming than it had been in the beginning.

Rehearsals started and all went well for a few days. Then Helen Spencer developed diphtheria, and despair set in again. This was a bitter disappointment. However, Mollie Kerr was engaged to take over the part and played it excellently.

Our next obstacle appeared to be insurmountable and reared itself up in the most unexpected quarter. Kate Cutler, for whom I had written the part of 'Florence', suddenly refused flatly to go on rehearsing. I have never quite known to this day what strange devil got into her. We were close friends and she had been my strongest and wisest ally through all the vicissitudes of *I'll Leave it to You* and *The Young Idea*. At all events she became surprisingly angry because, upon realising that the last act was too short, I had rewritten it, enlarging my own part considerably in the process. It was a painful and, I still think, unreasonable quarrel. Norman Macdermott was away for the week-end, and there was no one to whom we could appeal for arbitration. After a violent scene in which Kate and I both held our ground sturdily and refused to give way an inch, Kate left the theatre, and there I was, a week away from production, faced with two alternatives. I could either stick to my guns, in which case I should have to find a new leading lady immediately and rehearse her from the beginning, even supposing that I would persuade any first-rate actress to undertake such a task at such short notice. Or I could surrender to Kate by reverting to the original last act which I knew to be too short and lacking the correct emotional balance in the conflict between the mother and son. The fact that Kate seemed to imagine that I had rewritten it only in order to give myself better material as an actor made me extremely angry. I remember roaring out several grandiloquent phrases about my 'literary integrity', etc., which, although pompous, were certainly justifiable in the circumstances.

Gladys and I drove back to Ebury Street in my red car, much too fast and sizzling with indignation. When all rage was spent and blood had resumed its normal circulation, I decided, quite firmly and without passion, that neither then nor at any time in my life would I allow myself to be dictated to in the age-old battle between actor and author: a resolution, I am proud to say, that I have kept more or less shining and unsullied to this day.

In the meantime a new mother had to be found, and all through that night a grotesque ballet of middle-aged actresses whirled through my dreams. The next morning, having been forced to discard, for various reasons, all those who were even remotely suitable to the part, I decided to work from another angle and make a list of actresses as far removed from the type of 'Florence' as possible. This list was headed by Lilian Braithwaite. She was tall and dark. Florence should be small and fair. She was well-bred and serene. Florence should be flamboyant and neurotic. Lilian Braithwaite had been associated in the public mind for some years with silver teapots in Haymarket comedies. She was almost inextricably wedged in a groove of gentle, understanding motherhood. Her moral position was clearly defined, and her virtue unassailable. Even in *Mr Wu* a few years back, when by a hair's breadth she had, nightly for over a year, escaped dishonour at the hands of a Chinaman, she had still managed to maintain an air of well-bred integrity, all of which went to prove the foolish incongruity of casting her for Florence. On the other hand, there was the finally important fact that she happened to be a first-rate actress. And so, waiving aside all obvious objections, I telephoned to her and about twenty minutes later was sitting in her drawing-room in Pelham Crescent reading the play to her.

Before starting, I had explained the Kate Cutler situation and told her that before anything definite could be decided, Kate must be given one more chance to say either yes or no. Lilian also told me that she was about to start rehearsals for a new play, *Orange Blossoms*, in which her part was bad but her salary extremely good. She added, however, with a slight glint of her eye, that she had not yet signed the contract.

That being such a portentous interview, I am sorry that I cannot remember more details of it. I recall that the room was dimly green, and that there were well-arranged flowers and several silver photograph frames; I remember Gladys's hat, which was brown and perky; also her rather screwed-up position in an armchair. Lilian wore a far-away expression during the reading; she was looking out of the window beyond the trees of the Crescent, at herself in a blond wig, rather *outré* clothes, with perhaps a long cigarette-holder. I knew by the occasional nods she gave that she was liking the play and recognising the value of the part. At the end, without any quibbling, she said that if Kate refused finally, she would play it. I explained about the regulation salary being only five pounds a week at the Everyman, and that unless the play were successful enough to be transferred to the West End the engagement would only be for a fortnight; to which she replied that she was willing to take the chance providing that we let her know definitely within a few hours. It was a nice clean morning's work. There were no blandishments and no superlatives, no time wasted on inessentials. Gladys and I gulped down some sherry, dashed out of the house and drove straight off to see Kate. It was only a short way, but to our strung-up minds it seemed miles. By that time we had bolstered ourselves into the belief that Lilian was absolutely ideal casting for the part and must play it at all costs. This was actually unfair to Kate, but it provided us with a certain necessary impetus. We burst in on Kate and found her still angry and still adamant. This was, of course, a relief superficially, but I felt horrid and sad inside as though I were playing her a dirty trick by allowing her, and at this moment definitely encouraging her, to throw away one of the best opportunities of her life. But there it was. It had to be done. I told her that, after careful reflection, I had decided to keep the play exactly as I had rewritten it, and that I wished her to say finally whether or not she would play it. She said 'No, no, no,' with rising inflections, and that was that. Gladys and I left the house, thankful that the scene was over, and went back to Lilian for another glass of sherry.

Before the Monday morning rehearsal I had a stormy interview with Norman Macdermott, who, furious that an important decision had been made while his back was turned, struck the desk firmly with his clenched fist and said that Lilian Braithwaite was utterly wrong for the part, and would ruin the play, and that if she played it he would wash his hands of the entire production.

I tried to reason with him and was at length forced to remind him that as I had scraped up a good deal of the backing, the production was no longer his, anyway, and leaving him to his hand-washing, I went down on to the stage to rehearse Lilian.

That week was almost entirely beastly, and I should hate to live through it again. The weather was icy, damp and foggy. The roads were so slippery that driving to and from Hampstead was a nightmare. Gladys worked like a slave over the scenery and dresses, assisted by Mrs Doddington, 'Doddie', the housekeeper at the Everyman. Doddie was a darling; fat and warm and dressed in untidy black. It was she who kept the fire going downstairs in the subterranean cavern where we all dressed. The dressing-rooms were little more than cubicles with a passage running between them which opened out into a small draughty space in front of the fireplace on either side of which were two frowsy, comfortable settees. Here, at any time of the day or night, Doddie brought us cups of strong tea.

Lilian learned her part in two days and devoted the rest of the time to developing and polishing her performance, with a dry, down-to-earth efficiency which was fascinating to watch. It was the only brightness in those cold, hurrying days. I knew, after her second rehearsal, that she was going to be superb, but in addition to all the extraneous details I had to attend to I was dreadfully worried about my own performance. The play as a whole I had, of course, never seen, as I was on the stage myself most of the time. I had no way of telling whether I was overplaying or underplaying, or whether my emotion was real or forced. Gladys emerged seldom from the basement, and as Macdermott remained up in his office, there was nobody out front to give me the faintest indication as to whether I was going to be good, bad or indifferent. Lilian remained a rock and allowed me to dash my miseries and hopes and fears and exaltations against her. Over and over that last act we went when everyone else had gone and the lights were reduced to one working lamp on the stage. That memory is vivid enough, anyway. Those blank rows of empty seats in the foggy auditorium; Lilian and I wrapped up in coats and tearing ourselves to pieces. 'That speech was bad – let's go back' – 'I must start crying later, if I start too soon the scene's gone' – back again – then suddenly an uninterrupted flow for a little – 'It's coming this time' – triumph! – then back again just once more, to set it –

no life – no flow – despair! So on and so forth until gradually there began to grow into the scene the shape and reality we had been working for. Gladys came up one night towards the end of the week and saw it through. She was clearly excited by it, and we all went downstairs exhausted and drank tea by the fire.

The dress rehearsal staunchly upheld theatrical tradition by being gloomy and depressing to the point of suicide. The acting was nervous and unbalanced. The dresses looked awful, and the lighting was sharply unbecoming. The theatre cat made a mess in the middle of the stage, which everybody said was lucky, but which, to me, seemed to be nothing so much as a sound criticism of the entire performance.

An incident occurred which was remarkable only because it marked the first and last time that I have ever seen Gladys shed a tear over a production. At the end of the second act she appeared suddenly in my dressing-room trembling with rage and clutching a proof of the programme. The cause of her rage was a little paragraph which announced that the scenery of Act One and Act Three had been designed by G. E. Calthrop, and that of Act Two by Norman Macdermott. Considering that the whole essence of Gladys's scheme of *décor* lay in the contrast she had made between the highly-coloured modernism of the first and last acts and the oak-and-plaster simplicity of the country house in Act Two, her anger was understandable. True, Macdermott had contributed an idea for the construction of the fireplace, but apart from this the whole structure, colour and conception of the set had been Gladys's. We immediately went up into the stalls and tackled him about it, whereupon he said blandly that the complete set had been designed by him and that the programme must remain as it was. We then left him and went straight upstairs to his office, where we ransacked his desk and finally unearthed Gladys's original sketch with Macdermott's 'O.K'. scribbled across it in his own handwriting. We took it down to him triumphantly and he was very cross, and became crosser still when I said that I would not rehearse any further until the programme was changed. He ultimately gave in, however, and ordered his personal fireplace to be hacked out of the scene. This was done, and we were left with no fireplace at all for the opening night.

The next day Gladys was at the theatre early in the morning with the carpenter and George Carr, our stage manager, and by about seven in the evening, an hour before the play was due to begin, the set was fixed satisfactorily.

Meanwhile I was having a spirited duel with the Lord Chamberlain (Lord Cromer) in his office in St James's. He had at first refused point-blank to grant a licence for the play because of the unpleasantness of its theme, and it was only after a long-drawn-out argument, during which, I must say, he was charming and sympathetic, that I persuaded him that the play was little more than a moral tract. With a whimsical and rather weary smile he finally granted the licence, and with this last and most agitating of all obstacles safely surmounted, I jumped into my car and drove up to Hampstead to help Gladys with the set.

We spent a couple of hours with hammer and nails hanging pictures and tacking bits of material on to the last-act furniture, and at seven o'clock allowed ourselves a quarter of an hour to rush over the road and have some tomato soup, which, for the first time in the history of that particular café, happened to be so scorching hot that we were almost unable to drink it. Then back to the theatre again. Gladys changed into evening dress in my dressing-room while I made up. The call-boy called 'Half an Hour', then 'Quarter of an Hour', then 'Beginners'.

The stage was reached by a spiral iron staircase; I can feel the ring of it now under my feet as I went up, my heart pounding, to see that everything was in order and to listen, with a sort of dead resignation, to the scufflings and murmurings of the audience at the other side of the curtain. Gladys, with a tightened expression about her mouth, moved about the set arranging flower-vases and cigarette-boxes on small tables. George Carr made a few little jokes and animal noises in order to make us giggle and forget for a moment the lifts going up and down in our insides. Lilian appeared resplendent in pillar-box-red and a blond wig, wearing her 'emu' face, a particular and individual expression of outward calm masking inward turmoil. She was apparently placid – as cool as a cucumber. First nights were nothing to her, she had known too many of them! But yet there was a little twitch that occurred ever so often at the side of her jaw, as though she were biting very hard on something to prevent herself from screaming. Presently Kinsey Peile, Mary Robson, Millie Sim and Alan Hollis came on to the stage in various stages of alert misery. George Carr glanced at his watch and said 'Clear, please,' very softly, as if he were scared that we might all rush madly out into the street. Gladys gave one last hopeless look at the set. We all cleared to the side of the stage and, amid a sickening silence, the curtain rose on the first act.

That evening was altogether an extraordinary experience. There was a certain feeling of expectancy in the air, an acceptance almost that the play would be a success. The audience looked distressingly near owing to there being no orchestra pit and no footlights. Familiar faces suddenly jumped out of the darkness and accosted us in the middle of a scene. Lilian was cool and steady and played beautifully. I was all over the place but gave, on the whole, one of those effective, nerve-strung *tour-de-force* performances, technically unstable, but vital enough to sweep people into enthusiasm.

At the end of the play the applause was terrific. I happened to cut a vein in my wrist when, towards the end of the last act, I had to sweep all the cosmetics and bottles off the dressing-table. I bound it up with my handkerchief during the curtain calls, but it bled effectively through my author's speech.

The first person to clutch my hand afterwards was Michael Arlen. His face was white with excitement and he said: 'I'd be so proud, so *very* proud if I had written it.'

After him came the deluge. And a very gratifying deluge it was, too. There was little or no empty politeness about it. People had obviously been genuinely moved and Lilian and I held court for a long time until finally the last visitor went away and we could relax.

There it was real and complete, my first big moment. I don't remember exactly how I felt. I do know that I was tired. We were all tired. I know also that I recognised a solidity underlying all the excitement; this time I really had done it. The cheering and applause had been no louder than it had been for *I'll leave it to You* and *The Young Idea*. If anything it had been a trifle less, owing to the smallness of the Everyman Theatre. The back-stage enthusiasts had used the same phrases; their superlatives were still in my ears; the same superlatives as before; the same 'divines', 'darlings', 'brilliants', and 'marvellouses'. The same fervent embraces and handshakes; the same glistening eyes. But this time there was a subtle difference. Lilian said wearily: 'Do you think we are all right?' And I knew, and she knew that I knew, that that question was merely rhetorical, a routine gesture of diffidence. We were all right, more than all right. We were a smash hit.

– From *Present Indicative*.

Ann Davison Sails the Atlantic

ANN DAVISON

I suppose I should have been delighted by the interest in the venture which appeared to have snowballed whilst my back was turned, but in point of fact I was embarrassed. Fresh from the sea, I was in a pretty humble frame of mind, for whatever the conditions, a week or two on the water under that illimitable dome of sky will deflate any ego, and the concern for my welfare seemed exaggerated and unnecessary.

With what I then considered to be an excess of caution I prepared for a sixty-day trip.

There could be no turning back on this voyage. No change of plan. This sort of certainty was sobering. . . I did not know how I would react to absolute solitude. It is an experience few of us are ever called upon to undergo and one which few of us would voluntarily choose. It is almost unimaginable, because solitude is something that normally can be broken at will. Even being on one's own in undeveloped country, popularly supposed to epitomise loneliness, is not true solitude, for one is surrounded by trees and bush and grass and animals, all part of the substance of one's own living. But the sea is an alien element; one cannot live in it or on it for long, and one survives that little time by one's own wit and judgment and the Grace of God. When a man says he loves the sea, he loves the illusion of mastery, the pride of skill, the life attendant on sea-faring, but not the sea itself. One may be moved by its beauty or its grandeur, or terrified by its immensity and power of destruction, but one cannot love it any more than one can love the atmosphere or the stars in outer space.

From the Log of the *Felicity Ann*

Wednesday December 3rd 1952

0750 hours. Thirteen days at sea. Have been up since before dawn doing odd chores. Considering only have one meal a day extraordinary how washing up accumulates. Trade Winds blowing fresh. Feeling not so good these last few days. Don't know why; eyes have been bothering, sore from salt and glare, and I don't think the crack on the head from the boom last night helps much. Did not realise it had actually split open until this morning when tried to comb hair and found comb all bloody. Lack of exercise also beginning to tell. I don't want to eat, but get low and dispirited if I don't.

Friday December 5th

0630. Surface to find flying fish on deck. Felt honour-bound to cook it for breakfast having read so often that this is one of the perks of Trade Wind sailing. The fish are attracted by the lights of a small vessel and fly towards them. Find flying fish good eating, like fresh herring only not so oily. Split it like herring, took out backbone, and fried it in butter.

1200. Seas absolutely monumental. Haven't rigged steering device yet – don't feel this is the time to experiment.

Sunday December 7th

Ship steered herself all through the night and put up 45 on the log. The motion is fierce, very quick and erratic, and the sound of the water rushing past as heard from below is as if it was being poured very quickly from a giant and inexhaustible bottle. At last feel we are getting somewhere . . .

1200. Log 759. Took day off and read a couple of whodunits and feel better for rest. Whodunits in middle of ocean are even more improbable than ashore.

Monday December 8th

Surfaced dawn to find log reading 818. This is *joy* . . . to have her sailing on whilst I sleep. Leap out in morning to count mileage like enthusiastic chicken farmer counting eggs.

Tuesday December 9th

Surface dawn as usual. Delicious morning. F3 wind. No cloud. Hot sun. Fixed primus and went to town with fried potatoes and eggs for breakfast. Passed empty rum bottle – who are we following? . . . Later, passed lots of jetsam and ship debris. Strange how reassuring a few empty cans can be on the ocean.

Friday December 12th

Gorgeous golden sunrise with authentic golden rays. Fixed primus as wind abated and seas slightly easier. Also hungry. Cooked enormous breakfast of french fries, apple, and eggs. This to cover today and yesterday. The motion never really settles down and I don't think one can ever become used to it the way one becomes used to normal motion, it is quite unpredictable. Curtails activity. Takes over an hour and a half to prepare and eat breakfast, a very exhausting procedure.

Sunday December 14th

1200. Managed to get slight croak on radio last night. Fading badly. Suspect battery is going to peter out. Hot humid cabin is no storage place for dry cells. Hot day.

Monday December 15th

1200. The fish watch my washing up operations with evident interest. Four to five feet long, bright turquoise blue with electric blue fins and yellow tails. Gorgeous creatures. They swim close to the surface of the water and give the flying fish hell. Little fish like silver pencil dances madly on its tail on surface just by stern of ship, dodging death by inches, no doubt. Reflect gloomily marine life unequivocably grim. Two bosun birds visit ship with loud squawks and fly round and round mast shrieking ornithological oaths at one another.

Tuesday December 16th

Squalls all night. Continuous lightning and heavy rain. *Felicity*

Ann most prominent thing on this part of ocean. Speculate on effect of ship being struck by lightning.

Wednesday December 17th

Decide those colourful fish are dolphins. They are supposed to be good eating and easy to catch, but although there is a fishing line and strong hooks aboard, I cannot bring myself to try and catch one. They are too friendly and trusting. One comes every morning to see what I have to throw overside, and if I lower the canvas bucket on to his nose, he doesn't swim away but seems to like having his nose scratched. He has an engaging habit of rolling over and studying me searchingly with one eye.

1745. No wind. What did I tell you? Heave-to. Another night of lightning more terrifying than ever.

2112. Had just gone to sleep when awakened by shriek of wind and found the most awful black squall in full blast. Ship lying right over and lightning flashing all round.

This is very bad. Will have to reef.

Reef down on wet deck tilted at incredible angle. Wind takes your breath away like icy plunge. Work in dark as cannot hold flashlight as well as hold on. Lightning darts about apparently looking for us. Idiotically try and pretend not to see it.

Thursday December 18th

Four weeks at sea and not half way. Hideous night like those off the Portuguese coast. Leaves one so limp for the next day.

Friday December 19th

1245. Have just taken a look at the bottom, both sides as she rolls; *covered* with barnacles. This in only four weeks. So much for copper paint. Another factor to slow us down.

A new type of fish has also adopted the ship, small, flat, and black with prim little mouths. Trigger fish according to illustrations in fish book. One of them likes cigarette ends. Made scones for tea (two meals today!). Wind east F1. Advancing on America majestically at one m.p.h.

Bosun bird, going east, flies past ship without batting an eyelid. This very unusual as these birds take a great interest in *Felicity Ann*. So I give a piercing wolf whistle, whereon bosun bird wheels smartly round, flaps back to ship, dives and stalls about three feet from my head, looks sharply at me, decides against whatever he had in mind to do and flies smartly away again.

Saturday December 20th

1630. Plodding along at just under two – yet there is a nice breeze that ought to send us along better than that. Touched by despair tonight. If it blows hard enough to get us moving I am worried sick. But if it doesn't blow hard we get nowhere fast, and there is a hell of a lot of ocean to cross yet.

Sunday December 21st

0815. Just finished breakfast. Make a rule to have this before doing anything else, for if I don't I am liable to overlook eating altogether since meals have no social significance. If one doesn't eat, morale gets very low. There is apparently no end to this filthy weather.

0920. Have been dickering with twins for the past hour trying to get *Felicity Ann* to sail *anywhere* west of north, but wind is all over the shop now and it is pouring with rain.

Everything below is soaked and moulding and rotting, without so far as can be seen any chance of drying out. . . .

Monday December 22nd

Quiet night. Calm sea. Little wind.

1100. Wind pulling round to westward. We are making progress at one knot. ('Trade Wind sailing a wonderful experience?' Phooey!)

Tuesday December 23rd

Make chart up to date immeasurably depressed by infinitesimal progress. Wash up and bring in log line to scrub off the barnacles it has acquired over last few days. Wish could do same for bottom. Log line appalling sight and it took hours to scrub the little beasts off. Fish life abundant this morning. The cigarette-eating fish is here again, gobbling up the butts I throw overboard, and a blue-and-black-striped job about six inches long is scavenging barnacles scrubbed off the line. Stupid sort of fish, why doesn't he go browse off the bottom?

Suffer much from thirst these days. It is very hot and everything I do makes me sweat inordinately. The water temperature is around 80 degrees and the boat is virtually floating in a warm bath so the cabin is not only hot but humid. I have only to sit on the settee to have the sweat running off me as though I was playing endless games of squash. So I am thirsty. But water is limited. Water is the limiting factor of the whole voyage. At present rate of progress we should make the other side in about one hundred and twenty days from now and there is not enough water for that. Have rationed drinking to one pint per day, and can think of little else but when I can have the next drink.

1915. The dolphins were rather amusing when I got going on the engine today. They took up station alongside and swam by the ship like dogs walking to heel. Every now and then they would spot a bunch of seaweed or a flying fish and dart after it just like a dog going into a hedgerow or after a rabbit. Then they would look round to see where the ship was and come scampering back to heel.

Wednesday December 24th

1500. Running into plenty of dirt ahead again. Back painful. Lumbago ashore is not much fun, aboard a fussy little ship it makes the performance of the simplest task one of the most exquisite tortures this side of hell. We are a fine pair – I am hobbling and *Felicity Ann* no longer sails like a smart Bermudan sloop, but lumbers along like turn-of-century box-bottomed barge.

1925. Managed to get quite wonderful reception on the radio . . . bit of Christmas cheer from the BBC, but it faded right out at the critical moment for the time signal which I wanted for a chronometer check. The announcer said: 'In one and a half minutes time when it will be ten o'clock . . .' and the set went dead. Battery I am afraid. As near as I can get, the chronometer is ten minutes slow, and I reckon her average daily rate to be two seconds slow.

Thursday December 25th

What a Christmas. Opened a letter delivered to me at Las Palmas, marked not to be opened until December 25th, and a parcel given me by the Parks, also marked Christmas Only. The letter was a greeting card from home, and the parcel was full of messages and little Christmas objects. Somehow this thoughtfulness did not impart the spirit intended. I feel acutely lonely, saddened, and dispirited, desolated by the sensation of absolute isolation. Try to improve outlook opening tin of Christmas pudding for dinner, not having any turkey, but my one meal a day is breakfast and Christmas pudding is no good for breakfast, even on Christmas Day.

1200. Lat. 19 11N which seems reasonably correct. Figure we are making point-eight knots. Heat is stupendous. Sun burning hot without being oppressive. It would be perfect if only we were moving a little faster towards the West Indies. I read with real interest a booklet called *Survival at Sea* presented pessimistically before leaving Plymouth.

1615. Stop motor. Really, it has been a beautiful day and my back is much better. I drink to absent friends, pulling faces over the poisonous rum bought in the Canaries. So raw it makes you shudder for half an hour after swallowing. I should have tried before buying but naïvely thought rum was rum all the world over. Have no wish to forgo sundowner institution. It makes a time mark in the day and something to look forward to, though I notice it has a tendency to get earlier and bigger each day. I visualise my friends very clearly as I drink their health. As if they were present. I can even hear their voices.

Friday December 26th

0915. Oh, what a beautiful morning – black as your hat as far as the eye can see. Thunder, lightning, and no wind to speak of. *Felicity Ann* waltzing in stately circles. I am preparing the biggest breakfast ever, a monstrous dish of sausages and batter, which I just couldn't eat when it was fixed. Ah well, there are only 364 more shopping days to Christmas.

1040. Have read all books aboard two or three times, know all the adverts in the magazines intimately and have taken to studying the shipping announcements in Brown's Nautical Almanac.

Sunday December 28th
  1730. No wind.
  1815. No radio either. Tried out spare battery, but that is flat, too. Don't know that I have ever felt lower.

Tuesday December 30th
  1500. Threw the air plant overboard. 'Something to watch,' Dorothy Park had said when she gave it to me, and I have watched it hanging from the boom gallows gradually shrivelling to death. One has an inclination to invent superstition. . . . 'If this lives we'll get to the other side . . .' and there is no one to talk one out of it.
  1835. Made a queer batter from one spoonful of gofio and two spoonfuls of dried egg and ate the result with margarine and brown sugar and liked it very much indeed.

Wednesday December 31st
  0600. Surface reluctantly after wretched night, and the morning does not promise to be much better. Although not in the least hungry am preparing breakfast as it is doing something positive which is the only protection against apathy and despair.
  1700. Heave-to, absolutely beat. Today touched an all-time low.

Thursday January 1st 1953
  Woke at 0600 absolutely scuppered, not having been rested at all. I slept all right, but it didn't seem to do any good.
  1800. Log 1592. Heave-to, been running all day with reefed main and small jib and wind on starboard quarter. The seas were heavy and swell monstrous, 30 feet at best. . . . . Waves, I noted today, break in divers ways. There is the kind that bounces up to you like a large and friendly puppy (down, boy). There is the kind that slams down beside you with the ferocity of a large fat man trumping your ace, and there is the kind that grows bigger and bigger and bigger and topples over with a kind of hissing roar that is like nothing on earth. . . . Feel sick and dizzy tonight.

2100. Awakened by boom swinging and banging and find it is calm again. This is incredible. How can so much wind be turned off like water at a tap?

Friday January 2nd

1000. I feel dizzy most of the time and am completely at the mercy of uncontrollable emotional impulses. The least little thing can delight or distress beyond measure. Mostly it is distress and I have wept more in these last few days than I have ever done in my whole life and for such trivial reasons as failing to light the stove with one match.

1610. There is no wind worth mentioning. BUT – have discovered a bottle of gin I didn't know I had, hidden at the bottom of a locker. Treasure. CORN IN EGYPT.

Saturday January 3rd

Calm all night. Calm this morning, and now at 0750, it promises to be terribly hot. These are undoubtedly the doldrums, there can be nothing else to account for such conditions.

1000. Still glassy calm.

1200. A cigarette can thrown over hours ago is still alongside.

Monday January 5th

1715. *Felicity Ann* roared on all afternoon steering herself admirably before pretty fierce seas. Motion fabulous of course. Sky astern looks better and I keep telling myself the seas are easier, but I don't know. It all has the appearance of having once started it is prepared to go on roaring for ever. And what am I griping about – this is what I want, isn't it?

Tuesday January 6th

Restless anxious night as wind and sea continue high and I have developed a chronic worry condition. The twins would keep having flogging bouts and I could visualise them blowing out any minute.

0600. Flying fish for breakfast, a good-sized one, too. Deck is covered with tiny baby cuttlefish for some inexplicable reason.

Wednesday January 7th

Another harassing night. When I do sleep it is only to have these wretched dreams of fitting out a small ship for an ocean crossing, or such horrible nightmares I am afraid to sleep at all. And the twins keep flogging. Seas are savage this morning.

Thursday January 8th

Seven weeks at sea. A more restful night than usual, but maybe I am more tired – if that is possible – and care less. Living under these conditions, apart from the anxiety, is terribly wearing as the fantastic motion makes the smallest task the most prodigious effort.

Saturday January 10th

I don't know why the motion seems worse in the morning, maybe one has to get used to it every day. Small flying fish again for breakfast.

1345. Log 2106, observed position 13 58N, 52 35W. Afternoon sights always turn out queer and I always have a hell of a job getting them for some reason. If this position is correct, we are only 420 miles from Barbados. Broached last bottle of brandy, opened last tin of cigarettes, and finished last of potatoes for breakfast. So we had better be only 420 miles from Barbados.

1615. Feeling rather lousy this evening – too long sea voyage is telling physically as well as mentally. Have painful sty on eye, and sea boils are manifest in spite of vitamin tablets.

Sunday January 11th

Wretched night, hardly any sleep, as eye was very painful and I had to keep bathing it, and this morning it is a most sordid sight. Wind got up during the night, driving *Felicity Ann* like a scalded cat and the motion was worse than ever, if that is possible. An enormous flying fish was in the cockpit when I looked out, I heard it flop aboard during the night, and there was another smaller one on deck, so it was a very good breakfast indeed, though I am pooped after it as usual; preparing, cooking, and eating being a major operation and equivalent to a hard day's work ashore.

1200. Log 2195, day's run 95. We are certainly moving and the racket is appalling – only hope everything holds together.

[211]

H

Monday January 12th

1350. In one of the lulls the wind dropped away altogether as if someone had shut a door, and I heard a roaring sound in the distance like surf breaking on a shore, and looked out of the cabin to see astern and coming towards us at a tremendous rate a line of white stretching across the sea from horizon to horizon. There was no escaping it, and I watched, transfixed, from the cabin, looking aft over the stern. As it drew nearer it grew higher and higher, and as it caught up with us, towering, tremendous, roaring, and breaking, I ducked below and pulled the hatch over. The ship was picked up and thrown on her beam ends, and it seemed for a moment as if we had had it . . . Then *Felicity Ann* surfaced, throwing the water off her, and I looked out to find the cockpit completely flooded. But there were no more tidal waves coming along, thank Heaven. The confusion in the cabin was chaotic. After that sea, which I think must have been the result of a sea-quake somewhere, had passed, the wind got up again and went on blowing with increased vigour. And the rain came down in torrents.

1800. Incessant scream of the wind gets on your nerves so you could scream back at it. I do, and relieve some of the tension. It is much easier to be brave when there is someone to impress with your courage, but you cannot fool yourself, and on your own you are just plain scared.

Tuesday January 13th

Slept some last night, I was dead-beat and would have slept through atomic warfare.

0850. Breakfast almost insuperable task but managed somehow. Pineapple juice, omelette, and coffee, simple enough, but by the time I had finished I was drenched in sweat and worn out. It *looks* a much nicer day now, but haven't the energy to cope with it. If only it would let-up for a while – the frightful incessant motion, the frightful incessant howl of the wind, the frightful hissing seas.

1820. The situation is not improved by the appearance of three large sharks who have taken up stations beside the ship, one on either side, and one astern. One swam right up under the cockpit and rolled over to look at me in that fishy way they have with one eye. They look unspeakably sinister, seeming to emphasise the menace of the ocean . . . this ceaseless, tireless, lonely, loveless sea.

Thursday January 15th

Eight weeks at sea, the maximum time I expected to take for the crossing. Fortunately it is much quieter this morning, in fact it is perfectly all right and I should press on regardless, except there are villainous banks of cloud hanging about and I am so weak the thought of getting those warps in and sail up slays me . . . and those slippery decks.

1200. Log 2324, day's run 13. Heavy squalls and weather continues to look rough and unsettled. Try and take my mind off it by planning a farm in Cornwall . . . even got down to mortising the joints in the built-in furniture in the farmhouse.

About 1700, I was very heartened and encouraged by the most perfect rainbow I have ever seen; it spanned the sea in a brilliant arch with colours of a pristine purity all the lovelier for appearing after what seems a lifetime of grey. It gave me as big a lift as a landfall.

2100. Here we are again, blowing as hard as ever. Had to turn out and take in another reef, *Felicity Ann* pitching wildly in heavy seas. Then the jib sheet shackle broke and it was a wet and windy party smothering the jib and replacing the shackle. Wherever we make landfall, Hell, Hull, or Halifax, it will do me.

Friday January 16th

0700. Dreadful night and still blowing as hard as ever. Glass still low and no sign of a let up. Have just had a self-heating can of malted milk. These self-heating cans have been a godsend in bad weather, and I have lived on them these past few days. You simply prise the cap off the top of the can, thus exposing a taper to which you put a match or cigarette end, and the taper flares and fizzles out and a chemical reaction is set up that heats the can in four minutes flat. . . . God knows, I am bad enough with a hot drink, without one I would be flayed. Eye still very sore and swollen in spite of care and bathing.

1315. Sky clear at last, and the heat is scorching.

Saturday January 17th

1900. Very weak as if arms and legs were stuffed with sawdust, and every move requires monumental effort.

Sunday January 18th

0710. Awakened by fierce squall.

I do believe we have made landfall.

Can't identify it yet as it is only a faint shape on the horizon, part hidden by cloud. Perhaps it is cloud. If it is still there after I have had a cup of coffee it is land.

It is! And it couldn't be anywhere else but Barbados.

I have hove-to on the starboard tack, about eight miles off shore, so I can fill the lamps, tidy the ship and myself, get supper as have neither fed nor drunk today and feel pretty whacko . . . then we can go in in the morning all fresh.

And, anyway, *we have crossed the ruddy ocean.*

Monday January 19th

0330. Another ghastly night. No sleep on account of ships for I cannot keep the lights on in these conditions – they blow out as fast as I light them. We are being driven inexorably westward and the lights of the Island are sinking slowly but surely over the horizon. I don't see how we are ever going to beat back across this stuff, for the seas are running mighty high again.

1100. It is a brilliant sunny day with a hard blue sky. The Island is right out of sight, and there are no ships to be seen. Keep going on benzedrine.

1125. It is heartbreaking to have been so close and to have the prize snatched just when it was within grasp.

I don't think I can take much more.

1700. It has eased down a little and having suddenly remembered I haven't eaten anything since an omelette last night have come below and had two Carr's lifeboat ration biscuits with marmalade and a snort of poison rum. *Felicity Ann* steering herself meanwhile, close-hauled. We came here quickly enough but it is going to be a long,

long haul back. My eyes are both now terribly inflamed and I don't
see too well. For this reason if no other, I must try and get in somewhere. Am using up reserves . . . everyone has a breaking-point and
am rapidly approaching mine.

1800. At sunset I saw what I thought might be Tobago astern and
the Grenadines to leeward, but am so tuckered out I cannot think
straight and they might be anywhere. Anyway I don't want to get
too close until I find out . . . It's these bloody big seas that bitch us
and knock the way off the little ship.

I see double out of my left eye.

Tuesday January 20th

0750. Had cup coffee, last in tin, cup of cocoa, two biscuits, two
vitamin tablets, and a benzedrine for breakfast.

1000. A great dollop of ocean broke over the ship, poured through
the hatch and soused everything. I am soaked. Everything's soaked.
Blowing hard again and the seas are white . . . Unless I can get some
assistance I don't think I can make port. Am stupid with fatigue and
my thinking is warped.

1115. Discover the handbearing compass to be about 20 degrees
out . . .

Wednesday January 21st

0745. Tonight for the first time since the middle of the ocean it
is calm and we are lying hove-to off that curious mountain pinnacle
that rises for a thousand feet straight up out of the sea, Gros Piton
Point. I feel entirely different now with land and good weather on
hand. Fair weather sailor, me. Now wondering how to get into Port
Castries, St. Lucia.

Thursday January 22nd

This is really very funny. On account of having to sleep and eat
we are now 20 miles westward of St Lucia and have a long beat back.
Missed 'im! It looks as though I shall have to try and carry on to
Antigua as originally planned. I started sailing at 0630 but find I
should carry full sail. It is fantastic but I have not the strength to

get the last bit of sail up, and there is still one roll on the boom, but she is sailing along quite nicely in spite of that. And *still* there are no signs of ships of any sort.

Saturday January 24th

What is the matter with me? All my life I have wanted to see the West Indies and here I am sailing past island after island – for why? Because I picked on Antigua? Phooey. The description of Prince Rupert Bay and the town of Portsmouth makes enchanting reading in the West Indies Pilot, and there it is, only a few miles to east'ard . . . So hi-ho for Dominica . . .

0720. Start engine and turn for Prince Rupert Bay. Nearing the Bay we run into a flotilla of native fishing boats, built-up dug-out canoes heavily overcanvassed with what appears to be four bags and going like fun. Some of them pass close and the crews wave cheerfully. It is the most extraordinary sensation to see people after so long. It is sixty-five days since I sailed out of Las Palmas and last set eyes on a fellow soul.

1800. At anchor in Prince Rupert Bay, just off the jetty at Portsmouth, a fascinating little tropical town hiding behind the scrub and coconut palms lining the shore and dominated by the densely wooded mountains in the background.

*   *   *   *   *   *

I sat in the Cockpit watching the lights of the little village spring out like fireflies in the deepening dusk, and listened to the jungle chorus humming and drumming and ringing in the green-mantled mountains, which were quickly losing their identity in the dark velvet of a tropical night. I had no desire to go ashore. It was enough that it was there, warm and pulsating, solid and real, and belonging to me in a way no legal deeds or titles could surpass or diminish; for I was of the land and to the land had returned. And tomorrow, or the day after maybe, I would go ashore and walk on solid earth, and talk to people and become one of them again, and revert to my problems, none of which had been solved by this preposterous voyage.

But that was tomorrow. Tonight I was savouring an experience I had forgotten existed, symbolised by quiet schooners on quiet waters, a peaceful sea lapping a silent shore, the sibilant wind rustling the palm fronds: tranquillity.

– From *My Ship is so Small.*

Miss Frances Burney Writes a Book

FANNY BURNEY

1778. This year was ushered in by a grand and most important event. At the latter end of January, the literary world was favoured with the first publication of the ingenious, learned, and most profound Fanny Burney. This admirable authoress has named her most elaborate performance EVELINA; *or a Young Lady's Entrance into the World*.

A thousand little odd incidents happened about this time; however, they were none of them productive of a discovery either to my father or mother.

My aunt Anne and Miss Humphries being settled at this time at Brompton, I was going thither with Susan to tea, when Charlotte acquainted me that they were then employed in reading *Evelina* to the invalid, my cousin Richard.

This intelligence gave me the utmost uneasiness – I foresaw a thousand dangers of a discovery. In truth I was quite sick with apprehension, and was too uncomfortable to go to Brompton, and Susan carried my excuses.

Upon her return I was somewhat tranquillised, for she assured me that there was not the smallest suspicion of the author, and that they had concluded it to be the work of a *man*.

Finding myself safe, I ventured to go to Brompton next day. On my way upstairs, I heard Miss Humphries in the midst of Mr Villars' letter of consolation upon Sir John Belmont's rejection of his daughter; and just as I entered the room, she cried out: 'How pretty that is.'

How much in luck would she have thought herself, had she known *who* heard her. My aunt Anne told me a thousand things that had

[218]

been said in its praise. I must own I suffered great difficulty in refraining from laughing upon several occasions – and several times, when they praised what they read, I was on the point of saying: 'You are very good,' and so forth, and I could scarcely keep myself from making acknowledgments, and bowing my head involuntarily. However, I got off perfectly safe.

Chessington, June 18. I came hither the first week in May, and could not resist treating myself with a little private sport with 'Evelina'. I had promised *Hetty* that *she* should read it to Mr Crisp, but I wrote my excuses and introduced it myself.

I told him it was a book which Hetty had taken to Brompton, to divert my cousin Richard. Mr Crisp was so indifferent about it that I thought he would not give himself the trouble to read it, and often embarrassed me by unlucky questions, such as: 'Is it reckoned clever?' and 'What do you think of it' and 'Do folks laugh at it?' At length he desired me to begin reading to him. I found it a much more awkward thing than I had expected; my voice quite faltered when I began it, which, however, I passed off for the effect of remaining weakness of lungs; and, in short, the book, by my reading, lost all manner of spirit. I determined to leave Hetty the third volume, and therefore pretended I had not brought it. He was in a delightful ill-humour about it, and I enjoyed his impatience far more than I should have done his forbearance . . . For Mr Crisp, before my mother, very innocently said to Susan: 'O, pray Susette, do send me the third volume of *Evelina*. Fanny brought me the first two on purpose, I believe, to tantalise me.'

I felt myself in a ferment; and Susan, too, looked foolish, and knew not what to answer. As I sat on the same sofa with him, I gave him a gentle shove, as a token, which he could not but understand, that he had said something wrong – though I believe he could not imagine *what*. Indeed how should he?

My mother instantly darted forward, and repeated: '*Evelina*, what's that, pray?'

Again I jolted Mr Crisp, who, very much perplexed, said in a boggling manner, that it was a novel – he supposed from the circulating library – 'Only a trumpery novel.' . . .

Two days after I received from Charlotte a letter, the most interesting that could be written to me, for it acquainted me that my dear father was at length reading my book, which has now been published six months.

It seems the very moment almost that my mother and Susan left the house, he desired Charlotte to bring him the *Monthly Review*. She contrived to look over his shoulder as he opened it, which he did at the account of *Evelina; or a Young Lady's Entrance into the World*. He read it with great earnestness, then put it down; and presently after snatched it up again. He turned to Charlotte, put his finger on the word 'Evelina' and bade her write down the name and send the man to Lowndes, as if for herself. This she did, and away went William.

When William returned, he took the book from him, and the moment he was gone, opened the first volume – and opened it upon the ode.[1] How great must have been his astonishment at seeing himself so addressed. Indeed, Charlotte says he looked all amazement, read a line or two with great eagerness, and then, stopping short, he seemed quite affected and the tears started into his eyes; dear soul!

I believe he was obliged to go out before he advanced much further. But the next day I had a letter from Susan, in which I heard he had begun reading it with Lady Hales and Miss Coussmaker, and that they like it vastly. Lady Hales spoke of it in the highest terms, declaring she was sure it was written by somebody in high life, and added 'He must be a man of great abilities.'

What will all this come to? Where will it end? and when and how shall I wake from the vision of such splendid success? for I hardly know how to believe it real.

Well, I cannot but rejoice that I published the book, little as I ever imagined how it would fare.

August 3. Susan writes me word that when my father went last to Streatham, Dr Johnson was not there, but Mrs Thrale told him that when he gave her the first volume of *Evelina*, which she had

---

[1] 'To ——' which Dr. Burney recognised as intended for himself – in effect a dedication.

lent him, he said: 'Why, madam, why, what a charming book you lent me,' and eagerly enquired for the rest.

Dr Johnson's approbation! It almost crazed me with agreeable surprise – it gave me such a flight of spirits that I danced a jig to Mr Crisp, without any preparation, music or explanation – to his no small amazement and diversion. I left him, however, to make his own comments upon my friskiness.

I now come to last Saturday evening, when my beloved father came to Chessington. In his way hither he had stopped at Streatham, and he settled with Mrs Thrale that he would call on her again on his way to town, and carry me with him, and Mrs Thrale said: 'We all long to know her.'

I have been in a kind of twitter ever since.

London, August. I have now to write an account of the most consequential day I have spent since my birth; namely my Streatham visit.

Our journey was the least pleasant part of the day, for the roads were dreadfully dusty, and I was really in the fidgets from thinking what my reception might be.

Mr Thrale's house is white, and very pleasantly situated, in a fine paddock. Mrs Thrale was strolling about, and came to us as we got out of the chaise. She then received me, taking both my hands, and welcoming me to Streatham. She led me into the house, and addressed herself almost wholly for a few minutes to my father, as if to give me an assurance that she did not mean to regard me as a show, or to distress or frighten me by drawing me out. Afterwards she took me upstairs and showed me the house, and said she had very much wished to see me. But though we were some time together, she did not *hint* at my book . . .

Soon after Mrs Thrale took me to the library; she talked a little while upon common topics, and then, at last she mentioned *Evelina*!

'Yesterday at supper,' she said, 'we talked it all over. Dr Johnson repeated whole scenes by heart. I declare I was astonished at him. O, you can't imagine how much he is pleased with the book. But was it not droll,' she said, 'that I should recommend it to Dr Burney and tease him so innocently to read it?'

When we were summoned to dinner, Mrs Thrale made my father

and me sit on each side of her. I said that I hoped I did not take Dr Johnson's place – for he had not yet appeared.

'No,' answered Mrs Thrale, 'he will sit by you, which I am sure will give him great pleasure.'

Soon after we were seated, this great man entered. I have so true a veneration for him that the very sight of him inspires me with delight and reverence, notwithstanding the cruel infirmities to which he is subject; for he has almost perpetual convulsive movements, either in his hands, lips, feet, or knees, and sometimes all together.

Mrs Thrale introduced me to him, and he took his place. We had a noble dinner, and a most elegant dessert. Dr Johnson, in the middle of dinner, asked Mrs Thrale what was in some little pies that were near him.

'Mutton,' answered she, 'so I don't ask you to eat any, because I know you despise it.'

'No, madam, no,' cried he; 'I despise nothing that is good of its sort; but I am too proud now to eat of it. Sitting by Miss Burney makes me very proud to-day.'

– From *The Diary of Fanny Burney*.

Monica Dickens Practises Nursing

MONICA DICKENS

They had had several operation cases in the late afternoon and evening, and the last one, an old lady of seventy, had come back from the Theatre only just alive. 'She won't last long,' said Sister, getting up again to feel her barely perceptible pulse. 'I've rung up her people, but I doubt whether they'll get here in time.' Automatically, she straightened the sheet over the dying woman and left us. There was nothing more she could do.

Sister Adams was off that night, and Sister Gilbert came tiptoeing up at ten o'clock with Mrs Colley's relations. The husband was a humble old man with faded blue eyes and the walk of a man who has spent his life with horses. His daughter was thin and tired-looking, her face blotched with crying, but she had put on her best coat and hat and was clutching an enormous battered handbag.

'I've brought Mum's bag along,' she whispered. 'She can't bear to be parted from it, but they took her off in such a hurry.' They stood by the bed and looked speechlessly at the old lady, her nose high and pinched in her waxy face, the collar of the white gown much too big for her.

Chris wanted to look at her dressing, and the husband and daughter went obediently to wait in Sister's sitting-room. The old man sat forward in his chair, his elbows on his knees, turning his cap round and round in his hands, and the daughter sat politely, with her hands in her lap as if she were making a call.

Chris had her hand on Mrs Colley's wrist, frowning.

'Not long,' she said. 'Christ, I hate to stand by and let someone just slip off like this. Here – stay with her a minute. That Appendix'll be out of bed if I don't give her her morphia.'

The green-shaded light over the bed fell on the old woman's face. You could trace the outline of every bone in her skull and her nose was typically sharp and prominent, as if the face had fallen away from it. Her skin was cold and faintly damp, and her pulse no more than a tremor and then not even that. I listened for her breathing and called Chris over. 'She's dead.'

'I wouldn't swear to it,' she said, and stood pensively tapping her foot. 'Look, get the hypo. syringe and the coramine. It couldn't hurt to give her a shot.'

'I suppose I'd better call her people in,' she said despondently, when she had given the injection. 'Oh, damn, there's Chubby. What the hell does he want?' Chubby was Mr Soames, the little new House Surgeon, just out of the egg, with fluffy hair that never would lie down on his round head. He was on for all surgical cases to-night, and was just going round to see if it was all right for him to go to bed. As we watched Mrs Colley, one of her eyelids fluttered and for a moment her breathing was audible.

'My God,' said Chris suddenly, 'I wonder – ' She clutched hold of Chubby's arm. 'Listen,' she whispered urgently, 'couldn't we give her an intravenous? Couldn't we try it? Sister said it wasn't any use, but I don't know – *Please*, Mr Soames, do let's try. It seems awful just not to do anything when she's still alive.'

Chubby ran his fingers through his hair. 'I don't know,' he said, hesitatingly; 'it's not much good – ' Chris's eyes were sparkling at him, her face alive with urgency. 'All right,' he said and laughed nervously, 'I'll have a shot if you like.'

'I'll go and lay up the trolley,' she gabbled. 'Don't go away – I'll have it ready by the time you've scrubbed up. You put the electric heat cradle over her,' she told me, 'and tell her people they can't come in for a sec.'

'Is she ―― ?' asked the daughter, getting up as I went into the sitting-room. 'We're going to try something,' I said. 'It might not be any good, but ――' The old man was watching me like a trusting dog.

I wanted to stay and watch Chubby cut down into Mrs Colley's vein, where the saline was going to run in through the needle, but half the ward chose to be awake and kept me running about for the next half-hour. Mrs Davenport fussed and fretted and had me yanking her leg up and down five or six times. 'What's all that light at the top of the ward for?' she grumbled. 'A person can't sleep with all this running about.'

'We're trying to save someone's life,' I snapped.

'Poor soul,' she said. 'But me leg isn't right yet, Nurse, I don't know how it is . . .' I said something quite rude to her, I can't remember what, but it shocked her into silence, although she kept up a rhythmic, insistent moaning for as long as she could keep herself awake.

I went to hold Mrs Colley's arm for Chris, while she bandaged it to the splint to keep it still. Mr Soames was regulating the drip of the saline, his face flushed with excitement, for it was the first intravenous he had done since he had been here. Sister Gilbert came along to see why we had not rung her yet to say that Mrs Colley had died.

'I'll do the round while I'm here,' she said. 'All right, don't bother to come with me, Nurse,' and she tiptoed off down the ward alone.

When she came back, she found the three of us wild with excitement. Mrs Colley's skin was still cold, but it was no longer clammy. You could hear her breathing now; you could distinctly feel her pulse.

'Of course, it might be only a momentary rally,' Sister said doubtfully, but she obviously didn't think that.

'Keep her warm,' said Chubby, putting on his white coat, his chick's hair on end. 'I'll come back when I've finished my round. Let me know at once if anything happens, and for God's sake keep that drip running.'

'Tidy her up,' said Sister, 'and let her people come in.' While I was rearranging the sheets to hide a little blood that Chubby had split in his haste, I kept touching Mrs Colley, to feel her skin gradually losing its marble chill. Suddenly she opened her eyes and looked at me accusingly. 'Me arm,' she whispered, 'what you done to me arm?'

'Now you've got to keep that arm still, d'you hear? Don't you dare move it.' She raised a grizzled eyebrow at me.

'Hoity-toity,' she said faintly.

The husband and daughter came in, breathless with hope, glancing uneasily at the bandaged arm rigidly outflung and the gibbet-like saline apparatus. 'She may not know you,' whispered Chris, and Mrs Colley unhooded one eye. 'Think I don't know Dad?' she mumbled. ' 'Ere, where's me 'andbag? '

'Here you are, Mum.' Her daughter laid it on the bed under her groping hand. 'Ah, that's more like it,' she said, and drifted off into her Limbo again. They sat by the bed for a while, and presently they went into the sitting-room and had some tea. They wouldn't go home. Mrs Colley's pulse continued to be satisfactory.

Soon after Chubby had gone to bed, the saline tube blocked. We took the whole apparatus to pieces to try and eliminate the air bubble, but still we could see in the glass connection that it wasn't dripping through. We conjured with it for hours, trying different connections and new bottles.

Chris left me fiddling with it while she went to do a mastoid dressing. When Sister came down, Mrs Colley's colour was worse and her pulse weaker. 'Try rebandaging the arm,' she said. 'There may be too much pressure.' She spoke calmly, but I could see that she was as worried as we were. She gave Mrs Colley some more coramine, and then the telephone summoned her to another ward. I piled on more blankets, refilled the hot bottles, and tried the old lady with some oxygen.

The arm was exposed now, with the needle tied into the vein, but still the saline was not running. 'I believe we'll have to get Chubby out of bed to cut down again,' said Chris, and swore under her breath as she fiddled with the tube. I became aware that Mrs Davenport had been calling monotonously for some time and went to shut her up. When I got back, Chris was not swearing under her breath but humming triumphantly.

'Don't move, don't breathe,' she said. 'I don't know what I did, but I've done it.' One of us stayed with Mrs Colley all the time, watching her like a hawk, checking her pulse, keeping her arm still and regulating the oxygen. Presently, she was well enough to take half a feeding cup of tea and even to grumble that it was not sweet enough.

She got very naughty. That was the joy of it. As her strength returned, she began to throw her weight about, and we could not let her people sit with her because she became too lively if she thought she had an audience.

'What you done to me arm?' she kept demanding. 'Practising on me, that's all you girls are doing – practising nursing, and I won't have it.'

'You keep that arm still,' said Chris.

'Don't you order me about, Miss,' said the old lady. 'I'm very poorly. I'll have another cup of tea, that's what I'll have, and if I wants to move me arm, I'll move it, see?' Her voice rose to a squeak.

'Look here, granny,' said Chris. 'We saved your life. Now shut up.'

'Oh, don't be mean to her,' I said. 'I feel as if she were my child.'

'So do I. I feel marvellous about the old bird, don't you? We saved her life.'

'Chubby didn't do anything of course.'

'Oh, well, he helped, I suppose,' she conceded grudgingly, 'but I feel as if I'd done it all myself, don't you?'

Mrs Colley's husband and daughter had some breakfast and then they came in to see her. 'It's like a miracle,' the daughter kept saying, but they both had a bewildered air. They had steeled themselves to meet tragedy and now they had to get used to this new idea. We put screens round Mrs Colley's bed, because the Day Nurses were starting the work of the ward. When Sister came on, with every hair in place, she sought me out where I was doing a bit of rinsing in the sluice.

'Nurse,' she said, 'why haven't you put Mrs Colley's mattress and pillows outside the ward to be fumigated?'

'Because she's still using them,' I said, pushing up some hair with the back of a wet hand. It was one of the proudest moments of my life.

– From *One Pair of Feet*.

[227]

Aage Thaarup Makes Hats

AAGE THAARUP

Hat-making has projected me into all sorts of lively adventures. It has led me down many honeysuckled lanes. It has enabled me to scale more than one undreamed-of height.

I learned to make hats for all sorts of women. According to their personalities, the length of their skulls, and their pocket-books.

And I learnt something else; that the woman who is terribly confident that she knows 'just what suits her' generally knows least. Nowadays, when I get a customer like that, I simply say: 'Madam, here is my whole collection. I will have somebody show it to you.' Even if I am at the other end of the salon, I can tell whether she has chosen rightly or wrongly. And if the latter I am soon back again.

'Madam!' I say. 'Did you look at yourself from this side? Your forehead is too protruding for that one.' Or: 'That hat does not go with your nose. It is too . . .' I should like to add '. . . too much like mutton dressed as lamb', but of course one does not say such things.

But when a customer puts herself in my hands, then my interest in her is aroused. I am fascinated by any problem she may have, and will take endless trouble on her account. She can have a glass eye, two deaf-aids and three double chins; I can, and will, do something for her.

It is difficult to say where a hat begins and ends.

Of inspiration I make no special virtue. To me it is one of the easier parts of the business. It is as natural as living.

One can be walking down Piccadilly, one can be shopping for a pound of steak in the King's Road, one can be lying in one's bath;

something in a shop window, some chance reflection in the mind and an idea sidles in.

At a party, one is hungrily lending one ear to one person and the other to another. Across the space two words will wing towards each other, forge themselves together and evoke a picture that makes an idea. These are sunshiny moments. In an almost mesmeric trance one passes the olives or buys the pound of steak or hurries down Piccadilly.

The pretty girls at the party pass unnoticed, the butcher's levity unregarded. Sometimes I have even found myself with thirty minutes and two miles unaccounted for, but cosily wrapped in the cocoon of my mind is the grub that will flutter, as a butterfly, round my showrooms next week or next month or next season. It waits only for the handicraft of my workroom for it to be the first butterfly of that species.

If inspiration is lacking there is a sure way of courting it. The rendezvous is the stockroom. For, of course, as soon as one begins to be established a stockroom becomes a pleasant necessity. A place where the materials, the hoods, the spartra, the wire, the tulle, the feathers and the flowers are kept; all the appurtenances of hat-making. And when the lady dragon in charge can be prevailed upon to open all the cupboards it is an Aladdin's cave.

But at nine o'clock in the morning the cupboards will all be closed, the trestle tables bare. Perhaps one of the chairs is occupied, however, for it is at this hour that the travellers call. They come from the big wholesale importers and manufacturers all round Oxford Circus, Great Marlborough Street and Great Portland Street. Or they come from some little room in Soho.

They come with shiny bags and cases; with well-worn ones. With battered trunks, with bright, new-painted boxes. They come with crinkly, crumpled paper bags.

And their mien and step are just as diverse; as shabby, despondent and shapeless as some of the bulging fibre cases; as well-nourished and tanned as the hide ones; as perky and bright as the new-painted boxes; as faded and crumpled as the paper bags.

It is their living to trot round London selling their wares. And remembering the days when I, too, carried a paper bag, when I sat in Hyde Park and cried with exhaustion and frustration, how could I be less than sympathetic and polite to these honest people? But if politeness is automatic, it is also good business. One never knows what might be in that closed brown bag on that busy morning. It might be just *the* morning when that particular bag carries the most beautiful idea of the season.

Some mornings there will be straws from Switzerland, another day a flower from France, a piece of velvet from Lyons or satin from Milan. These come from the big people.

But it is the little person who interests me. The tiny Czech woman; a frail little thing, a refugee. Her large brown orbs peer sombrely from their blue-white surround, the worn hands clutch a much-used paper bag. But open it, and there is revealed an exquisitely made ornament.

Or the little old gentleman with the silver moustache. Old! He must be a hundred; he climbs my stairs with difficulty, shuffling his feet and wheezing a little. But once in the stockroom, he shows a grace, an old-fashioned grace that makes one feel slightly humble. He knows I like only the best material, and, so honest is he and so transparent, one can almost tell from his grip on his bag whether he has something good or only something indifferent to show me. I can see him now, the glint on his spectacles, and the confident handling of the bag on a good morning; the faint look of shame when he has something not quite first-class.

The quickening of inspiration is a magic moment. But a creative artist needs skilled manual help and it remains for my work-people actually to construct the hat. And on their talent a great deal depends.

My method is to speak with each girl, whether she is just starting at sixteen or is fifty-nine and an 'old' girl. I like to explain the job to her personally; I like her to feel that she has her part in the hat's creation.

And when I find talent, when I find a girl who has got 'it' . . . I throw my own hat into the air. I do everything I can to encourage her. It is I, who cannot stitch a hat elastic into place, who should make the tea!

Hat-making is a bit like sculpture. You take this bit of spartra or millinery material and shape and mould it. All the time your eye and hand tell you whether you are succeeding. I can go into my work-room, pick up a hat and, though a girl may have worked on it for ten hours or twelve hours, I can see immediatcly if she has lost some-thing. It may be a bit too wide on this side or too shallow on that; lopsided or uneven.

Well, it is a dull November morning and it is time to think of spring shapes. There may be snow on the ground, there may be an influenza epidemic, but the hats must look very fresh, very gay; tender, disarming.

I have made the shape; shall I make the hat in Swiss straw, in braid that is only half an inch wide? Shall I take an exotic straw that came from Java, or Singapore, or Panama; or a piece of linen made in Ireland, a piece of Paisley cotton? Or shall I use French satin; an Italian straw hood, or my favourite, a Leghorn? A beautiful Leghorn, flaunting a handsomeness that no other straw has. Alas, I have too few of these.

I decide. And then, if I am in a practical frame of mind, I think of a customer. There are some I know who will like to have a hat from me whether it is April or October and whether it is made in Berkeley Street or Bywater Street.

So I think of Mrs Mitchell. Mrs Mitchell likes navy, navy with a touch of white. I make my hat with Mrs Mitchell in mind and when the snow has gone and there are crocuses in the parks and the first spring sunshine is 'x-raying' every wardrobe door, I telephone Mrs Mitchell.

'I thought of you in November. It is a little thing in navy and white. Am I right?'

'Yes, Mr Thaarup. I'll be along tomorrow.'

I may have no one in mind. I may choose an Italian straw braid in pale leaf green simply in revolt against the murky gloom outside. Shall I trim it? I will. Because I think trimming suits English women. Perhaps I will make the trimming interchangeable so that the hat can be sober for church on Sunday morning, gay for tea in the after-noon.

So I am standing with this green hat in my hand! I go into the stockroom and ask the stockroom-keeper to open the cupboards that are hiding the spring flowers. There are snowdrops, crocuses, violets; moss roses which I love; and mignonette which I love even more. There are dandelions, there are blooms so varied that a seedsman's catalogue would be put out of countenance. The flowers must look real. . . . The rose petals can be exaggeratedly velvety, the lily-of-the-valley blossoms a little bolder and the leaves even cooler than in nature; the anemone stamens more pollen-laden. But real, even if with the reality of dreams. . . . Shall I try this one, or that one?

Expecially in making hats for Royal ladies do flowers present difficulties.

For a flowered hat, though it might very properly become the occasion, still risks the hazard of vying with the bouquet which is almost certain to be presented to the Royal lady. La France roses might look enchanting on the hat, but how can one foretell just what the little pig-tailed girl or blushing 'deb' will contribute to the picture? She may present a glorious arrangement of white lilac; but, perhaps, a bunch of sweet peas!

So, I always advise any lady who is likely to receive a bouquet to have her hat flowerless; instead, a simple tulle or veiling trim.

Is there any place like a milliner's salon for meeting different types of women? I sometimes wonder, rather irreverently, whether a confessional box gets as varied a sample of femininity.

Mrs Claude Beddington would, I know, have allowed me to speak of her as a 'character'. She came one day – on whose recommendation I do not know – sweeping into my tiny salon clothed ('disguised' would perhaps describe her state better) in a voluminous mackintosh cape. A cape was a rare thing in those days; this one, according to Mrs Beddington was the envy of all her friends.

Besides being a great personality, Mrs Beddington was an astoundingly good-looking woman. Her skin was fair, all milk and roses, and she had quantities of dark, very dark hair.

'Young man, I hear you are talented and I want you to try to create for me. But I want nothing inspired by anything later than the fifteenth century.'

Bang. It was a command.

I cudgelled my brain. I searched the history books. I settled on a Viking inspiration.

The hat should be a tricorne, I decided, so I made it in grey silk with blue wings sticking out like ears from either side. The hat was not contemporary; it was not a 'pretty' hat, not even picturesque. It was made with the finest workmanship, and I knew it was just what Mrs Beddington wanted.

She swept into the salon, blue cape and all, and put on the hat.

'It's a masterpiece,' she said.

I got to know Mrs Beddington better, and I copied that Viking hat perhaps a dozen times. But her husband was a great yachting man and there was always some exciting trip being planned, to Bermuda or Florida or some warm sea. So naturally I made yachting caps too – always, of course, with a 'difference'.

Later, when, alas, Mrs Beddington had lost her husband, I was again asked to go to see her. 'I've lost everything! Everything!' she said. 'But I shall need some more hats.' What spirit that woman had.

Another and quite different sort of customer at that time was the lovely Evelyn, Lady Alington. Probably the oldest lady ever to climb my tiny staircase, she was rather of the period of Queen Alexandra. So gracious, so much a lady of the old school. She brought her maid; she bowed to the smallest liftboy or little nobody in the business.

She was beautiful; and she was very properly, as I think women should be, proud. She chose her hats with the greatest appreciation of what became her, and what was intrinsically good and beautiful.

And how kind she was. Surrounding her were always numbers of nieces and grandchildren. 'Eileen,' she would say, or 'Jennifer, go along and see that nice little Mr Thaarup. I will pay.'

I made hats for this wonderful old lady for many years. Her charm was inestimable, her graciousness unbelievable. And when, alas, she died, there remained still one more gesture of kindness: her maid arrived one morning with two big boxes of feathers, ribbons and veils. Her ladyship had asked her to bring them to me, because she knew that I had difficulty in finding trimmings during the war.

It is sad to recall the passing of another outstanding woman. But

[233]

how alive, how magnificently alive in those days was the incomparable Nellie Wallace!

I first saw her at the Palladium on that first visit of mine as a young boy. Surprisingly she was playing Juliet. Not a pretty Juliet, but, nevertheless, a very exciting one. But now she came to me for some hats to wear in her character sketches. They were all deliciously exaggerated things. Extravagant ostrich feathers to wear with bootees; a Robin Hood hat to go with a crinoline; and all sorts of other amusingly inappropriate pieces.

Then came the *famous* hat. The cockney hat that became her trade mark. A tiny, tiny brown hat with a big, big feather. The original, she told me, she had picked up in the market place at Nottingham where she first started performing on the public stage. And she had had it for 'donkey's years'. It had to be renewed.

'I'll try,' I said.

I got a bit of felt and a long pheasant feather; I copied that hat exactly. But Miss Wallace was too great an artist to let it go at that.

'It's got to have a worn look,' she said.

So we took it down the stairs, rolled it in the gutter, trod on it a little, sat on it – and got it just right.

I copied this hat several times more and always remembered to get the 'patina'.

You could never tell what you were in for with Lady Oxford. One could generally expect some forward-looking idea; equally it could be something startlingly practical with an almost Victorian flavour. Coming down from the workrooms one day, I found Lady Oxford being shown some hats by a young sales-girl. It was a cold day and the sales-girl had a rather short frock and, of course, nylon stockings – or were they silk in those days? Lady Oxford always wore ground-length dresses, and as I came in I heard her say: 'You silly girl! You'll catch your death of cold. Now you be sensible, as I am.'

And she lifted her skirt and showed black and white striped football stockings reaching to the knee. The odd thing is that they looked right!

A hat that was interesting to make was one for Frances Day. She came to my showrooms in Grosvenor Street in slacks, her flaxen mane flowing and her huge pet dog bounding at her side. It was about the time that she was enchanting everyone with a lovely little song, 'It's d'lightful, it's d'licious, it's d'lovely'. I am sure that even those Londoners who had not heard her singing it on the stage would nevertheless have had a recording of it, for those were the days when everybody played the gramophone.

'I want a hat for Ascot,' said Miss Day.

'It's d'lightful. It's d'lovely. It's d'lirious.' The refrain spun in my mind. Miss Day showed me a sketch of the frock she was to wear.

'I want to look like a nun,' she said. One never can tell!

I like to think I have been conscientious always, and certainly I have had some outstanding rewards. This was one of the loveliest. Out of the blue it came, as unexpectedly as it was esteemed:

The telephone rang. 'Can Mr Thaarup be in at three o'clock to receive Her Royal Highness the Duchess of York?'

I put down the receiver, not quite in a panic, but not very calm.

I made my small salon ready, found a few extra nice hats. My stock was still not so very large; would the Duchess want a pink hat or a black hat, a felt or a straw?

Then, of course, there were the stairs. Everything was quite presentable, almost elegant up to the second floor, but after that there were bare boards. Quickly I borrowed a little strip of red carpet and secured it with drawing pins.

I showed the Duchess and her companion into the lift – so small I had to squeeze into it myself in order to close the gates, then pressed the button for the second floor.

'I'm sorry,' I said lamely. 'There's still a little further.'

Would the little bit of red carpet look decent? And above, the Jacob's Ladder, and my little room in grey? The black and white matting on the floor, the chromium chairs?

Nervously I drew aside the tweed curtain draped across my stock cupboard. A pink hat toppled out, and the Duchess smiled. The cold spell was broken.

Whenever I recall that first visit of Queen Elizabeth the Queen Mother, I remember that smile; that amazing flow of warmth. The feeling of sensitivity and graciousness that immediately put another human being at ease.

I showed a few berets and some other new hats. I explained about the Jacob's Ladder, I excused the fire jugs. I think I even admitted to Her Royal Highness the borrowing of the bit of red carpet.

No dreams that these first hats of mine for the Duchess of York would lead to my making so many more for her as Queen of England. Hats that would accompany her on proud ceremonies in Kingdom and Empire in peacetime, or would play their part on heartening tours amongst her people during wartime. And again, more hats for her as the still beautiful Queen Mother.

In those days my hats were for the Duchess of York, a charming young mother of Scottish royal lineage with two small and lovely children, the Princesses Elizabeth and Margaret Rose, who sometimes would gravely watch the hat-fitting ceremony.

– From *Heads and Tales.*

PART FIVE

It's Your Father All Over:

A Procession of Husbands

Father Brightens the Sick-Room

CLARENCE DAY

Throughout Mother's illness, Father hadn't been very much troubled. But now that she was beginning to get well again, he felt quite alarmed, for he realised at last, as he watched her, how feeble she had become. He kept patting her hand and saying 'Dear Vinnie', and telling her he couldn't stand it.

Mother was pleased by his being attentive. When she saw other women being fussed over by their husbands, she often wished she got more of such attentions. But she was not really the kind of woman to linger much over endearments. She liked things of that sort to be electric, and to come in quick flashes, and pass. She hadn't time or patience to give herself up to long interchanges.

So after Father, who wasn't very inventive, had patted her hand twenty times, she snatched it away in annoyance and said: 'Stop it, Clare! That's enough!'

'Get your hat and stick, dear,' she added. 'It's time you were starting.'

Mrs Nicholas was giving a tea which Mother wished to hear all about, and she had coerced Father, much against his will, into saying he'd go. What had made him consent was his desire to do something for her. She said that if he told her about the tea it might brighten her up, and he felt that she probably needed a little amusement.

He looked spruce and handsome in his formal cutaway coat. Mother smiled at him. She felt she was being generous to Mrs Nicholas, and executive, too, to send Father there in her stead – such a distinguished-looking, ruddy, agreeable man would be a help at any tea. It would be pleasant for Father, besides. She only wished she could go, instead of sitting in bed with nothing more interesting to look forward to than a chicken broth. Things tasted so good at a tea.

'Anything I can do for you while I'm out?' Father asked her.

'Yes, Clare,' she said suddenly, 'there *is* something I'd like. Do bring me some of those little sandwiches Mrs Nicholas has – they'd be nice with the broth.'

'Sandwiches and *broth*?' Father said in dismay.

'No! Just sandwiches,' Mother said. 'Those little thin sandwiches. Bring some in your pocket.'

'Oh, some sandwiches, eh?' Father put on his high hat, took his stick and gloves from the table, and left.

He enjoyed himself more than he expected to at the tea. Met some men he knew, and was spoken to by a great many ladies whom he knew more or less. It made him feel expansive and jovial to be kept busy responding to all of them.

He was on guard, however. There were some women present whom he knew of old and took care to avoid: women who talked every minute, or who had masculine airs, or who dressed like old frumps. But he picked out a good corner to sit in where there were none of these persons, and where he could be gallant in his jolly way to others of a much nicer kind. And their daughters. He had a cup of tea, too, and a plate of sandwiches that one of the attendants had given him.

As he munched them appreciatively, he remembered that he was to get some for Mother.

He looked around to see where the sandwiches had come from and observed a long table at the other side of the room piled high with delicacies. But how could he possibly march up to that table publicly, and amaze everyone by juggling the sticky things into his coat-tail pocket?

One of the young girls was asking him a question. He turned to her to respond. As their conversation went on, his mind went back again, once or twice, to the sandwiches, but he didn't see how he could go over there and put a supply in his pocket. It would be an odd thing to do. He had never done such a thing in his life. It had never even occurred to him to do a thing of that kind. He was sure that Mother would understand how impossible it was when he told her.

He had too good a time to leave early, and he stopped at the club for a moment before walking leisurely home.

Mother's broth had been brought up to her and she was lying there, waiting. She heard him let himself in the front door and put away his hat and things in the coat closet. He seemed to take forever to do it. She heard the closet door shut. She tasted her broth. It was flat. But Father's step was coming along the hall to her room now, at last.

He beamed cheerfully at her as he entered and started to sit down in a chair.

'Don't sit on my sandwiches,' she warned him.

He half put his hand to his coat-tails, then remembered, and frowned.

'Oh, Clare!' Mother cried disappointedly. 'Didn't you bring them? 'It's been so tiresome sitting here waiting. Didn't you even bring one?'

'Now wait,' Father said, 'wait a moment and let me explain.'

'Weren't there any there?'

'Yes, but —— '

'You *forgot* them!'

'No! I didn't forget them!' Father said crossly.

'Why didn't you bring me some, then?'

'Will – you – let – me – ex – plain?'

'Never mind. I'm tired,' said Mother, 'and I knew you wouldn't anyway.'

'I insist on your listening to me,' Father shouted. 'I intend to be heard.'

Mother lay back on her pillows, looking deeply hurt and closing her eyes.

'The table was at one side of the room,' Father began. 'Over here, say. There were the sandwiches, there. I remembered you wanted some, and I noted where they were, several times. But – they – it was impracticable, Vinnie. In short, there was no way to do it.'

'What did you do all the time, then?' Mother sighed. 'Who did you see?'

'I saw everybody,' Father said. 'I had a very nice talk with – er – Mrs Fisher. No, Folsom? Wait a moment. What is that woman's name? She's a cousin of Mrs – well, I can't remember, but I know the name perfectly. Finley. No not Finley. Anyway, she lives on Park Avenue.'

'Oh dear,' Mother said. 'And who else?'

'Well, let me see. Mrs Palmer, of course.'

'Mrs Palmer! Why, she's in the South.'

'Oh. Well, maybe it was Mrs – er – what's-her-name then. The woman whose uncle owns that ugly house on Quaker Ridge.'

'I don't know who you're talking about.'

'Why, yes, you do. You've seen him fifty times, damn it. The man who drives that lopsided pair of flea-bitten greys.'

'And you talked to *him*?'

'No! The confounded blatherskite. He wasn't there. I talked with his aunt, I tell you. His niece I mean. The one who looks like an Eskimo.'

'Can't you tell me about *anybody* who was there? Anybody at all?'

'I can't remember all their names. No.'

'Well, Clare!' Mother said. 'I hope you spoke to Mrs Nicholas.'

'Yes, I did. We had quite a talk.'

'What did she have on?'

'Let me think, now. Something fuzzy, I remember. With chains.'

'What colour was it?'

'I think it was some shade of green.'

'That's funny. She wore that green dress when she received with her sister, last month.'

'Maybe it wasn't green. Perhaps it was purple.'

'Oh, Clare!'

'Good God!' Father roared. 'Don't be so unreasonable. I can't give you an account of all the little details of every stitch she had on. I'm not a damned couturier, Vinnie.'

'But you aren't telling me a thing about anybody,' Mother wailed. 'I did hope you'd bring home a little news for me, even if you didn't remember my sandwiches.' She looked at him sharply. 'Did you eat any yourself?'

'Yes,' Father said, recollecting the taste with pleasure. 'I had several. They were very nice.'

'*Oh, Clare!*'

'Don't begin on that again,' Father said. 'I *wanted* to bring you some, Vinnie.' He searched his mind perplexedly for a way to explain. But he didn't quite understand, himself, why he hadn't brought those sandwiches home. He looked helplessly at her.

'You never will do anything that you think isn't "suitable",' Mother said irritatedly.

'Why, of course I won't,' he said, frowning. 'Why should I?'

'Not even for me?'

'Oh, damn! Oh, damnation!' said Father.

– From *Life With Mother*.

Fear

ROBERT LYND

I am afraid of so many things that I ought not to have been surprised, on taking rooms in a little cottage in Buckinghamshire, to find myself living in terror of the landlady. I was afraid to be late for breakfast, afraid to be late for lunch, afraid to be late for tea, afraid to be late for supper – she resolutely refused to cook me a hot dinner – and a little nervous even of being late going to bed. I do not think she meant to frighten me, for she was an honest, Christian woman, but she liked having her own way. She even compelled me to eat what she liked. In a sense, she always allowed me to choose, but I always found that in the end I had to choose exactly what she had chosen that I should choose. 'What about lunch to-d'y, sir?' she would say to me, lingering in the doorway, a large, dark, smiling, intimidating figure, after she had put the breakfast on the table. I weighed the rival charms of various delicacies in my mind, almost tasting them as my thoughts lingered on them. Then, as my wants are of the simplest and I wished to give the woman no trouble, I would suggest tentatively: 'What about a roast chicken and apple tart?' Her eyes with the dark rings under them would be quite expressionless as her massive head began to shake on her massive shoulders with a faint wobble of doubt. 'I've got a nice bit of cold 'am,' she would say meditatively, fixing me with her eyes and turning up the corners of her mouth in a joyless smile. As I did not really care much, I said: 'Good! Cold ham and apple tart will do splendidly.' Again her face lengthened, and the massive head once more began to shake from side to side with a faint wobble on her massive shoulders. 'I'm afryde I can't do pystry,' she said mournfully. 'Got no time,' she explained, swelling on the last word with emphasis and raising her voice as she uttered it. And then she would add, with a sickly smile of reproach at me for forgetting what I ought to have been old enough to remember: 'There are only twenty-four hours in a d'y, y'know.' 'Oh, well,' I would say, a little shamefacedly, 'make whatever gives the least trouble.' She became almost winning at that. 'Wot do you s'y to a little stewed rhubarb?' she would entice me, her hand still on the handle of the door. 'Splendid!' I told her. 'That's right,' she said, nodding as if in approbation of a child that had been naughty and was now good; 'stewed rhubarb and shype.' Now, though not particularly fastidious about food, I can honestly say that I almost hate blancmange, so that I said to her hurriedly: 'Oh, don't trouble about the shape. Stewed rhubarb will do splendidly.' She became almost genial under the sacrifices I was making, one by one, to her convenience, but she absolutely refused to accept this one. 'Oh, you shall 'ave your shype,' she told me, wagging her head jocularly as she disappeared through the doorway. And I did.

One of the great disadvantages of being a coward is that one is constantly having to eat things that one does not wish to eat. One is not free from this necessity even at home, if one happens to be afraid of the servants. I remember, during the war, being very much afraid of a cook who was at once so brawny and so mysterious that we suspected her of being a deserter from the army disguising himself as a woman. One thing was certain: she was not a cook. At least, she did not know how to make soup. She did not know how much salt to put in; she did not know how much pepper to put in. And, as a result, each of us was confronted at table with a bowl of hot and greasy water, which first scalded the lips, then pickled the tongue, and, finally (so lavish had she been with the pepper), scorched the throat, so that at the end of the first spoonful everybody was breathing like a dog on a hot day. Now it is easy enough for one person to get out of eating soup. All you have to do is to explain that you have been forbidden soup by the doctor. A cook cannot consider that an insult, and she may even sympathise with you as an invalid. This soup was so bad, however, that even our guests (of whom there were two present) seemed unwilling to go on with it, and it would obviously have been impossible to persuade the cook that a large number of men, women, and children, under forty, were all such dyspeptics as to have been forbidden soup by their doctors. To make such a pretence would have been hardly less insulting than to ring for the housemaid and tell her to take the stuff away. This being so, there was no alternative but to dispose of the soup in some manner other than by eating it. Luckily, there was a second scullery in the house, and, though in order to reach it one had to go along a passage which would be visible to watchful eyes in the kitchen, there was a faint hope that the cook might not be looking. See us, then, one by one, guests, children, and all, tiptoeing along the passage, trembling in fear of demon eyes, each carrying a little bowl of soup, pouring it as quietly as possible down the sink, and hurrying furtively and feverishly back to our places at the table. How happy we felt when we were all safely in our seats again, our empty bowls before us, without having suffered a single casualty! To have outwitted the cook and the housemaid in this fashion seemed at the moment the supreme triumph of our lives. When the next course arrived, though I have no doubt it was as vilely cooked as the first one, we were so hilarious as a result of the success of our stratagem that we ate it as though it had been ambrosia. Fortunately, after a few days, the cook had stolen so many things that she decamped, leaving as little as she could but a memory of prodigal pepper behind her. Even to-day, when I think of her, I find myself gasping gently.

It is one thing, however, to make away with a bowl of soup in one's own house and quite another thing to make away with a blancmange in lodgings. I thought at first of opening the window and throwing the blancmange into a thick bush. I would have given it to the birds if I had been sure they would eat it. Then I considered the possibilities of the fire. If I could only have been certain that blancmange was one of those things that burn quickly! I pictured to myself, however, the little flat, white dome of blancmange still slowly sizzling on the top of the logs when the landlady came into the room to clear the things away, and I had not the courage to face the situation. Even if I were to beat it with the poker, I knew that I could not beat it so as to make it look like anything but blancmange.

'Wy, wot 'ave you been doing to the fire?' the landlady would have said; and I am not one of those silver-tongued people who could have charmed her into believing that the blancmange had got there by accident. You may wonder why I did not wrap it in a piece of paper and throw it into a field later in the afternoon, but, though such a course is possible – and has even, I believe, been taken with rabbit and with suet pudding – it seems to me alien to the spirit of blancmange. If I were to put a parcel of this kind in my pocket, I should be sure to forgot it. In the end, I braced myself to the inevitable. I ate the blancmange. It was even worse than I had feared; but it was not so bad as offending the landlady. After that I tried to avoid any recurrence of 'shape' by standing out against all invitations to 'choose' any kind of stewed fruit for any of my meals. My landlady might try to allure me with: 'Wot would you s'y, sir, to a few stewed pru-ins?' but, guessing that they would be served with 'shape', I assured her warmly that all I wanted was biscuits and cheese.

By an evil chance I fell a victim to the landlady's wiles again one day when, as we held our usual after-breakfast conversation, I happened to remark that I supposed she was kept fairly busy all the year round. 'Oh, yes,' she said, taking up the bacon dish, 'I'm gen'rally pretty full.' She nodded sagely. 'People know where they'll be comfortable,' she assured me; 'they soon find out where they can get good food – good food and good, plyne cooking,' she added, without even the shadow of a smile. She lowered her voice to a confidential tone and a brightness came into her face. 'I tell you wot some of 'em like,' she said – 'a nice boiled suet pudding with a little nice treacle. Wy, you 'aven't 'ad it yet, I don't think! No. Just fancy! Wy, wot *can* I have been thinking about? I tell you wot, sir, you shall 'ave a little treat to-d'y. Yes, you shall 'ave it – a nice little boiled pudding with some nice treacle.' It was in vain that I protested that I was a man of few needs and besought her not to give herself unnecessary trouble. 'No trouble at all,' she assured me; 'and, if it is, well, once in a w'y, wot does it matter? Life's myde up of troubles,' she added; and, as she swept out of the room, I could hear her murmuring, mechanically: 'Yes, you shall 'ave it.' And I did. When it appeared I confess I once more looked longingly at the fire, but again the thought that either the smell or the sizzle of a slab of burning pudding would betray me to the landlady frightened me. I was so demoralised by this time, indeed, that I should have felt guilty even if I had done the thing up into a parcel and taken it away to hide it in the woods. I had no will, though plenty of wish, left. Therefore, I ate a slice of the pudding, and congratulated the landlady on her cooking. 'That's right,' she said, as if commending a child for swallowing a dose of medicine; 'you shall 'ave it agyne.' And I did.

Now it is a curious fact, worth the notice of psychologists, that, if I went back to that neighbourhood again, I should go back to the same landlady, simply because I should be too great a coward to go anywhere else. I dare not pass her door if I stayed at a rival lodging-house. I should be afraid that she might be looking out of a window or standing at the gate, thinking things she was too civilised to say. And this fear of landladies, I believe, is not at all uncommon. I have known men who were very uncomfortable in their lodgings but who went on living in them because they had not the courage to give notice. When I was a boy, I knew an old gentleman who used to say the most ferocious things about his landlady behind her back, but who was all smiles and obeisance as soon as she came into the room. He was in the tea trade and had a square beard and scandal-seeking eyes and walked with his toes turned out so far that his feet progressed sideways in the fashion to which Charlie Chaplin has since accustomed us. I used to meet him at 'high tea', for he lodged in the same house and had his meals at the same table as a medical student who was a great friend of mine. The old gentleman used to sit at the head of the table, and as soon as the landlady had disappeared would denounce her because of the draught that came in under the door and swept round his ankles. He declared that he would leave if she did not have this remedied. Then he would pour himself out a cup of tea, and, after the first sip, would begin muttering an ever-increasing stream of blasphemies. 'If I have told that woman the right way to make tea once,' he declared, wrathfully, 'I've told her a hundred times. You can't make good tea without first rinsing the pot with hot water. She knows that as well as I do, but she won't do it. I sometimes wonder whether she's only a lazy slut or whether she does it to annoy me.'

He angrily dipped his spoon into the cup and removed several floating tea leaves. 'I don't like either to hear or to make use of strong language, Mr Lynd,' he said, with the hairs of his eyebrows bristling, 'but that woman's a bitch.' She came into the room at that moment with a butter-knife she had forgotten. The old man's aspect changed in an instant to a smirk of greeting. 'I was just looking for the butter-knife, Mrs Triggs,' he would say to her, with a nervous snigger; 'thank you very much.' Then, when she had left the room, he would cock an eye at us, half in fear and half in hope, and say: 'Do you think, did she hear what I said?' Even if she had heard him, however, I do not think she would have turned him out – she despised him too much to care what he said. I have never heard greater contempt in a woman's voice than on one occasion, when the medical student suggested that Mr Brown might one day marry and leave her. 'And who under God,' said she, as though the suggestion were that of a lunatic, 'would marry *him*?'

Poor man, I used rather to despise him myself. Since then, however, I have lived in lodgings in Buckinghamshire, and, looking back on him, I love him as a brother.

– From *The Blue Lion*.

Miss Paddleford

ERSKINE CALDWELL

It was the middle of the August afternoon when Harry Emory got back to his office at the canning factory after lunch and he felt drowsy and sluggish and downright lazy in the summer heat.

As usual on such occasions, which occurred several times a week during the canning season from early June to late September, Harry had eaten too much and drunk too much, and he dreaded to think about the way his wife, Clara, was going to chide him again about his constantly increasing weight and girth when he went home that evening. Clara's remarks about his romantic appeal were becoming bitterly taunting and sarcastic.

Harry Emory had spent nearly three hours with a wholesale commission merchant from New Orleans who had come to Sawyerville to buy a car-load of canned fresh-shelled brown-eyed peas. As he was accustomed to doing, Harry closed the sale and had the signed contract in his pocket within fifteen minutes. The remainder of the time, except when they were eating, had been devoted to drinking whisky and swapping stories with the commission buyer.

As soon as Harry went into his office at the cannery and sat down at his desk, Miss Paddleford came into the room and held a slip of paper with several names and phone numbers neatly typed on it. It was times like that when he wished his secretary would not be so thoroughly and aggravatingly efficient, although he knew that it was because Miss Paddleford was so efficient and businesslike that the canning factory, of which he had been the superintendent and general manager for the past twelve years, operated so smoothly and profitably. Miss Paddleford had been in charge of his office for the past seven years and he earnestly hoped, for the sake of his own job, that she would be there for ever.

Sleepily blinking his eyes, Harry took the slip of paper from his secretary and gazed at it indifferently.

'Anything else, Miss Paddleford?' he asked then.

'No, Mr Emory,' she replied crisply.

'Well, I've had an exhausting business conference and we'll call these people back later,' he said, dropping the paper on his desk. 'Maybe not till tomorrow.'

'Very well, Mr Emory,' she said as she took a step backward, her severely efficient expression unchanged. 'Is there anything else, Mr Emory?'

While he was shaking his head slowly from side to side, Miss Paddleford turned around and walked primly back to her office in the adjoining room.

Through partly closed eyes, Harry watched Miss Paddleford sit down at her desk and begin typing again. He could see vaguely the white blur of her starched high-necked blouse and the hazy outline of her chestnut-coloured hair. For a long time he sat there wondering if there had ever been moments in her life, even in the privacy of her bedroom, when she was not wearing a high-necked blouse and did not have her hair combed tightly against her head. He knew very little about Miss Paddleford other than that she was thirty-six years old, that she lived with and supported her widowed mother, and that she had never been married. At the close of the canning season in late September he always gave her a month's vacation, with pay but, in order to save money and not be extravagant, she always stayed at home in Sawyerville instead of going to the beach or elsewhere.

Continuing to gaze drowsily at Miss Paddleford in the next room, and lulled by the rhythmical sound of her typewriter, Harry leaned back in his chair and thought about some of the stories the New Orleans commission buyer had told him at lunch. He had heard some of the stories before, but many of them were new to him and, as he recalled them now, unusually funny. He liked one story in particular – it was about a young secretary who went to New Orleans for her vacation and forgot to lock her hotel door the first night – and when he recalled it now, it made him chuckle to himself over and over again.

Closing his eyes and listening to the lulling sound of Miss Paddleford's typewriter, he wondered if she had ever found herself in such a predicament. He shook his head. Miss Paddleford was such a prim and proper person that it was too far-fetched to imagine her ever permitting herself to get into such an odd situation. And yet, he thought, if Miss Paddleford should take off her heavy-rimmed glasses and insist that he call her Nell instead of Miss Paddleford, it was entirely possible that she would be just as enticing and seductive as the young woman who forgot to lock the door of her hotel room. The more he thought about it, the more probable it seemed. And, strangely enough, he remembered that there had been times during the past seven years when he had seen her take off her glasses and carelessly cross her legs as though the customary formal atmosphere of the office had ceased to exist. Each time that had happened, as he recalled vividly now, she had had the appearance of an attractive and sportive young woman of twenty-two or twenty-four who left no doubt in his mind that she would be delighted to accept an invitation to spend a week-end in New Orleans. . . .

Miss Paddleford got up from her typewriter and came into his office with a slip of paper on which she had neatly typed several names and phone numbers. Harry glanced casually at the paper and then dropped it on his desk.

Leaning back in his chair, he looked up into her sparkling blue eyes.

'Nell, I'm going to drive down to New Orleans this afternoon on a business matter,' he told her, 'and I was wondering if you'd like to spend the week-end there.'

'Oh, I'd love to, Harry,' she replied with a delightful eagerness, removing her glasses and smiling expressively. 'I was hoping you'd ask me, and now you have!'

'It's something that came up suddenly, Nell, and I hope you haven't made other plans for the week-end.'

'Oh, it's such a thrilling surprise, Harry – of course I'll go! Will we be staying at that wonderful hotel in the French Quarter – the one with the beautiful ironwork balconies all around it?'

'Yes, Nell, that's where we'll stay,' he assured her. 'I have a few things to attend to here at the cannery before I can leave, so I suggest that you drive down right away in your own car. You'll be there within a couple of hours from now, and that'll give you plenty of time to freshen up before I get there.'

She ran to his side of the desk, putting her arms around his neck, and kissed him fervently.

Harry patted her fondly while she was kissing him.

'I'll be waiting for you, Harry,' she said with breathless excitement as she ran from the office. 'Don't let anything keep you too long!'

After she had left the office and gone home to pack her suitcase, Harry wondered why he had waited so long to spend a week-end with Nell in New Orleans, and he made up his mind to do it more often after that.

Before leaving for New Orleans in his car, he had to find the assistant superintendent and leave some instructions so that the cannery would operate smoothly while he was away. In addition, since it was Friday, he had to sign the pay-roll. All of those details took time, but when everything had been attended to, Harry cleared his desk and got into his car and drove out of town as rapidly as he could.

It was shortly before dusk in the balmy summer evening when he reached the hotel in the French Quarter, and he hurriedly took a shower and changed his clothes. When he was ready twenty minutes later, he called the hotel desk clerk and asked for Nell's room number. After that he walked briskly to the elevator and went up to her room.

Harry knocked lightly on Nell's door, and she opened it immediately. He was a little startled at first, because he had not expected her to be wearing her heavy-rimmed glasses, but after he had walked into the darkened, perfume-scented bedroom he realised that she would want to be wearing something of the kind when she opened the door for him. Besides, he had not recognised her momentarily, seeing her for the first time with her chestnut-coloured hair floating airily about her head and when she was not wearing one of her starched high-necked blouses, but as soon as she closed the door and locked it securely, she took off her glasses and placed them on the table. After that, there was no uncertainty in his mind whatsoever. From head to toe, she looked exactly as he had always imagined her to be.

'I know you want a drink right away, Harry,' Nell said, throwing her arms around him and hugging him excitedly, 'but I've just got to kiss you first.'

Harry took her warm slender body into his arms and kissed her mouth and cheeks and neck for a long time. After a while, with a reluctant sigh, Nell drew away from him and went to the table where glasses, a bucket of ice, and several bottles of whisky were neatly arranged. After making their drinks, Nell sat down beside him and squeezed his hand affectionately.

'Harry, I'm so thrilled and happy to be here like this with you!' she whispered to him with an ardent tremor in her voice as she snuggled into his arms. 'If you only knew how bored and lonely I get at the cannery, you'd know how I feel now. Now I can be my own passionate, affectionate self. It's heavenly to come to New Orleans and be all alone with you like this. It's what I've dreamed of all these years. And now at last it's come true!'

Harry patted her understandingly.

'You know something, Nell?' he said after a while.

'What is it, Harry?' she whispered.

'I'd like to be here every week-end with you the way we are now, but being superintendent of the cannery is a big responsibility, and I have to stay close to the job. If it weren't for that, though ——'

'Harry, let's move that old canning factory to New Orleans!' she said, sitting up and shaking him excitedly. 'Don't you see? If we moved it from Sawyerville to New Orleans, we could be together like this every night!'

'Move the cannery from Sawyerville to new Orleans!' he said, startled by the suggestion.

'Of course, Harry!'

'But where would we get fresh-shelled brown-eyed peas to can?' he said, shaking his head. 'Everybody in New Orleans eats brown-eyed peas, but nobody here grows them. We wouldn't have a source of supply for the cannery, Nell.'

'That's simple,' she said at once. 'We could can something else instead.'

'What?'

'Shrimp.'

'Shrimp?'

Nell nodded.

'But I'm a brown-eyed pea man, Nell. I don't know a thing in the world about shrimp.'

'You could learn, Harry.'

'But, Nell, I'm forty-seven years old. A man can't get out of brown-eyed peas and into shrimp at my age.'

'If you really and truly liked me, Harry Emory,' she retorted, pouting delightfully, 'and sincerely wanted to be with me all the time, you'd find a way to do it.'

He stroked her shoulders soothingly, hoping that she would remain calm.

'Listen, Nell,' he said to her, speaking with all the earnestness he could bring forth. 'You know I am very fond of you. I think you are wonderful – devilishly fascinating. But, just the same, there are other considerations ——'

'I know what you mean!' she cried, angrily hitting his chest with her fists. 'You're thinking about that wife of yours! You think more of her than you do of me!'

'Now, Nell,' he pleaded, 'please don't talk like that. Let me explain——'

The ringing of the phone suddenly filled the room with a shrill noise. Harry tried to ignore it, but the persistent ringing prevented him from thinking of anything else.

'I guess you'll have to answer that, Nell,' he said unhappily. 'It's going to keep on ringing till you do.'

Nell got up to answer the phone while Harry raised his glass and drank some more of the whisky. He gazed at her longingly over the rim of his glass as she crossed the room with an artfully enticing sway of her hips and stood erectly beside the table.

When Nell turned around, she picked up her heavy-rimmed glasses and put them on. Startled by her sudden transformation, Harry stared at her in bewilderment.

Nell handed him the phone.

'Mr Emory,' she said crisply, 'Mrs Emory is calling.'

'What – what did you say, Miss Paddleford?'

'Your wife is on the phone, Mr Emory. Mrs Emory wishes to speak to you personally.'

Harry grasped the phone that Miss Paddleford was thrusting at him. Rubbing his eyes, he sat up erectly in his chair.

'Thank you, Miss Paddleford,' he said as she turned and walked primly to her office in the adjoining room. He continued looking at her until he heard the familiar sound of her typewriter, his eyes blinking at the sight of the white blur of her starched high-necked blouse. 'Oh, hello, Clara, dear,' he spoke hurriedly into the phone, wondering why Miss Paddleford's chestnut-coloured hair appeared to be more tightly combed than ever before. 'Yes, dear, I'm just getting ready to leave the office. I'll be home in fifteen minutes. Good-bye, dear.'

– From *Gulf Coast Stories*.

Cartwright and the Need for Sleep

OLIVIA MANNING

My husband Cartwright would describe himself as a realist, but he is not above harbouring certain illusions. One of these used to be that he did not snore: or if he did, it was in such a manner no reasonable person could be disturbed by him. In any case there was a cure. He snored only when lying on his back, and, at a request to turn over, would turn over and peace would be restored. There was a time when this was true.

Once, during the war, he had to share a tent on a desert survey with a man called Donaldson. Before they left Cairo I said to Donaldson: 'I'm afraid Cartwright snores slightly. He only does it when he's tired, of course, and only when lying on his back. If you say to him "Turn over, darling," he'll turn over and be quiet.'

'Must it be "Turn over, *darling*"?'

'Nothing else is effective.'

The next night Donaldson was wakened by Cartwright's snores. Sitting up in bed he commanded: 'Turn over.'

Cartwright remained flat on his back.

'Turn over, Cartwright.'

No move.

Then, reluctantly, in the fiercest tones, Donaldson said: 'Turn over, darling,' and with the slow, inevitable movement of a wave, Cartwright turned over and slept in silence.

The time came when this formula ceased to be effective. When Cartwright turned there would be a short peace, then the noise would start again. When I could endure it no longer I would wake him up.

'Darling, wake up. You're making a frightful noise.'

'Me? Impossible. I was lying on my side.'

'That makes no difference nowadays.'

'But any doctor will tell you that people can't snore on their sides.'

'Well, I should know better. I've been awake since midnight.'

'The trouble is, darling, you're becoming neurotic. I wasn't even asleep. I was just lying thinking. I had my eyes open.'

'Then you not only snore on your back and on your side, you snore with your eyes open.'

'You're being ridiculous. And *please* don't wake me up again.'

One day he discussed the matter with a scientific friend who said he had done research on the problem of snoring. People, he said, snored when lying on their backs because the tongue fell against the soft palate, causing it to vibrate. He lay on the floor to demonstrate his theory. Cartwright insisted on my watching the performance. The scientific friend, flat on his back, snored furiously, then rolled over on his side and ceased to snore. His tongue, he said, had fallen into its natural position, so snoring became impossible.

'Now are you convinced?' Cartwright asked me.

'Of course I'm not.'

'Darling, you're being unreasonable.'

Like many people addicted to theory he was badly betrayed by experience. He did not, needless to say, lend himself willingly to experience. The occasion was forced upon him. It happened last year when he was invited by a student body to lecture on Scottish Drama at the Edinburgh Festival. He travelled north with his three fellow lecturers. They arrived to find that owing to Festival overcrowding it had been possible to book only two rooms for the four of them. Each room, however, contained two beds, so no great hardship was imposed on the lecturers. Cartwright was to share with a very large, good-natured man called Peabody, and was pleased rather than not by the prospect. So sociable is his nature that he finds it a strain to suffer even a night in solitude. His only fear was that Peabody would object to his reading in bed. I sometimes objected – usually when, having been too busy to absorb them during the day, he rattled his way through a collection of newspapers.

'I read in bed a bit,' said Cartwright; 'hope it won't disturb you.'

'Nothing disturbs me.'

'That's splendid. My wife's rather a light sleeper.'

'I sleep like the dead,' said Peabody. 'I'm off as soon as I put my head on the pillow and I don't wake up till morning.'

Another theory held by Cartwright is that human beings need very little sleep. Sleep, he believes, is a superstition of mind. He needs no more than four or five hours. Night was the time when he 'caught up with his reading'.

Cartwright is a busy man made more busy by the fact he gives so much time to his friends. Before leaving for Edinburgh he had been too busy to make notes for his lectures. He might have made them on the train, but with three companions willing to listen to him all the way, work would have been a waste of opportunity. He intended settling down to it on arrival, but the others were in jovial mood, inclined towards an evening of good food and drink, and Cartwright was easily persuaded to join them. They were all wine drinkers, but they felt they owed it to Scotland to drink what they kept calling 'the wine of the country'. They had an evening on whisky, which is generously served in Edinburgh. By the time they reached their rooms Peabody was so drowsy he had to be assisted to bed. He was asleep even before his head touched the pillow.

Cartwright, drowsy or not, had now to apply himself to his lecture notes. He sat up in bed surrounded by books on the Scottish Drama which he had supposed, before this time, to be non-existent. Although he is not a silent man, he likes quiet when he works. He had just uncapped his fountain-pen when Peabody gave a first snore. It was slight and brief. Cartwright ignored it. That, he supposed, was the sort of noise he occasionally made himself. It need disturb no one. The first snore, however, was followed by a much louder one. Then, as though, after a trial attempt, an engine had got under way, there was a crescendo of snores that ended in a spluttering roar like the bursting of a water-tank. This climax achieved, Peabody set out to achieve it again.

I might find such a noise disturbing, but Cartwright decided he did not. He fixed his eyes on his text-book. He was concentrating. Peabody repeated the water-tank theme a dozen times before Cartwright realised he was unable to understand a word he read. He looked appealingly at Peabody, then remembered that people snored only when on their backs. Peabody was flat on his back. He must be turned upon his side.

Cartwright ordered him: 'Turn over, Peabody.'

Peabody did not move.

'Turn over, darling.'

This famous formula had no effect on Peabody. He was an unmarried man. Cartwright decided to move him by force. He rose and started tugging and pushing at Peabody. Cartwright is a big man, but Peabody was much bigger. He was a dead weight. At last Peabody was moved on to his side, but as soon as he was left unsupported he slid round again on to his back. This happened half a dozen times.

There was only one pillow on each bed. Cartwright realised he must sacrifice his as a prop for Peabody. When he wedged it in, Peabody's vast body remained on its side.

Cartwright returned to bed to work. He had read half a dozen lines when Peabody spluttered slightly, then gave a preliminary snore. Cartwright could not believe his ears. Peabody snored again, then settled to a new theme, a rhythmic trumpeting on a deep note. Cartwright gazed at him. It was true – Peabody was lying on his side and snoring. After some moments he decided the trouble was he had put Peabody on the wrong side.

He rose again, then, tugging and pushing, rolled Peabody on to the other side and wedged the pillow back again. Now he would have peace in which to work.

Peabody, perhaps disturbed by the experience, remained silent slightly longer than before. Cartwright was just congratulating himself on having achieved quiet when Peabody snored. Not possible. Cartwright's heart sank. He paused in apprehension. Soon Peabody's snores were rising again to full blast. It was as though a procession of elephants, emerging from jungle into sunlight, trumpeted in turn. It was a monotonous procession bringing not even the relief of an exploding water-tank.

Cartwright had to admit that people did snore on their sides. This extension of knowledge brought no comfort. Still, it was not

Peabody's fault. Anyone might snore. The reasonable listener did not permit himself to be disturbed by such a trifle. Cartwright kept his eyes on his book and again told himself he was concentrating on work. But he was not. When he was not listening to Peabody he was fabricating excuses for Peabody or telling himself that he had, after all, chosen to work at night. Anyone else would be asleep. At the thought of sleep he realised how tired he was. He had travelled that day from London to Edinburgh. He had dined well and drunk deeply. He had a heavy day's talking behind him. He realised that human beings did, after all, need some sleep. He needed it now.

He decided to leave Scottish Drama until the morning. He turned off the light and settled down to sleep. But he could not sleep. The snores vibrated through his head. As sleep overcame him a roar would buffet him back to wakefulness. He was in the midst of telling himself he could not blame Peabody – when the benignity of his nature suddenly collapsed beneath him. He fell into fury. He sat up and put on the light. He shouted: 'Peabody, for heaven's sake, shut up!'

The shout seemed to stun Peabody. He was silent for a full minute, then, grunting and spluttering, he recovered himself. He struggled round as though against fearful odds, then, lying spread-eagled on Cartwright's pillow, he started out again upon the water-tank theme.

Cartwright, seldom made angry, can, on rare occasions, touch upon frenzy. He touched upon it now. He picked up one of his shoes and bounced it upon Peabody's belly, shouting: 'Shut up! Shut up!' The shoe caused no more than a moment's hiatus in sound. The second shoe did not even do that.

Cartwright opened his book again. He read one paragraph half a dozen times. He could make nothing of it. Somewhere a clock struck three. He had made one lecture note: 'Where's your Wullie Shakespeare now?' What the answer was he neither knew nor cared. He wanted only to sleep.

At four o'clock he decided he could bear the water-tank theme no longer. He rose and crossed to the other bed. Standing there he snarled: 'Peabody, I hate you!' Then he set about turning Peabody back on to his side. When he again held his pillow in his hand he was filled with a wild, exultant desire to smother Peabody's snores beneath it. Overcoming this, he wedged it behind the body again and stood and listened until Peabody was well back into the elephant theme.

Back in bed, Cartwright began to shiver with weariness and frustration. He put out the light and tried again to sleep. He covered his ears with his hands. They did no more than take the edge off the noise. After an hour or two he shouted: 'For goodness' sake, Peabody, shut up!'

At intervals, to relieve his almost unendurable exasperation he, bawled out: 'Wake up, Peabody, or I shall wring your neck,' or '. . . fling you out of bed,' or '. . . brain you with the electric fire.'

Peabody slept, sublimely unaware of these dangers.

Some time after dawn exhaustion overcame Cartwright's senses so that the snoring came to him as no more than an attendant of dreams. Sometimes it seemed the rhythm of the 'Flying Scotsman', sometimes the engine of a ship, sometimes the ruthless hammer-blows of a man driven to exterminate his tormentor.

A cheerful Scottish voice broke in on all this to say: 'Come along, now, sir. You wanted to be wakened at eight o'clock sharp.'

Cartwright struggled up in bed and took his breakfast tray on his knee. He was due in the lecture room at nine-thirty. He might, if he ate and dressed hurriedly, have half an hour to give to Scottish Drama.

He was in a stupor. The wardrobe looking-glass showed him his face, drawn, ghastly, moist-looking, the eyes rimmed with red and oozing tears. He could not keep from yawning. He looked at his breakfast with disgust.

Sitting up in the other bed, Peabody was aglow with health and eating with appetite. He met Cartwright's glance with a coy smile.

Cartwright, who had had it in mind to make some wryly humorous reference to his disturbed night, now decided to say nothing. What was past, was past. He simply said 'Hope you slept well?'

Peabody's coy smile grew more coy. 'I hardly like to mention it,' he said, 'but – you know what, Cartwright? You talk in your sleep.'

– From *My Husband Cartwright*.

The Whipping

HIRAM PERCY MAXIM

My besetting sins were teasing my sisters and breaking things around the house. Finally a day came when I did a thing which my mother felt was beyond her.

She had a full-length pier glass in her room which extended from the floor to the ceiling. It had a white marble base with a flat place on the latter which extended out into the room about a foot. Little Florence discovered that a large glass marble would bounce beautifully off this base. One day she was bouncing her marble in front of the pier glass, and it occurred to me that it would surprise her very much were I to snatch the marble while it was in the air. I edged up, and when I was within reach I made a quick pass to snatch the marble. But I miscalculated. Instead of closing my hand upon it, I struck it with my hand and knocked it against the pier glass, which it broke.

I told my mother, and when she came upstairs and beheld her broken mirror she sank into a chair and wept. I was desolated. It hurt me inexpressibly that I should be the cause of my mother's weeping. She told me that I had got beyond her control and that she would have to turn me over to my father for a good whipping; that I paid no attention to her, and as things were going there was no living with me.

Turning me over to my father for a good whipping was a brand-new idea to me. I could not remember that my father had ever laid a hand upon me, except possibly once when I was very young indeed, when he tapped me gently with the tongue of his draughtsman's T-square. This was very light and very thin and stung for a moment. It would not bruise. It is an admirable instrument for administering a little corporal punishment.

That evening after my father had come home he was led up to the broken pier glass and shown my latest and worst offence. It appeared to prostrate him utterly. He sank into a chair, held his head in his hands, rocked back and forth in exquisite agony, and gave several similar indications of being completely undone by the spectacle. He made it an extremely painful scene for me and I certainly did feel low in my mind. My mother told him that I was getting entirely out of hand and that he must give me a good whipping or I would break everything in the house besides making them all thoroughly miserable. Father said he was too prostrated to undertake the whipping then, but that he would attend to it after supper.

Supper was a doleful affair. I had never sat through such a nerve-wearing ordeal before. I was in the deepest disgrace and everybody, including little Florence, was sunk in woe. I had never been so thoroughly unhappy.

After supper my father announced that he would read his paper first, and when he had finished he would take up the whipping matter. I had never had a whipping. My mother had spanked me many times, but I did not regard that as a whipping. I wondered what it would be like to be whipped. I waited patiently until my father had finished his evening paper, sitting in a deep gloom meanwhile, but with no fear or terror. My woe was born of having broken my mother's pier glass, which she treasured, and of throwing the whole family into gloom.

When my father had finished his paper he got up briskly, saying: 'Well, now. Come along, Percy. Let's attend to this whipping business.' He led the way out into the back yard where we visited my mother's shrubs and bushes, from which a suitable whip was to be cut. My father had his pocket knife open, ready to cut when he found a stalk that met the requirements. He explained to me that it was necessary to find one that had just the right length and thickness and straightness. If it were too short it would not have enough spring. If it were too long it would have too much spring and would break. If it were too thin it would be weak, whereas, if it were too thick it would bruise, which of course would not do.

We searched and searched without finding anything that just suited. I became interested in the problem and pointed out several likely-looking sticks which appeared as though they might answer the exacting specifications. He discussed my selections with me, examining each one with care. After spending quite a time at it, he finally decided that the best thing to do would be to cut several and try them. He cut a long thin one, a long thick one, a middle-length one, and several other compromises. This made five whips. I was very much impressed with his technique. I could see that between all of the whips it was more than likely that one would be found which would suit much better than possibly could be the case were one only to be selected by guessing. I did not recognise it at the time, but I had received my first lesson in engineering rescarch.

After all had been prepared and whittled down smooth he said: 'Now come along up to my room and we will try them.' He led the way to the third-floor front, which was his room. Arrived here, he took off his coat, his collar, and necktie and rolled up his sleeves. I was a bit concerned at this, for it suggested that a whipping must be something calling for considerable activity. He laid the five whips on the bed and, taking one at a time, he smote the coverlet. The savage whir and the succeeding whack sounded all over the house. He put real muscle into it. The long thin whip broke. He explained that he had expected this to happen, for the stick was too thin for its length. The thick one made a fearful whir and whack when it hit the coverlet. We rejected this one because it was evident that it would bruise. Later on I heard my mother say that she never suffered such horrible nervous strain in all her life, listening to the savage whir of the whip and the awful whack as it struck. She imagined my little body might be receiving these blows; but as I did not cry out and as she could hear me talking calmly afterwards, she assumed that I could not be suffering very acutely. I firmly believe that most of this bed-whacking business was for my mother's benefit, as she sat downstairs trying to read.

When we had whacked the bed coverlet for a long time, testing the whips and breaking most of them, my father was far from being satisfied. He sat down on the edge of the bed and outlined in his clear way the problem as it confronted us. Said he: 'What we need is something fairly long, very strong, and yet very light. It also must be very springy. Where can we find such a thing which we could use for a whip?'

We thought and thought. By this time I was as keenly interested in the solution of the problem as though someone else were to receive the whipping. I suggested a baseball bat, but in the same breath I pointed out that it was unsuitable, although I pointed out that it would hit awful hard.

'Oh, *much* too hard,' he replied. 'Why, you could break a man's back with a baseball bat, and kill him.' He recoiled at the suggestion of a baseball bat.

'I suppose a broomstick would be too stiff, too,' I ventured.

'Altogether too stiff and too heavy. It would break bones and be very dangerous.'

There was a long pause here while we both thought. Then an idea occurred to me. 'Gosh, Papa! I know the very thing. That thin cane of yours.' Among his walking-sticks was a very thin one which I used to admire.

'By Jove!' he exclaimed. 'That's a good idea. Go and fetch it.'

I remember hurrying downstairs to the clothes-closet in the butler's pantry where the canes and umbrellas were kept. As I ran through the reception-room, being in my usual hurry, I had to pass my mother. She seemed much surprised to see me hurrying to the clothes-closet She asked me what I was after. I answered:

'We're trying to find a good whip. We're going to try the thin cane.'

She asked something else, but I was much too busy to stop just then and explain. She afterwards said that my being in such a hurry to find a cane with which to be whipped seemed one of the most extraordinary things she ever heard of.

When I returned with the thin cane my father whacked the coverlet with it with all his might. It made a particularly savage noise. My mother must have winced when she heard it. After whacking the bed coverlet until my mother was ready to fly out of her skin, my father shook his head and handed the cane to me, asking me to try it and say what I thought. I had noticed him putting a lot of 'beef' into his blows, so I decided to put in all I had. Getting the best grip I could, which was difficult on account of the curved handle, I whacked the bed coverlet for all that was in me. It only made a fair noise and my father feared my mother might not hear it. He told me to put more 'beef' into it. I wiped off my hands, took a fresh grip, took careful aim, and belaboured the coverlet with all my might. When my father expressed disappointment over the weight of my blows, I explained that the curved handle got in my way and that no one could hit hard, with the handle where it was. My father was not satisfied and we went into executive session again. It was quite apparent to me what was required, but we would have to do a lot of searching around to find just exactly the thing. It must have appeared this way to my father, too, for he finally said:

'Well, I guess we shall have to give up the whipping, Percy. We can't seem to find the right whip. But, anyway, you understand that you must be more careful around the house and that you must not make so much trouble for Mamma, don't you; and you will begin to-morrow morning and try to be a better boy, won't you, Percy?'

I was very deeply impressed by the way he said it. He was asking me as a favour to him and to Mamma to do something. I realised that it would be very mean indeed of me to fail to do as he asked. And it would be yet meaner not to try to make things more pleasant for Mamma. So I said: 'Yes, Papa. I will.' And then we went downstairs and explained to Mamma that the whipping matter had to be called off. I am glad to be able to say that I kept my promise in pretty fair shape, as time proved.

– From *A Genius in the Family*.

Groucho

ARTHUR MARX

When he took the family out to dinner at a restaurant, Mother could always count on him for big jokes, especially if the restaurant was crowded, and he hadn't made a reservation, and the head waiter didn't recognise him.

'Name, sir? There'll be a short wait.'

'Jackson,' Groucho would usually reply. 'Sam Jackson. And this is Mrs Jackson, and these are all the little Jacksons.'

Jackson was his favourite *nom de plume*, and Mother would always do a slow burn whenever he used it at a time like this. She knew that if he'd give the head waiter his real name we'd probably get a table immediately.

'Grouch!' she would whisper. 'Tell them who you are.'

'Why should I?' he'd reply. 'If I can't get in under the name of Jackson, then I don't want to eat here. I don't like restaurants where you have to be a celebrity in order to get in.'

'Then you should have made a reservation,' she'd say. 'You just can't walk into a restaurant on a Thursday night without a reservation, and expect to get seated right away if you don't tell them who you are.'

At this point we'd either leave for another restaurant, or else he'd appear to give in to her request and tap the head waiter on the arm. 'My wife wants me to tell you who I am,' he'd say. 'My name's not really Jackson. It's Schwartz, and I'm in the wholesale plumbing supply business. And this is Mrs Schwartz, and all the little Schwartzes.'

If the head waiter thought he was peculiar, the waitress, when we'd finally be seated, would consider him completely mad.

[268]

'Miss,' he might begin, glancing up from the menu, 'do you have frog's legs?'

'I'll ask the chef,' she'd reply.

'No; you're not supposed to say that,' Groucho would explain in a patient tone. 'When I say: "Do you have frog's legs?" you're supposed to answer: "No, rheumatism makes me walk this way".'

She'd nod, bewildered, and he'd say: 'Okay. Now let's try it again. Miss, do you have frog's legs?'

Her face would go blank. 'It isn't on the menu. I'll have to ask the chef.'

He'd shake his head. 'Now you've spoiled it. We'll have to start all over aga——.'

'Grouch,' my mother would interrupt. 'This girl is busy. Why do you waste her time with such foolishness?'

'It's not foolishness. It might come in very handy to her some day. Supposing vaudeville comes back and she wants to get up an act. Look at the shape she'd be in with this sure-fire material.'

Groucho would rather do anything than admit he's wrong – even if it means risking his life.

I knew of no better example than the time back in 1927 when his stubbornness was nearly responsible for wiping out the entire Marx family and a Swedish nurse named Sadie.

It was on the day we were bringing my mother, our new baby, Miriam, and the nurse home from the hospital in New York City, where Miriam was born.

Groucho, in his anxiety to get Miriam home safely, was driving very slowly and cautiously, even for him. And when we approached the railroad crossing in Great Neck, he slowed the Lincoln to such a snail's pace that it stalled – right on the tracks.

He stepped on the starter several times, but the engine wouldn't respond. At that moment we heard the familiar tooting of a Long Island Railroad train approaching from around the bend.

'The 3.02 is right on time,' remarked Groucho, glancing calmly at his wrist watch.

'My baby!' screamed Mother. 'Let's get out of here.'

'And leave a $6,000 car on the tracks?' replied Groucho. 'Not I. These cars don't grow on trees, you know.'

'I don't give a damn about the car,' said Mother hysterically.

'Well, I do,' replied Groucho. 'She's got a lot of miles in her yet. She just flooded, but I'll get her started. Just be calm, everybody – be calm!'

But nobody was calm, and he *couldn't* get the engine started. And when the train came into view, Mother grabbed Miriam from out of the arms of the nurse, alighted from the car and urged the rest of us to run for our lives, too. Sadie and I did, but Groucho remained at his post, refusing to be swayed by female hysterics.

As the train drew closer, Groucho suddenly shouted out of the window: 'Hey, Ruth – in case I get killed, the key to the vault is behind *The Works of Shakespeare* in my study!'

Mother shuddered and refused to look. Groucho was quite pale himself, but as I mentioned before he's a pretty stubborn fellow. He sat there, grimly trying the starter, and out of the corner of his eye watching the train come closer and closer.

I often wonder what would have happened if the train hadn't turned out to be a local that had already started to slow down for Great Neck Station before it ever rounded the bend . . .

At home Groucho didn't approve of fancy service at the dinner table. All he asked for was good, simple cooking. It angered him to have to wait for the meat, the potatoes, and the vegetables to be brought in one at a time on separate platters and passed slowly around the table by the butler.

'What became of the potatoes?' he'd bellow impatiently after he'd helped himself to the meat and the butler had disappeared inside the kitchen for a moment. 'Has that guy got lost or something?'

'Give him time, Grouch. He probably had to wait for Hazel to dish them out.'

Groucho would give him another ten seconds, during which time he'd be glowering at the meat on his plate. If the butler hadn't returned by then, there would be another explosion.

'This is a hell of a way to have to eat,' he'd say in a loud tone.

'By the time I get the potatoes and vegetables, my *meat*'ll be ice cold. Why can't we just put all the food on the table at once and help ourselves? That's the way we did it when we were kids.'

'No one does it that way any more.'

'Why not?'

'It just isn't done.'

'Well, what about the families where they don't have anyone else to pass the food? I'll bet *they* get the meat and the vegetables at the same time.'

'That's different. But if you're going to have someone to do the serving, you might as well do it right.'

'Who cares what's right? I'd rather be poor if I have to go through life getting my vegetables fifteen minutes after my meat. Who are we trying to impress, anyway?'

In those days Groucho was still pliable enough to make certain concessions to the female sex which he wouldn't dream of making today.

One of the many concessions he wouldn't make was eating by candlelight. My mother, like many women, felt that candles added a soothing, romantic atmosphere to the dining-room. Groucho felt they were something for the Dark Ages.

It was quite a shock to Mother to see his reaction the first time she tried lighting our dining-room in Great Neck with candles only.

'What's this – a coal mine?' he said, walking straight to the electric light switch and flipping it on. 'I have to see what I eat. Candles are for tea-rooms and gigolos.'

If they had company, he'd allow my mother to have the candelabras lit until the guests entered the dining-room and were seated. Then he'd announce: 'If you've all seen the candles we'll dispense with them immediately. We just want you to know we have them.'

The chances are that he wouldn't even leave the candelabras on the table. He'd put them on the sideboard. He hated to have anything obstructing his view of the person across the table from him. Table floral displays were also an anathema to him, particularly if they were tall. 'Who's buried under there?' he'd remark, and soon the flowers would be on the sideboard alongside the candlesticks.

In addition to the fact that he insisted on the dining-room being as brightly lighted as a movie set, he had – and still has – some pretty eccentric eating habits. In the thirty-two years I've known him, I don't believe he's ever sat through an entire meal without complaining about the food, the service, or both.[1] And he'll complain no matter where he happens to be eating – at your house, his house, or in his favourite restaurant. He's not at all biased that way.

Another thing Groucho always insisted on at home was eating at a 'reasonable' hour. Nothing upsets him like having to wait until eight-thirty or nine for his dinner (even if he isn't a bit hungry before then).

If he discovered, after several dinners at someone else's house, that his hosts were habitual late eaters, he'd make a mental note of it. The next time he was invited there he'd have his dinner at home first, despite my mother's protests that it was impolite and that he wouldn't like anyone to do that to him.

'No one has the right,' he'd tell her, 'to invite you to dinner at seven o'clock and make you wait until ten before giving you something to eat.'

If he found that a couple he knew were habitual late arrivers, he had his own way of curing them of the habit. He'd start dinner without them . . .

Mother thought this was impolite, too, but Groucho said; 'When I tell people seven o'clock, I don't see how they can misunderstand me to mean a quarter to eight. My diction isn't that bad. I can be heard in the last row of the balcony.'

He also expects his guests to leave at a reasonable hour. He doesn't like to have them hanging around until three or four in the morning. He wants to go to bed.

He'll never tell anyone to leave, however, if his guests persist in ignoring his yawns, he'll stand up and make the announcement that he's tired and going to bed. 'You people stay as late as you like. You know where the liquor is – enjoy yourselves.'

'You'd be surprised,' he once told me, 'how many people stay and have a hell of a time after I go to bed. One of these days I'm

1 Or the company. – GROUCHO

going to throw a party and never come out of my room at all. It'll
be a smashing success.'

Groucho was a family man who could play neither bridge nor
croquet, and whose main interests were his children, his work, his
books, his guitar and a large coterie of close friends.

The only time he was willing to make an exception was when he'd
get an invitation to play poker with the crowd who, in the mid-
twenties, used to congregate at the Hotel Algonquin: Dorothy
Parker, Heywood Broun, Woollcott, Benchley, F. P. Adams, George
Kaufman, Harold Ross and Robert Sherwood. But he was never very
good at the game, nor was he especially interested. He merely used it
as a device to be with these people, who were such poker addicts
themselves that frequently the only way he could spend any time
with them was to participate in their card games.

'And besides,' adds Groucho, 'that group was fun to be with
in spite of the fact that they took their cards seriously.'

Once, after we moved to California, Groucho, in an unwitting
moment, let Norman Krasna talk him into taking bridge lessons.
Krasna couldn't play either, and he thought it would be nice for
the two of them to learn together. So they hired a bridge teacher,
who came out to our house in Beverly Hills one evening after dinner.

The teacher was a prim, middle-aged woman whose name was
Cynthia Jones. She sat down at the table with Krasna and my mother
and father, and started out by saying: 'Now, the first thing we do is
to deal thirteen cards to each person.' She dealt the cards. 'Now we
arrange the cards in our hands according to suits – hearts, spades, and
so on.'

'What does a spade look like?' asked Groucho, completely dead-pan.

Very patiently Miss Jones explained to him about the different
suits.

'Why do we have to call a spade a spade?' asked Groucho. 'Why
can't we call a diamond a spade for a change? That's the trouble with
this game. It's too reactionary. What this game needs is young blood!'

Miss Jones cleared her throat. 'As I was saying, the first thing we
do is arrange the cards according to suits.'

'Why do we have to do that?' asked Groucho.

'Because that's how you play the game.'

'That's how *you* play the game, you mean.'

'No; but those are the rules.'

'Whose rules?'

'Well, we're going to play the Culbertson system.'

'What right does he have to dictate to me how we're going to play bridge?' asked Groucho indignantly. 'This is my house. Let him play the Culbertson system in *his* house if he wants.'

'Grouch,' urged Mother, 'we're paying this woman for lessons. Let's listen.'

'How much are we paying?' asked Groucho suspiciously.

'Five dollars an hour,' announced Miss Jones.

'It's too much,' said Groucho. 'We could have bought Culbertson's book for a buck and a quarter.'

After about an hour of suffering through his interruptions, Miss Jones thought they knew enough of the fundamentals to try playing a hand. At this point they recessed, while Mother went into the kitchen to get a pitcher of ice-water and Krasna excused himself to go to the washroom.

Alone with the teacher, Groucho leaned over to her and said, 'Miss Jones, how about you and me blowing this joint and heading south over the border? I know a nice little motel in Tijuana. Of course, we won't have enough people for bridge, but we can play two-handed strip poker.'

Miss Jones promptly collected her things, streaked for the door, and was never heard from again.[1]

– From *Groucho.*

1 That's not true. She sent me a bill.–GROUCHO

Uncle William

BERNARD SHAW

. . . There was my Uncle William, a most amiable man with great natural dignity. In early manhood he was not only an inveterate smoker, but so insistent a toper that a man who made a bet that he would produce Barney Shaw sober, and knocked him up at six in the morning with that object, lost his bet. But this might have happened to any common drunkard. What gave the peculiar Shaw finish and humour to the case was that my uncle suddenly and instantly gave up smoking and drinking at one blow, and devoted himself to his accomplishment of playing the ophicleide.[1] In this harmless and gentle pursuit he continued, a blameless old bachelor, for many years, and then, to the amazement of Dublin, renounced the ophicleide and all its works, and married a lady of distinguished social position and great piety. She declined, naturally, to have anything to do with us; and, as far as I know, treated the rest of the family in the same way. Anyhow, I never saw her, and only saw my uncle furtively by the roadside after his marriage, when he would make hopeless attempts to save me, in the pious sense of the word, not perhaps without some secret Shavian enjoyment of the irreverent pleasantries with which I scattered my path to perdition. He was reputed to sit with a Bible on his knees, and an opera glass to his eyes, watching the ladies' bathing place in Dalkey; and my sister, who was a swimmer, confirmed this gossip so far as the opera glass was concerned.

But this was only the prelude to a very singular conclusion, or rather catastrophe. The fantastic imagery of the Bible so gained on

1 An instrument described by Berlioz as a sort of brazen bullock.

my uncle that he took off his boots, explaining that he expected to be taken up to heaven at any moment like Elijah, and that he felt that his boots would impede his celestial flight. He then went a step further, and hung his room with all the white fabrics he could lay hands on, alleging that he was the Holy Ghost. At last he became silent, and remained so to the end. His wife, warned that his harmless fancies might change into dangerous ones, had him removed to an asylum in the north of Dublin. My father thought that a musical appeal might prevail with him, and went in search of the ophicleide. But it was nowhere to be found. He took a flute to the asylum instead; for every Shaw of that generation seemed able to play any wind instrument at sight. My uncle, still obstinately mute, contemplated the flute for a while, and then played Home Sweet Home on it. My father had to be content with this small success, as nothing more could be got out of his brother. A day or two later, my uncle, impatient for heaven, resolved to expedite his arrival there. Every possible weapon had been removed from his reach; but his custodians reckoned without the Shavian originality. They had left him somehow within reach of a carpet bag. He put his head into it, and in a strenuous effort to decapitate or strangle himself by closing it on his neck, perished of heart failure. I should be glad to believe that, like Elijah, he got the heavenly reward he sought; for he was a fine upstanding man and a gentle creature, nobody's enemy but his own, as the saying is.

Still, what sort of gravity could a boy maintain with a family history of this kind?

– From the Preface to *Immaturity*.

PART SIX

Beauty and the Beast

The Music Lover

ROWENA FARRE

Animal lover though I knew Aunt Miriam to be, I decided after some thought not to inform her in my letter that I had become the owner of a young Common Seal, but to take my pet back unannounced as a 'surprise', trusting that Lora's affectionate nature would win Aunt over to the realisation that a home without a seal lacks a vital member of the family party.

A fortnight later I set off on the two days' journey home to our croft in the wilds of Sutherland, to which Aunt Miriam had retired after twenty years of teaching near London. Already Lora weighed thirty-eight pounds: a bulky parcel wrapped up in a tartan rug.

Bringing up a seal was no light task. As a pup she had a bottle four times a day. My first mistake was to allow her to have it on my lap. This privilege once accorded she had no intention of relinquishing it without a tussle. Even when fully grown, measuring some three-and-a-half feet and tipping the scales at over three hundredweight she would still try and scramble up on to a stranger's lap. Once on my return from a walk I went into the parlour to find Lora entrenched on a breathless and terrified lady visitor.

'She started to bark each time I tried to make her get down and . . . I wasn't sure if seals bit . . .'

I promptly ordered a reluctant Lora on to the floor.

Allowing her to sleep at the bottom of my bed was another mistake. A seal pup on one's feet is one thing, but a fully-grown seal quite another. It took me several weeks to train her to lie on a low bamboo couch at nights and to refrain from surreptitiously trying to clamber back on to the bed.

When on dry land seals move by pulling themselves along on their flippers. No sooner was she past infancy than Lora started to waddle after me round the croft and trail me over to the byre. If I set out on a walk her wails of protest at being left behind would pursue me into the distance. I decided that I must train her to become more independent and capable of amusing herself. We possessed a small rowboat which was kept in a sheltered inlet of the lochan. One day, seeing that the weather was not likely to turn squally, I took her out in it and dropped her over the side. In a moment, she was swimming vigorously, diving, twisting, and circling the boat with incredible swiftness. From a slow-moving, awkward creature she had turned into one of the utmost grace and speed. Each day henceforth she spent many hours swimming with the otters in the lochan. Should we want her, a call from us would usually bring her to the shore. Seals have no ear conches yet they possess very acute hearing.

Now that she had discovered her true element and was growing older our food problem was eased considerably, for she hunted her own fish. At nights she had a supper consisting of dog biscuits soaked in milk and oil.

I began teaching Lora to fetch and carry different objects and to take the mail from the postman. Directly she caught sight of his figure coming up the hill she would start towards him. On meeting, he would place the letters in her mouth and she would follow after in his wake. There was one unfortunate occasion when, busy over the teacups we did not notice her progress, and halfway to the croft, she decided to go for a swim in the lochan taking the mail with her. That bundle of letters was lost for ever and aye.

Lora's musical talent came out early. Whenever Aunt Miriam or I struck up on the piano the other animals would take no notice. Not so Lora. She would wriggle over to the instrument, lean against it or (more inconveniently) the player's legs, and listen with an expression of intense concentration and joy which was quite flattering, swaying now and then with her whole body to the music. When the music stopped she would sit quietly for several minutes, still under its spell. Her reactions to my singing, however, can only be described as humiliating.

A relation had sent me a mouth organ and book of songs for a birthday present. After a preliminary scale or two, I started off on 'Men of Harlech'. Whereupon she broke into a roar. Seals have perhaps the largest vocal range among mammals. Their repertoire includes grunts, snorts, barks, peculiar mewing, hisses, and a wail which often rises from a deep bass to a treble. The roar turned to a hiss. I took no notice but my reedy efforts were soon outclassed. Then I had the idea of letting her sing on her own to my accompaniment: she made valiant efforts to follow the music in a tuneless wail.

She began to pester me for the mouth organ. I was playing it outside the croft one afternoon and, growing weary of the grunts and whines and a heavily whiskered nose pressed against my face every so often as she attempted to wrest it from me, I finally acknowledged defeat and placed it in her mouth. From that moment she considered the mouth organ to be hers. Having gained possession of it, she found to her annoyance that it emitted no sound in spite of being gnawed with vigour. So she started tossing it up into the air and catching it as though it were the ball, and then, her annoyance increasing, rolling on it. All to no effect. Taking the instrument in her mouth once again she gave a loud sigh of desperation. This produced a blast of noise from the mouth organ and galvanised Lora to fresh efforts. I set off for a walk. When I returned there were most curious sounds coming from the rear of the croft. Lora had learnt the blow-suck method and there she was, blowing and sucking feebly, in a state of almost complete exhaustion, for she had been doing this, apparently, ever since I had left her. From that day onwards it became her favourite toy.

A young friend of mine, after visiting us, sent her a toy trumpet. Lora soon learnt to render ear-splitting blasts on this when it was held for her. Another admirer sent her a small xylophone complete with beater. She would hold the beater in her front teeth and bang any note to which I pointed. Her self-imposed practising on these various instruments drove us almost to distraction at times. It became necessary to put them out of her reach and allow her to play them only for short periods in the evenings.

At my school down south I had made and learnt to play a simple bamboo finger pipe. The tone was pleasant, but the range of notes only extended an octave so the number of tunes which could be played on it was limited. We had been at the croft well over a year before I troubled to unpack it. On hearing the sound of pipe music Lora – who was sitting outside shaking a tin which a thoughtful guest had filled with pebbles for her – came in, dropped the tin on the floor, and sat herself in front of me. Though I have no knowledge of séances, it appeared to me that she went into a light trance; her eyes had a far-away look and she seemed quite oblivious of everything except the music. As long as I continued to play she sat there, still and absorbed, never attempting to sing. And this was the way pipe music always affected her.

Having seen the effect piping had on her I began to use subtler methods. While Lora was going over the National Anthem for the umpteenth time on the xylophone, whacking each note with verve if not always with accuracy, I would start playing the pipe. She would glance up, the beater would drop from her mouth, and in a moment she would be spellbound, sitting with her eyes half closed. Still playing, with never a let up, I would sneak away her toy and place it on a shelf. When the music stopped and she opened her eyes and gazed about her, she would look mildly surprised at finding her plaything gone but on these occasions she never whined for its return. The piping had fulfilled its purpose – for ten minutes or so at any rate.

After a time we were forced to the rather humiliating conclusion that friends came on visits mainly to get acquainted with Lora; our company, peace and quiet, the beauties of the countryside were little more than sidelights.

'Where is she?' a guest would ask, the moment he had dumped down his suitcase and gulped a cup of tea to revive himself after the rigours of the journey.

'Out in the lochan.'

The guest would take a quick look at the rolling sea of hills, rocks and pockets of water stretching in every direction to the far horizon, and then – 'Well . . . can't she be got in?'

We would stroll down to the lochan, the guest carrying the trumpet in readiness, and we would stare across the sheet of water, devoid of any sign of animal life. I would call and presently we would see the small, dark speck of her head coming towards us, with perhaps a smaller one near by belonging to an otter. In less than a minute she would be ashore and the trumpet pressed against her mouth. Her boisterous good nature and love of showing off before visitors made her ever ready to play.

A certain uncle of mine took a great fancy to her. At his home outside Aberdeen he used to hold monthly *ceilidhs* (musical evenings) at which local talent used to perform. Uncle Andrew became obsessed with the idea that Lora should be a guest at one of these *ceilidhs*. He felt sure his musical friends would appreciate her gifts and delight in a performance from her. Ever one to make light of difficulties, he assured Aunt Miriam that the lengthy journey to Aberdeen with a seal could be easily accomplished. Shortly after he had visited us he arrived one evening in his brake to collect Lora and me. We set off early the following morning. I had packed two suitcases, one containing my belongings, the other Lora's instruments and her mackintosh. Uncle informed me that he had got in a large supply of fish, biscuits and oil.

On the evening of the *ceilidh* I led her into the drawing-room where it was to be held. My feelings about the forthcoming proceedings were dubious. A well known singer of mouth music (unaccompanied singing) was coming and had consented to start the evening with a song. A melodeon player was to take the platform next, followed by Lora giving an exhibition of xylophone playing. That was to comprise the first half of the evening.

There would be a break for supper. During the second half, amongst other attractions, Lora was to sing to my piano accompaniment. So far so good.

The guests started to arrive. Lora, the most sociable and extroverted of creatures, greeted them warmly. I suggested to Uncle, as the first artist took her place at the far end of the room, that I should shut Lora into his study until it was her turn to perform. But he and several of the guests vetoed this suggestion at once. She must stay. The singer smiled charmingly and started off with the assurance of a professional. She managed to sing a few notes of an old Hebridean air before the inevitable happened; Lora raised her head and roared her way from a deep bass to a seal top C. Even a full Covent Garden chorus would not have been able to compete with that, and the singer wisely gave up there and then. The audience were hysterical with laughter. They had not heard anything as good as that for a long while. When a certain amount of calm had been restored someone suggested that Lora be allowed to perform first and the human faction later; thus she would get her little act off her chest and be willling to listen to others. It was blatantly apparent that he had no knowledge of seals whatsoever, but by then she was out of my hands and being stage-managed by others. She was lifted bodily on to the top of the piano by two stalwart males so that the audience would get a good view of her, and the xylophone was placed before her. I stood by her side ready to point to the notes in case she should be overcome by a sudden fit of nerves at the sight of so large an audience and momentarily forget her piece. My presence proved unnecessary. She took the beater from me and started off with aplomb on 'Baa-baa Black Sheep'. The audience strained forward. I caught murmurs of – 'Yes, I recognised that bit.'

'Quite incredible . . .' and 'Isn't she playing "Danny Boy" now?'

'No, I'm sure she isn't. Oh, perhaps she might be . . .'

Loud applause greeted the final slither of the beater along the length of the instrument which denoted the end of 'Danny Boy' and was followed by vociferous calls for an encore.

The turn ended somewhat more soberly with a rendering of the National Anthem.

The melodeon player got up. I began to realise why professional actors so heartily dislike children and animals taking part in a play; when they are around nobody else gets a look in. His misgivings proved to be correct. With great good humour he walked back to his seat defeated and Lora again took the platform, this time to play the mouth organ.

After supper I managed to inveigle Lora into Uncle Andrew's study and close the door on her. The study most unfortunately was not soundproof and when the music started her piteous wails at being excluded from the proceedings drew the attention of the guests. Someone went along at once to let her out.

In a final attempt to keep order I made her sit by my side and told her severely to be quiet. The result was no less disastrous. Seals have free-flowing tear ducts and Lora, overcome with frustration at not being allowed to take part, sat with tears pouring down her face. Whereupon the sympathetic guests pleaded on her behalf and the other performers generously allowed her to take the platform yet again. The evening finished with a singsong in which Lora outsang the rest of us. But I was assured by Uncle that the *ceilidh* had been a great success.

– From *Seal Morning*.

My Birds

LEN HOWARD

I always remember the words of an electrician who once called to attend to fittings in my Sussex cottage. He stopped in amazement before my doorway, watching countless birds flying down from the trees to perch on me. He had looked an ordinary man with a work-a-day expression until he saw these birds, then his whole countenance seemed to alter, his face glowed, his eyes shone and he kept murmuring: 'How wonderful!' Then he said: 'But why shouldn't it be like that? It ought to be like that.'

There are, of course, great difficulties in living as I do, in continual company of numbers of birds. The practical ones are many, such as cleaning up, having things spoilt, the rooms always looking as if prepared for the sweep with newspapers spread over furniture and books covered with cloths: then the disturbance of sleep, for they hammer furiously on the panes if I shut the windows at dawn to keep them outside when the nights are short, and they do all they can to prevent my concentrating upon anything except themselves. But there are even worse problems. Cats and magpies!

Most mornings recently I have been awakened at five o'clock by a Great Tit making agitated flights to and fro from my bed to the window while uttering loud alarm cries. He is telling me to come out quickly, the Magpie is endangering his young, so I leap from bed and chase off this enemy with a stick. I return to bed, but soon there is more trouble, the Blackbird calls me up by agitated 'tchinks' close to my window, and again I go out to frighten away the cat by flinging a jug of water at it with a big splash.

There are often injured ones among my many birds, dependent

upon me for their recovery. In one way and another my birds demand attention from dawn until dusk. They do all they can to hinder any concentrated work, – while I am trying to write this page some are perching on the typewriter, some pulling at my hair, others flying to my hands and falling off as I start to tap the keys. There is one other person who knows from experience how demanding my Great Tits can be. This is a man named 'Old Harry', who, like me, loves all the wild creatures. He lives in his own little hut in a spinney about ten minutes walk from my cottage. One of my Great Tits this year was crowded out of my garden and she nested in his spinney. Until her young were hatched she used to fly back to me every morning and evening, urgently demanding a good feed. Then this kind old man, who feeds the birds, became the victim of her imperious ways. 'Proper tart, she is,' said Old Harry; 'she calls me up at dawn by tugging at the blankets and pecking at my face. You can't stop her and you've got to give her all she wants, and quickly too.' I knew at once from his description which bird it was, for this was exactly how the little tart had always treated me.

Perhaps it is because of my intense love for birds that they come to me quickly and I have not found any difficulty in gaining their confidence. . . .

It seems evident that birds can communicate with each other by slight inflections of voice and of movement, because I find those that know me well understand much by their sensitive interpretation of my voice or least movement. For example, when Great Tits want to peck at my butter dish, which they know is usually forbidden, they perch a little way off and look first at the butter, then at my face, hesitating although longing to help themselves, for they have a passion for butter. If I say 'come on' coaxingly, they confidently step up and eat it. If I say 'no' just a little sternly they remain where they are, but continue to look pleadingly at me and then at the butter. A shade crosser 'no' sends them hopping farther off; an angry 'no' makes them fly to the open window, but if I quickly call out: 'Here, come on,' in a very coaxing tone, they at once return and if I keep quiet, inch by inch they hop along the table towards the butter, still eyeing me for further signs of objection. . . . They interpret correctly any sign of objection or encouragement in voice or movement.

Birds are able to distinguish individual humans from afar, for those that are tamest often fly across meadows and along roads to meet me, apparently spotting me from tree-tops. It is not my clothes that are responsible for their ability to recognise me, for on one occasion I left home by the road, wearing a blue coat and head-scarf and returned across field-paths in a green mackintosh and hood, purposely pulled low over my face. Both had been purchased while out, but the birds flew as usual to meet me, recognising me from across two long fields. In winter, when very hungry, several Great Tits have sometimes flown to a nearby bus stop to meet my return bus on the rare occasions when I take this double-decker which passes my house to the country town. I presume they watch me get into it and remember this when two hours later the bus returns.

Close watch is kept over all my movements, and I find they often know what I am going to do from seeing my preparations. For instance, one winter when my hot-water supply failed I took weekly afternoon baths at a friend's house. After the third time Great and Blue Tits had learnt where I was going when they saw my basket filled with bath gear; directly I started out they flew on in front, along and across the road, and perched in my friend's garden to await my arrival, their purpose being to get a feed from my hand before I disappeared. . . .

Their reaction to humans varies according to the person. Some people who come to my cottage always induce fear, others they treat with comparative friendliness and enter the room while they are there without concern, although they never behave quite normally until alone with me again.

Many Great Tits are indoors with me for much of the time during autumn and winter, and I find it necessary to provide toys for them, otherwise they choose a pastime that inflicts damage to something of value to me. Before I knew that Great Tits liked toys I found one of four celluloid parakeets (from a Christmas tree) missing from its perch on a holly bough in my room. That same day I saw a Great Tit fly to the holly, knock one of the remaining parakeets on to the floor, then, holding it with one foot, begin hammering, pecking and pulling the bird in mock-ferocious manner, often picking it up and turning it over, probably because this made it rattle. Having succeeded in tearing its side open, the Tit flew with it out of the window. Until all these toy birds had been disposed of, the Tit had no eye for anything else in the room. Some clever imitations of Blue Tits, made in felt, were ill-treated in the same manner, but if nothing as realistic and exciting is in sight, Great Tits will seize my ink-bottle stopper and, knowing this to be forbidden, fly quickly out of the window with it while I am filling my pen. When wanting to cork the bottle I see the Tit on the lawn or a tree branch, ill-treating the stopper as he did the toy parakeets and stuffed birds. These were not regarded as live things, merely as toys that amused him and something on which to vent high spirits.

Unfortunately, it is not only the ink-bottle stopper they destroy. When they see me writing, dipping my pen in the inkpot, their favourite way of attracting my attention is to upset the ink. They do it deliberately, then escape my wrath by quick flight out of the window. They have various ways of trying to divert me from writing, often hammering on my skull, and sitting on my shoulder to pull my hair and tweak my ears, this meaning they want nuts and cheese. If I refuse to be bullied into noticing them sometimes one of them will walk on to my page and carefully lift my nib from the paper, looking up at me while doing it. This forces me to stop, so the Tits have won! The writing of this book provides good Tit sport. Many of my notes are on loose sheets; these they watch me place in order on the table beside the typewriter, then they fly up and purposely scatter pages to the floor. Another game is to perch on the roller of the typewriter when I pause for thought, and if my hands are not held over the page, they tear a hole in the last sentence while I am thinking of the next! Occasionally a Tit taps a key sharply with his beak but, luckily, the resulting movement he finds alarming.

One of my Great Tits' toys is a covered glass jar containing sea-shells. They pluck off the lid, pick out the shells and chuck them with a sharp twist of their heads either down on the floor or across the room, always watching them fall with interest. Matches are treated in the same manner and often when I have been out I return to find matches strewn all over the room, the box having been pulled open and lying in two halves on the floor.

One of the great charms of House-Martins is their playfulness. They have fun even in the cradle. I have watched a young one stretching half its body out of the nest to play with a smaller Martin in a neighbouring nest. Twittering excitedly, with head craned forward, it just managed to touch the tip of the other baby's beak. The smaller one entered into the fun and bobbed up from its nest to take the kiss, both withdrawing directly afterwards. Then the bigger one, behaving excitedly, began poking its brother – or sister – as if trying to egg it on to join in the fun, but getting no response, the merry Martin again turned to the neighbouring baby and, with a terrific effort, heaved almost all its body outside the nest, with eager twitterings touching the small one's beak. This touch or kiss was received with obvious amusement by the little one, who repeatedly retired into its nest then bobbed up again to thrust its head forward for another touch of beaks. The game continued for some time, the enjoyment of the Martins so infectious it was impossible to watch without laughter.

One winter, when I was ill for two or three weeks, Tits amused themselves on the bed every day in a variety of ways. Some played at possession of me, so it seemed, and displayed while walking about all over me, tails fully spread, wings half-opened and drooped, heads stiffly held up, their beaks pointing to the ceiling. They muttered queer language to each other while displaying, and their expressions were so humorous it was impossible to watch without laughter. It was obviously all in fun, the birds entering into the game were not at that time disputing for territory, for it was early winter. Another amusement was to slide down the slopes of my pillow, which miniature alpine sport some seemed to enjoy. They climbed to the top, then slowly slid down without moving their feet. Occasionally they rolled on the bed, two together with feet interlocked, quarrelling over a piece of cheese. They became very tyrannical when I had no more cheese to give them, especially Baldhead, who is a determined bird with a sharp beak. When he stood over me with his threatening look, demanding what I was unable to give, there was need for complete submergence under bedclothes. If I put out my head to breathe he pounced at my nose and gave a few sharp pecks to my cheeks so the sheet had to be quickly pulled over my head again. But his wits were as sharp as his beak; he tried to get at me by tugging at the top of the sheet, lifting the edge and squeezing himself underneath until he reached my hair which he pulled vigorously, while the other Tits walked over the sheet above my face, giving occasional pecks to try to remove it.

If they think I have any peanuts they start chucking away other food given them and pester me persistently for nuts until I take them to the cupboard where these are usually kept, and let them see for themselves the nut-tin is empty. They then understand and remember there are none until they see a fresh supply arrive. When Baldhead is shown the empty tin he looks very cross, the sudden change in his expression very noticeable, and he flies out of the window with a peculiar twitch of his tail which he gives when annoyed. But he soon returns to perch on my shoulder and accept some cheese.

Many ornithologists at the present time say that bird and human mind are completely different, and that the former have not such emotions as love, hatred, jealousy, etc., clearly defined. It is thought they react automatically in set patterns of behaviour according to the stimulus. . . . After the incidents I have witnessed during eleven years of observation of individual birds at close quarters, I cannot think that their mind is so remote from ours. It seems reasonable to think that they have some resemblances although, of course, many differences . . .

I am continually seeing birds faced with situations new to them and it has been my experience to find that unless they are paralysed with fright they act intelligently, the degree varying according to the individual as well as the species.

One of my Great Tits, Smoke, this year chose a large petrol tin for her nest. It being hung aslant, she skidded on the slippery surface when she took in her first bits of moss, so she began bringing some small sticks for a foundation. This is unusual for Tits; they choose moss, wool or other flexible material easily taken through the small entrance of a nesting-hole. These sticks presented a problem that Smoke had to solve for herself; they were longer than the width of the entrance to the petrol tin. The first one she brought was held in the middle and three unsuccessful attempts were made to force it through the hole, but she found it was too long and would not yield to pressure. She hopped to a perch in front of the tin and stared at the hole with an intent expression for a moment, then went back and deliberately stretched her head back – away from the hole – turned it to one side so the stick was in a lengthwise position instead of across the entrance hole, and successfully got it through. It could not possibly have been chance, for the pose of stretching back and twisting her neck was most unnatural. It must have been a deliberate action, which appeared to be the result of her concentrated stare at the entrance hole. Every stick was then taken through in this same manner. Many such problems are continually confronting the nest-builder; they are solved by the individual intelligence of the bird.

Naturally, many actions in the daily round of a bird's life are automatic – so are many of ours.

– From *Birds as Individuals.*

My African Cats

PAULETTE LLOYD GREAME

Much as I had always wanted to keep a lion, I still of course had a lot to learn about them, and it was a revelation to me to see how quickly these so-called savage creatures could become devoted to human beings. I am not for one moment trying to pretend that they are easy pets, swiftly tamed and as artless as dogs; nor to imply that all you have to do is show affection for a lion and it will lie down and serve you. On the contrary, however charming a lion may be 99 per cent of the time, there is always that 1 per cent of unpredictability for which you must be prepared.

However, it is true of all 'tame' lions, I think, that their moods are very much governed by the moods of the people with whom they are in contact. More than any other animals they react to one's own mental state. That is why, of course, it is widely said that if a keeper or a trainer develops a fear of one of his animals he is no longer safe with it. The lion senses his fear and takes advantage of it. But the same thing can apply in reverse. For instance, normally Sinclair was incredibly patient with animals but now and again he lost his temper. It was strange to see how terrified our enormous pair of pets could be. They wouldn't go near him when he was in a rage and I used to have to make it up with them.

Once, when Romeo and Juliet were about a year old, I was the one to get angry. I found my favourite lamp, a wrought iron one with a very nice shade that I had brought all the way from Europe, lying on the sitting-room floor, the shade torn to shreds. Two cubs, trying to look innocent but with that certain wary look about them that always meant a guilty conscience, were eyeing me from a distance.

I lost my temper and made for the lions with a whip in my hand. Of course they escaped me and, too furious to see the funny side, I started to chase them madly round the room, brandishing the whip. It was absolute bedlam, for the lions roared with fright, I roared with anger and Sinclair roared with laughter.

So far does this strange *rapport* between lions and humans extend itself that I could tell the state of my own nerves by watching Romeo's eyes. If I was inclined to be edgy but hadn't realised it myself, I realised it when I saw how he was looking at me. And when that happened I took no risks, as much for his sake as for mine.

Much as I loved them, there were occasions when they became exclusively Sinclair's lions. 'Will you please take your lions out of my sitting-room before they wreck it completely,' I said icily to Sinclair when I first realised that respect for my possessions was something that Romeo and Juliet didn't have and had no wish to learn.

Eventually I became resigned to their occasional moods of destruction because I really loved the lions much more than I loved my inanimate possessions.

One day when Romeo and Juliet were getting on for two years old Sinclair came across a small ad in the *East African Standard* that interested him enough to make him read it out loud.

'Tame and friendly lion cub. What offers?'

He looked at me guardedly. 'Of course we have two,' he said casually, 'but the ad is nicely worded.'

We found the owners of the lion just about to leave for Mombasa but there was no lion with them. They had lost him on the way. They were confident, however, that he would turn up because he had been lost near a Public Works Department camp and the men there had promised to look out for him.

We went away from the station with the most awful feeling of let-down. Now that we hadn't got him we knew quite definitely that we wanted him.

Sinclair, never one to let the grass grow under his feet, suggested a visit to Abdul Wahid's zoo so we took off for that emporium and came away with a three-week-old ball of fluff that gazed at us inquiringly with the opaque and short-sighted eyes peculiar to lion cubs. Sinclair had bought her for me, and I named her Ting-a-ling and took her straight off to spend the first part of her evening in the grill room of Torr's Hotel and the second part at a movie. Lying full length, she fitted exactly into my lap and she slept blissfully through the whole performance.

Of all the lions I have known Ting was by far the nicest creature and the only one of our big cats that we would honestly call house-trained. Right from the start I let her sleep on my bed with an old turkish bath sheet folded many times underneath her to serve as a diaper. We went to bed early on the farm and for the first few weeks I forced myself to wake up at about 11 p.m. to pick Ting up and drop her out of the window on to the garden. She soon learnt the reason for this rather callous treatment and after that she could last out the night.

Ting-a-ling had to be fed on the bottle at first and anything more adorable than a tiny lion cub pulling away at a baby's bottle is hard to imagine. She could manage a little raw minced meat as well but she was too young for much of this virile diet.

On their first introduction to Ting, Romeo and Juliet eyed her rather warily but they made no attempt to hurt her and they soon got used to her. They were too big to play with such a baby, and Bonny, the Scottie, took up rather a hoity-toity attitude about yet another lion in the house, but Ting found a friend in my cat, Minna. Smaller though lumpier than Minna, she was a lively but sweet-tempered playmate and the little big cat and the big little cat had the most wonderful batty games together, Minna always displaying that incredible gentleness and tolerance that a grown animal can show to a very young one. Of course she had the superior speed and agility. Ting's method of transport was a drunken lurching waddle, and she often lost her balance.

It was wonderful to have a young cub about the house again. Romeo and Juliet never ceased to be a source of pleasure and fun to us but they did cease to be the constant companions they had been at first. Lions, like other pets, *will* grow up, and grown-up lions are, let's face it, not quite such easily handled followers as very small ones.

You can take a tiny cub to the movies but you can't take a fully grown beast.

When Ting-a-ling had been with us for a month a telegram arrived saying that the missing lion from Uganda had been found and was being brought to Nairobi by a Mrs Le Geyt and would we please meet it.

'Now we've done it,' I said to Sinclair. 'Four lions in the home.'

Once again we drove lionwards to Nairobi where we met Mrs Le Geyt with Kitgum, a six-month-old lion, about the size of a large spaniel, on a leash. We all went off to have tea and I am afraid our entry into Torr's Hotel had all the characteristics of an explosion. The lion was strong for his size and was pulling tremendously hard on his leash. He burst into the hotel hall with the rest of us gasping along behind. You cannot keep lions and remain inconspicuous, I find.

By this time Romeo and Juliet had outgrown their boiler-house bedroom and spent the nights in a run we had constructed for them out of an old chicken run. Every day about twelve o'clock when we had finished our morning's work, we used to go to the run to bring them into the house. We had found that wherever one of the pair went the other would follow.

The ridiculous Juliet used to walk towards the house on her hind legs, one paw in Sinclair's hand and the other in mine, and Romeo would amble along behind us. It must have been quite a sight.

Once indoors they stayed in the house, with occasional enforced visits to the garden, until it was time to put them in their run again for the night.

The lions were protection as well as company. With Ting-a-ling sleeping on my bed, Kitgum in a box just outside the window and Romeo and Juliet in a flimsy run only a little way off, I felt no fear at all. I knew that no interloper would dare to try his hand at breaking into such a fierce household for he couldn't be expected to know, as I did, that at the slightest sign of danger the lions would have been under the bed in no time at all.

Luckily my houseboys were very good about the animals, although they did cause a lot of extra work. I rather had the impression that the natives got a sort of reflected glory from working for *Mzungus* (Whites) who were crazy enough to keep lions, and they put up with dirty floors and smeared windows, overturned vases and occasional puddles because of the extra cachet that being on intimate terms with lions gave them among their friends.

Sometimes in the evening if the cubs hadn't come home on their own I would tell Wanjohi to go out and find them. He would walk down the drive calling: 'Kitgum! Ting-a-ling!' as if he were calling in a couple of domestic cats or dogs. But the system worked; soon he would reappear with the two cubs ambling along beside him, a wonderful sight for any stranger to have seen if one had arrived at the farm at that moment.

When I went up to bath and change before dinner I was usually accompanied to the bathroom by Ting and Kitgum. When they lost sight of me in the bath, they stood up with their front feet on the edge of the tub, looking for me; and happy at having found me again, Kitgum would lick my back, nearly taking the skin off with his rough tongue.

The last thing Wanjohi did at night was to take Kitgum to his box and it used to amuse me that despite her love for him, there was always a slightly triumphant look on Ting-a-ling's face when Kitgum was taken out on his lead. Her expression quite clearly said: '*You* sleep in a box outside but *I* sleep on a bed.'

As a matter of fact there were moments when I wished Ting didn't sleep on a bed. As she grew she found that there wasn't quite as much room as there used to be and it became a scramble as to who would get into bed first and letch on the lion's share. She was supposed to sleep at my feet but she always managed to get a little higher every night, until one morning I found her head on the pillow beside mine. I resigned myself to this, but she next developed an unpleasant habit of stretching as she woke up and as a lion puts his claws out when he stretches, I used to be awakened by one large paw being thrust into my face and the other into my neck, all claws out. It was a startling way of beginning a new day.

One morning the boy bringing my early tea greeted me with, 'Memsahib, Romeo is in the chicken run.' I shot out of bed, dragged on a coat and rushed out in one of my rare rages with Romeo. I found him blessedly outside a hen coop housing 150 birds, walking up and down, up and down. I yelled at him from a distance, 'Romeo, get out of there,' as I ran towards him.

He knew perfectly well that he was doing something he shouldn't and at the first sound of my furious voice and the sight of my flying figure, he slunk out of the chicken run and, fortunately for me, straight to the door of his own run which I quickly opened to let him in. I had had visions of spending the day trying to get Romeo into his run and I was so relieved when he went home more like a lamb than a lion that I didn't scold him. I should have done though, for I found afterwards that he had already paid a visit to a breeding pen, with the direst results. He hadn't left a bird alive. I am afraid lions are not good poultry-farmers; and they're not good gardeners either; if I had a specially prized plant or seedling that I was particularly cherishing, I could almost bet on it that fat Romeo would select that spot on which to have his siesta. Poor Romeo! He could never understand my tantrums when I tried to move him off my precious garden.

Twice a week I went into Nanyuki to rail the eggs. I drove the Bedford with Ting sitting beside me on the seat and Wanjohi on the back of the lorry with Kitgum on a leash. Sometimes I used to finish off the day's work by going into the Sportsman's Arms bar and Ting came in with me but poor Kitgum, owing to his now considerable size, stayed outside with Wanjohi. He never liked this but I didn't realise how much he resented it until one day he caught a glimpse of me through one of the bar windows. He got very excited and I could see Wanjohi couldn't hold him back much longer so I rather hurriedly addressed the officer who was sitting in the window. 'Would you mind changing seats with me?' I said. 'My lion is coming through the window at any minute.'

The bar was cleared with the speed of lightning and Kitgum leapt through the window with one powerful jump, making little grunts of joy at being with me again. Somehow, after this I didn't feel we were very popular in the bar so we all three took our leave.

– From *With Lions by My Side.*

Lamb's Tale

REBECCA WARREN

'We're having a bad time with the ewes.'

'Ewes?' I lifted a sleepy eye and simulated interest; but my mind was still coping with the announcement that Charles and Sheila had made no less than forty gallons of the dandelion wine we were drinking.

'Yes,' Sheila went on. 'It's all bottles. I'm sick of the sight of bottl e – and teats.'

'Bottles?'

'Bottles of milk for the lambs. I suppose you wouldn't like one?'

Like a LAMB? Did she say a lamb? All my weariness left me – a dear little cuddly curly lamb for me! 'Oh,' I cried. 'I'd love a lamb. . . . Martin!' I called. 'Sheila has just offered us one of her lambs. Please say yes.'

The following evening Charles stood in the doorway of our sitting-room. He had a broad smile on his face and a small white bundle in his arms. 'Here she is,' he said. 'Here is her bottle and teat. She is ready for a feed now. Every four hours for a day or two as she is delicate.'

In one movement I was across the room and had gathered the small woolly animal to my chest and was gazing into its eyes. 'Ma, ma,' it said, looking up at me. I looked at Charles.

'Is it really for me, for me to keep?'

'Certainly, she's yours to do what you like with.'

'I shall call her Sheila after your wife.' It was the greatest gift I could think of at that moment. Charles looked rather nonplussed but he laughed again and then said: 'Well, I must be off. What with the weather and the lambing, we are up to our eyes at the moment. Good luck.'

In another moment we were alone. I was alone with my baby and Martin, who was standing open-mouthed by the fireplace.

Such a glow of motherly possession I had then, I could have gone through fire and water for that helpless little thing. I sank down in a chair by the fire and then I looked up at Martin and spoke.

'Well, Daddy, don't just stand there. Go and warm some milk for Sheila's bottle.'

Martin's throat worked convulsively once or twice before sound came out, and when it did come, it lacked its usual authority. 'S-S-Sheila? Milk?' he croaked, and, with one bewildered look at me and my lamb, he walked as though in a dream, into the scullery.

We made a nest of straw by the fire for Sheila and I sat up late that night gazing at my new possession and wondering if she would be all right if I went to bed. Supposing she slept all through the night and died in her sleep for want of food. All sorts of doubts and anxieties I worried myself with and had almost decided to spend the night in a chair when an ominous growl from Martin upstairs made me jump to my feet and, with many a backward look, go to bed.

I had set the alarm to waken me for her bottle but, long before the alarm went off I was aroused from a restless doze by a weak 'Ma, ma' from down below. Heavy with weariness I swung my legs out of bed and fumbled for my slippers. 'Mother's coming!' I called in the darkness of the bedroom. 'Mother's coming!' Another low growl caused me to hush this little monologue and I shuffled out of the room.

Martin always got up first in the morning to make the early morning tea. He also let the dog out and cut up the meat for the cats. It was my peak moment of the day to lie there luxuriating in my warm bed, whilst I heard Martin busying himself below. I lay and listened to the water running into the kettle, to Martin grumbling at the dog and angrily chopping meat up for the cats; he was not at his best at this early hour but he meant well. That morning there were new noises, the pitter-patter of little hoofs, the conversational, Ma ma, to which I could hear Martin's chatty answer directed to me upstairs. 'That damn lamb! Get OUT!'

Smiling fondly, I lay there listening; a new addition to our family, Sheila, Miss Sheila, how I would cherish that little being. She would be the most perfect lamb that was ever born. 'That DAMN LAMB' I heard again from down below. Why, I thought, she was one of the family already, Martin had taken to her at once. Miss Sheila Lamb, Miss Sheila Damn Lamb? It had a distinguished ring about it; Miss Sheila Von Damn? Yes, that was it, I could see her in her pen at the London Cattle Show, her white eyelashes framing her big dark eyes, her rosette pinned to her pen; FIRST PRIZE, MISS SHEILA VON DAMN LAMB.

At that moment my day dream was shattered by an angry voice calling up: 'Tea's ready!'

Still smiling I floated down the stairs eager to see my family. At the bottom Martin met me. He had a shovel in one hand, a brush in the other, a white enraged look on his face, and there was a strong smell of disinfectant on the air. He seemed beside himself with emotion and began speaking at once: 'IT IS BAD ENOUGH MAKING THE TEA, LETTING THE DOG OUT, CHOPPING UP MEAT FOR THE CATS, WITHOUT HAVING TO DO THE MUCKING OUT AS WELL – THAT DAMN LAMB.'

'Von damn lamb,' I corrected him kindly as I stooped to pick up the little thing from where it stood nibbling at his dressing gown; 'Miss Sheila Von Damn Lamb.'

Martin changed colour and a look of indescribable fury suffused his face; he began to stutter 'V-V-Vot d'you mean, von damn lamb? Von damn lamb is more than enough, von more damn lamb and I QUIT!'

Later, when peace was more or less restored, Sheila had had her bottle and we were sitting over our morning tea, I had a brilliant idea. Martin had said 'She-can't-stay-in-here-it-isn't-hygienic' and I had said 'She-can't-go-outside-it-is-snowing-again-you-know-Charles-said-she-was-delicate-she-is-only-a-baby.' Baby! That was it! That was the answer!

'Martin,' I said, 'will you be going into Town today?'

'I could do.' Martin was still sullen. 'Why?'

'I would like to go in with you, that is all. I wouldn't keep you,

I should be back here in half an hour.'

We, the locals, called it the Town, although actually it was just a one-eyed country place that was little more than a village. It had a few seed shops, agricultural implement shops and haberdashery shops dripping with dungarees and jeans. It had, however, one thing that at that moment filled me with hope. It boasted an excellent baby shop. Many a time in the past had I been in there to purchase a little something for the offspring of our friends. It was barely two hours later when I skipped up the stone steps and pinged the door bell.

'Oh, *please*,' I said to the gaunt elderly woman behind the counter, 'do you stock soluble diapers?'

'What size?' she replied calmly.

I breathed a thankful sigh. 'Oh, the largest size, I should think.'

'What age is the baby?'

'Two days old, but she is quite big; she is a lamb,' I gushed.

The woman gave a sceptical sniff. 'The smaller ones would be better.'

'No, I think I will have the largest. Six packets, please,' Sourly the the woman stacked them up on the counter. 'Now,' I said, 'I want some plastic panties. Large ones.'

Stubbornly the woman produced a minute pair and put them before me.

'Bigger!' I cried laughing, 'much bigger; those are much too small.'

The woman gave me a peculiar look. 'Two days old you said; are you sure?'

'Quite sure,' I said again. 'She's *so* sweet. She's a lamb.'

'Is she yours?'

'Oh yes, we've called her Sheila.'

The woman came round the counter and pulled up a tall wooden chair. 'You'd better sit down,' she said quietly.

I sat down whilst she fumbled among the boxes and eventually produced (with another sniff) a large pair of pale pink panties scattered about with little rosebuds. 'These are the largest I have.'

I sprang from my seat. 'Oh, aren't they sweet? Those will do beautifully, just the right size. I can cut a hole in the back for her tail.'

'What's the matter with the old girl?' said Martin when I skipped joyfully out of the shop and into the car. . . .

She had come to the shop door and was peering earnestly out at the car!

How impatiently I sat in the car on the return journey, and with what quick fingers I cut out the tail hole and bound it with some pink bias binding. Then, with my baby on my knee, I popped her into her knickers and tucked a soluble diaper inside. Sheila took to those panties without a backward glance and swaggered about on her wobbly legs, swinging her tail as though she were showing off.

They were the perfect answer. I found that it was quite easy to slip out a soiled diaper and tuck another one in without taking her knickers off, and when there was a gleam of sunshine in that continuous inclement weather I would take them off and let her out for a little scamper in the garden.

She was too young to nibble green stuff but she would skip about, doing an occasional *entrechat* or a *croisée* with astonishing agility and grace. She would leap high into the air with her little hoofs flashing like polished ebony in the sunlight and with, as ever, a benign smile on her mouth and a mischievous twinkle in her bright dark eyes. With the advent of her panties it seemed the natural thing to do to call her 'Baby'; she was so pretty, so curly, and so very young.

For two days at least I had to abandon all but the absolute essentials of housework; the rest of the time I devoted to making bottles and feeding the lamb, changing diapers and KEEPING THE PEACE. How I stroked, talked to and cajoled those animals into a semblance of friendship, and what a semblance it was, what a veneer. An inadvertent stumble from a not-too-footsure Baby, a little cry of joy when she saw her bottle, and the work of hours would be destroyed; the two Siamese cats and the dog would rise up *en masse* spitting and growling, their eyes flashing hate.

The animals had certainly let me down. I had imagined that Mitti would have welcomed her with open arms as a cuddly replacement for all those little kittens she had missed. I had imagined that Singhi, the loud-voiced, the hearty, would have welcomed her as an untiring playfellow; and Gunter, I thought, would have welcomed Sheila's warm woolly side to put his head on, as they all jockeyed for position round the fire. But no, it was not to be. Singhi the brave, the bully, was a trembling jelly of fear. On the first day he took his food outside and would only peep through the door at hourly intervals to see if that horror, that nightmare, were still there. On the second day he did come into the house but crept about under the furniture, a cringing cowardly thing. His coat was permanently staring and his eyes more crossed than ever and entirely unblinking; he seemed afraid that if he closed them for a split second that lamb would pounce on him and tear him limb from limb. Mitti, the small thoughtful one, was not so frightened; she developed a habit of peeping into Sheila's ear when she was asleep as though she wanted to find out what went on inside that woolly mass.

Gunter remained for ever consumed by an all-absorbing passion of jealousy. He would prance up to Baby wagging his tail and exuding a lying spirit of friendship and, when he was within easy masticating distance, he would snap off a mouthful of woolly fur. We smacked him, we thumped him, we shut him out in the cold, but it was of no avail. His attitude, though more tolerant as time went on, never became better than *sour*. He would stare at her plastic knickers, his lips curled up in disdain and a dozen times a day he would go to his ditty box and check the contents.

The fact that Gunter's heart was weak made the situation more difficult. He would work himself up into such a state of hate and agitation that we let him get away with far more spoilt behaviour than we would have done had he been in normal health. However, as time went on, the situation improved and in about two weeks from the time we had Baby the animals had accepted her as an unpleasant, smelly member of the family.

There was no doubt about it, Baby did smell; it was not an unpleasant smell, but as the weather improved and she went more and more into the garden she would come in in the evening, damp perhaps after a shower of rain, and settle down quietly by the fire. There would then assail our nostrils a smell of warm woollen winter underwear. Baby loved the fire. She would lie stretched out on the hearth, positively basking in the heat. As her coat grew thicker and longer there was no doubt that she became somewhat warm. She would pant and gasp through her little mouth and her fat sides would go up and down so fast that I would get worried and feel that a heart attack from her, too, was imminent. Then I would take her by her legs and tail and drag her away from the fire, but soon Baby would decide to go back. Too lazy to get on to her feet, she would rise to her knees and, in this strange position, like a cripple begging for alms, she would knuckle her way to her former place right in front of the blaze.

How that lamb grew! One minute she was a tiny thing that we had to stoop down to feed and then, it seemed overnight, she was, with her black ears waggling with glee, helping herself to toast from the breakfast table. She had a most arrogant swagger; she had a beautiful tail and, as though conscious of this, she would swing her behind from side to side as she walked. Should she be up to one of her many naughty tricks the view of Baby from the back gave her a nonchalant, don't-care attitude that made Martin shout 'THAT DAMN LAMB!' a dozen times a day.

Baby was a nibbler; she believed in tasting everything and she found almost everything [to her] taste. We did the sitting-room together in the mornings. Whilst I did the carpet and polished the surrounding tiles, Baby did the ash-trays. With a loud clashing of her sharp white teeth she would grind up all the cigarette ends and then lick round the trays until they were as clean as new pins. I had to make sure that her industry did not go too far; if she *did* come across a packet of cigarettes she could open them with a little nibbling movement of her lips and have the cigarettes eaten before I had noticed what she was doing.

'Naughty Baby,' I would cry, giving her furry face a sharp tap.

But the weather was really improving now. Baby was able to spend more and more time in the garden. She wore a blue leather collar round her neck and we tethered her by a long rope to an old garden fork. When she had eaten all the sprouts and grass tips from one position she would give her call and I could tell by the sound of it that she was ready to be moved.

She had lots of different tones in her voice. She had the conversational sound, which she used when I was working in the garden; a long calling note which said 'is that you?' to which I would answer: 'Mother's here, dear.' Then she would mutter among the grass as though she were telling me about some tasty snack which she had just enjoyed, and her tail would jerk up and down with pleasure, like a puppet on a string. When the dusk began to creep over the garden and Martin came back from his work, Baby would shout excitedly; she knew and welcomed the sound of *his* car. Then we let her off her rope to do a tour of the garden with us before we went indoors. Indoors at last, she would settle herself down with a tasty newspaper.

'Is that today's newspaper she is eating?' Martin would sigh wearily from his seat.

What with the two cats, the dog and the lamb, there wasn't much hearth to be seen. I used to slip my feet out of my shoes and bury my toes in Baby's warm wool; as for Martin, 'Pull up an animal and sit down,' was his favourite bit of sarcasm if we had any evening callers.

We were sitting around the fire one chilly spring evening, the cats, the dog and the lamb obscuring the hearthrug as usual. Martin and I were reading when, upon the quiet air, came an entirely new sound; a sound that caused Martin to drop his book, the cats to leap to their feet and the dog to start up with a visibly pounding heart. It was a strangled choking noise for all the world like a human being about to vomit. Only Baby remained unperturbed. She lay there, her feet tucked in, smiling and staring at the fire. I saw her throat move and the terrible sound came again and then, with a convulsive gulp, she began to chew.

'Martin!' I cried in delighted surprise, 'look at that. She has just brought up her first cud.'

'I shall bring something up if she does that often,' snapped Martin. . . .

All that night we had those astonishing sounds, and every time she did it the animals leaped wide-eyed to their feet.

'My God! That damn lamb! How long is this going on?' was Martin's comment.

'Don't be intolerant,' I protested. 'She is only just beginning, aren't

you, darling?' I tickled her chin fondly and Baby gazed up.
'Ma, ma, GULP!' she said.

Many people had been to see Baby. They all came with a jolly laugh and said: 'We've come to see this famous lamb of yours.'

There would be a prolonged all-staring pause and then the inevitable remark: 'What are you going to do with her eventually?'

I endured this for so long and then I evolved a wonderful come-back: 'EAT HER' I would say quite calmly. And then I stood there enjoying the ensuing, shocked silence.

What we were going to do with Baby eventually really was a problem. It was so difficult to find grazing. Take the onions for instance.

'Baby,' I cried, 'what have you been doing?'

Baby made no answer but attempted a staggering step towards me. She had eaten all the grass in a complete circle round the fork. 'There's a good girl,' I said, and then I saw the onions. The first row, which, thank heavens, was all she could reach, were cropped off so close to the ground that they looked like a row of tubby little sunken ships with just the tips of their hollow funnels sticking above their earthy sea. As I looked at them I went cold with horror. Martin's pride and joy, nipped off in their prime.

'Baby,' I whispered, 'what have you done!' But Baby didn't care. Baby seemed to have completely seized up; she was beyond mass peristaltic movement, let alone repentance. She gave a feeble 'mama' of indifference.

Martin was in a jolly mood that night. He made a cheerful crack and scratched Baby under the chin as he said: 'Was Dad only joking then?' But, when we arrived at the onion bed, all joking stopped. Martin stood in silent contemplation and Baby turned her head away as though nauseated by the very smell of onions. Nothing was said as we all trooped back to the house. Baby with her knickers on, knickers that were now so small that they stretched over her rear like an inflated balloon and the little flowers that had once been rose buds were now so expanded that they looked like small, full-blown cabbage roses, cavorted over the furniture and Martin went into the little cloak room to use the telephone.

'Well, that's settled,' he said when he came back. 'The lamb returns to the farm tomorrow morning. It is not your fault, Becca; it is not the lamb's fault, but we just haven't got the grazing she needs. She is getting too big for nibbling at the paths and borders, and we can't leave her on the lawn, the grass is too short. Besides, it is time she mixed with her fellow sheep.'

It was about two months later that the telephone bell rung and Martin came back to say that Sheila had asked us to join them for Sunday luncheon as it was Charles's birthday. We were there at twelve o'clock and, as lunch was not until one, the dandelion wine began to flow. I was daintily sipping mine from a wine glass, but Martin and Charles were quaffing theirs from tankards, and as they drank their faces began to glow. When their very hearty laughter rang out I thought that in this old room of the farmhouse they resembled a painting of men quaffing ale in a tap room in the reign of Charles the First.

'Take no notice of Charles,' said Sheila when Charles's laughter rang out again loud and long. 'He was at the dandelion before you came.'

It was just one o'clock when Charles led me into the dining-room and we all sat down at the table. We had soup first of all and with the soup some more wine and, all the time, Charles kept on laughing.

'Charles!' said Sheila, 'behave yourself.'

'Ha, ha, ha,' choked Charles. 'I can't help it.'

Charles was still laughing when the leg of lamb came in, and he stood up to carve. When he began to put the slices on the plates he appeared to be convulsed with mirth. 'One of our own,' he choked; 'one of this year's lambs.'

Suddenly I felt the colour drain from my face and, apprehensively, I looked over at Martin. Martin was looking down at his plate and deliberately, it seemed, avoided my eye. I saw him, though, pushing his meat under his vegetables.

I looked at Sheila wonderingly and then she laughed too. 'Take no notice of Charles,' she said again, 'he is always like this after dandelion wine.'

I went through a pretence of eating, but my plate was so untouched that I had to plead an acute headache and, as soon as we could, we left.

As Martin slipped the car into gear and we began to move away my tears began to flow. 'Don't be so silly, Becca,' Martin tried to sound convincing. 'Old Charles wouldn't do a thing like that.'

'B-b-but,' I choked, 'why was he laughing. He laughed more than ever when he carved the lamb.'

'It was the dandelion wine; you heard what Sheila said.'

'But she began laughing too. Why did they laugh like that? Oh! Martin.'

As I wiped my streaming eyes I looked out of the window and, on my side of the car I could see a field of sheep.

'Martin,' I cried, urgently, 'stop the car!'

Martin pulled up quickly and looked out.

'Isn't this one of Charles's fields?'

'Yes, it is.' Martin opened his door and got out.

In a flash I, too, was out and we both leaned over the gate. I had to blow my nose very heartily and clear my throat, but at last I was able to call. 'Baby, Baby, come to mother.'

Some of the sheep stopped their grazing and lifted their heads for a moment, their jaws working as they chewed and stared. 'Baby,' I called again, 'come to mother.' Once again the sheep, with blank, unfocused eyes, stared at me.

'Come on,' Martin pulled my arm, 'she will have forgotten you by now.'

I looked up at him in anguish. 'Baby! Forgotten me! You don't really mean that, do you? You think as I do that we have eaten her for lunch!'

'Nonsense,' Martin's voice sounded miserable. He went round the car to get in; as he walked he turned to have one last look. 'Wait a minute!' he said, then he hurried back to the gate. He took a deep breath: 'HEY YOU, STOMACH!' he yelled at the top of his voice. I leaned out of the window and stared earnestly across the field.

As I looked, a large fat matronly figure from far across the other side gave a glad cry of 'Ma-ma,' and, at a most undignified lope, headed towards the gate.

'Come on, Stomach,' said Martin, 'come to Dad!' He turned to where I was now standing beside him; he dragged a packet of cigarettes from his pocket in readiness for Baby's arrival.

'Look at that,' Martin's voice was thick with emotion. 'Dear old Stomach knows her Dad.'

– From *A Lamb in the Lounge*.

PART SEVEN

A Nest in the Country

Country Etiquette For Mother

VIRGINIA GRAHAM

Humouring the Hostess

It is well to remember that although the ostensible purpose of your visit to the country is that you should enjoy yourself, society imposes limits on the amount of enjoyment you can reasonably expect, and it is etiquette here, as in other spheres, for joy to be paid for. An effort, however small, to be companionable and indeed useful to your hostess will earn her lasting gratitude, for although she may have asked you down 'to have a good rest', it will not have been her intention that you should lie speechless, in a torpor, for forty-eight hours. Either she will have other guests to whom it is expected you should pass a remark every now and then or else, living as she does during the week solely in the company of cocker spaniels, she may need verbal encouragement herself . . .

Remember the houses of others are invariably much colder than your own, even if the thermometer states otherwise, and the richer the hosts the colder the house. This does not mean, however, that ladies should wear cardigans over their evening dresses or balaclavas at breakfast. Neither does it mean that guests are at liberty to shut windows or light fires. The temperature of a house is sacred to its owners and should on no account be mentioned except in the privacy of the bedroom. This applies also to the bath water. If a hostess, knowing she has taken all the hot water, says: 'I'm afraid, darling, you had an ice-cold bath?' it is then just permissible to reply in the crypto-affirmative, *i.e.*: 'No, honestly, it was awfully nearly hot enough.' This is what is known, quite simply, as good manners and, though perfectly useless thermostatically speaking, maintains that atmosphere of goodwill so necessary in human relationships.

It will be the firm intention of your hosts to take you, as soon as possible, *away* from their homes. Remember, they do not know what on earth to do with you and have been arguing about it for weeks, so do not be difficult and announce that all you want to do is to sit still and look at the view. They are irrevocably determined you should be entertained, and it is a matter of little importance whether you wish to be or whether you don't. In point of fact, life being what it is in the country, it is they who wish for entertainment and the perfect guest provides the perfect excuse. So be prepared for all sorts of pursuits, probably far removed from your interests and certainly far removed from an armchair, and enter into the spirit of them with grace if not with pleasure.

Pleasuring the Horse

If you have to give a horse a lump of sugar or a slice of carrot, see that it is placed strictly in the centre of the palm of the hand and keep your thumb well back. Owing to the extraordinary length of a horse's nose and the curious position of its eyes, it cannot really see what it is doing and imbibes nourishment by touch system. Sugar, carrots and thumbs are all one to it until they are actually in the mouth when, presumably, they taste differently, so keep the digits as much together as possible so as to form an oblong pink plate. Few horses have eaten a whole hand in one mouthful.

Deforestation

There may come a moment when you will be invited to dismember a birch tree with a pair of secateurs. On no account should you lay a finger on an axe, neither should you attempt to blaze a trail or open up a vista, for it is a gentleman's prerogative to destroy, and there is nothing more irritating for him than to see a lady cutting down a large tree with the best axe, particularly if she is doing this speedily and accurately. A lady's place in forestry, as well as in all other human experiences, is in the rear, clearing up the mess left by the gentlemen.

Hunting

A meet can be one of the loveliest sights in the world, but it is curious how often it takes place in a blizzard. The main thing to strive for, as a pedestrian, is balance. To be too much in the centre of things is to get kicked. To be cowering behind a car is to invite scorn. The very best position to assume is half-way up the bank of a ditch with a small, low car stationed just in front. Leaning the elbows on the roof of this modest rampart it is possible to converse with those on horseback without coming in contact with any part of the horse. If, however, at any time a horse should show an unquenchable desire to suck the sleeve of your coat, it must be permitted to do so, within reason. Reason stops when it uses its teeth . . .

In no circumstances whatever should a fox be invited into a car, as this not only muddies the rugs but also wrecks the fox's day.

Hounds are never called Rover or Jock like other dogs, but are christened more with an eye to alliteration than to any individual characteristic; thus in one pack you may have everything from Daphne to Dreadnought, and in another anything from Maud to Majestic. It is a rare pleasure for a lady to be able to look fearlessly into the eyes of another lady, even though she be on four legs, and say loudly and clearly: 'Bitch!'

Shooting

The real reason why ladies go out shooting is that they follow the food, few hostesses being either willing or able to provide a meal at home as well as a meal *al fresco*. Shooting lunches are invariably good, but never fail to be draughty . . .

After luncheon the gentlemen, flushed but usually able to stand, take up positions in various exposed parts of the landscape, and it is etiquette that there should then crouch beside them at least one female.

Ladies are sometimes hit on the head by moribund birds and almost always hit on the nose by expended cartridge cases. They are also often trodden on by a gentleman seeking to take a high bird, and they are sometimes, though seldom, shot dead by the gentleman next door. There is no pleasure, however, without a spice of danger, and the sound of feathered bodies bouncing on the ground, the smell of gunpowder and the beauty of the wintry trees lashing themselves against the steel-grey sky should be sufficient reward for any perils endured.

Fishing

In the case of fly-fishing a gentleman often places himself thigh-deep in the middle of a river and all that a lady can do is to sit on the bank and look . . . As a gentleman will stay anything up to three hours in the water, a lady must have some very beautiful thoughts to sustain her meanwhile, and frankly it is only she who deems each movement of the beloved's wrist a thing of joy, and each little puff from his pipe as part of some divine plan, who can survive the appalling ennui of such a vigil.

Occasionally a gentleman will allow a non-angling lady to 'have a go', and it is then etiquette, when the line is dangling weakly two inches out from the bank, for the lady to hook the largest fish that has ever been seen in the Dee since 1892. Unfortunately it is not etiquette for a lady to land this fish. Many attempts have been made to keep hold of the rod. . . . 'Damn you, I hooked it and I'm going to land it or lose it, I don't care which, but it's MINE!' As in all purely physical battles between the sexes, however, the gentleman, if he dare be so called, wins . . . Ladies have to be very much in love to stand this sort of thing, and many a romance has thus swirled away down the rocky path of a Scottish river to be lost in the soulless sea.

At the Dance

There is no sadder time in a lady's life than when she is staying in a house in which a dance is being given. During the long day before the night, while the furniture is being rearranged and room after room becomes uninhabitable, it is borne in upon her that even in the unlikely event of her enjoying the damned thing, the very last guests – yes, even the one who is doing tricks with a champagne bottle and the other who has just drunk its contents – must have left the house before she can go to bed. Time and again during the evening she will find herself sitting out with a gentleman on two gilt chairs planted exactly outside her bedroom door, but though she may gaze wistfully at its panels, and even perhaps fondle its knob, she must never, never cross the threshold. Down she has to go again into the confusion, into the *macédoine* of strange faces and convivial noises, while up here, separated by a plank of eau-de-nil wood, there is a little pool of quiet in which doze the old familiars; the toothbrush, never before so dear; the hot water bottle in its shabby cover; the nightgown; the softly ticking travelling clock . . .

Mothers of daughters who have just come out should take particular care to disregard their young, and should these disappear for several hours must remain in a state of refined coma on chairs near the band. Gone are the days when mothers could have six suppers in succession, and they must be thankful when an elderly beau brings them a bridge roll stuffed with meat paste, leaning, on the same plate, against an emerald green jelly. Manual and facial signs to their offspring should be studiously avoided, for mothers are always irksome things and when, by pointing meaningly at their own shoulder-straps or ostentatiously fluffing out their greying hair, they seek to draw their children's attention to straying underclothes and plastered fringes, they are too tedious for any words. However, though maternal contact is undesirable, should a daughter's knickers fall off in the ballroom a mother is permitted to fold them up and put them in her bag.

On Giving in Gracefully

There are burning loves that can consume all hazards in their paths, and when a lady sees that her daughter is adamantly resolved to marry the stoker on the 9.15 to Carlisle and that nothing she can say or do will stop her, then let her give in gracefully. Grace is a virtue which a lady would be wise to hold on to. Let it go for a moment and she becomes a woman, which, as any woman will tell you, is a very depressing thing to be. Thus shall a lady, the last bridge burned, the last raft sunk, go down with colours flying and take into her arms the stoker with his dear, black face. Let her pronounce him, loudly, from every convenient housetop, to be an absolute treasure, and let there be no nonsense about going to bed with flu on the day of the wedding, no words of recrimination, no tearful warnings, and no sobbing on the bosoms of talkative friends. The courageous acceptance of inevitable disaster is always becoming, particularly when the two main tragedians are quite certain the disaster is delightful.

Humouring the Aged

It is etiquette to be courteous to the aged, however offensive or tiresome they may be, and though they may slander your friends, dismiss your servants and beat your children with hard malacca canes, no word of censure must be permitted to pass your lips. The reward for this unnatural restraint comes when you yourself reach the age of indiscretion; the age when you no longer fear the censure of others or care a hoot in hell for their opinions; when being kind is no longer a matter of expediency or are manners the stepping-stones to success. On that joyful day when you realise that you are too old to worry about anything except the next meal, you in your turn can cast off the trappings of polite society and be free to express the sentiments you so patiently damned when you were younger.

In order not to rob the aged of these long-awaited pleasures it is kinder not to assume that they are mentally deficient or decrepit. Although theoretically it is etiquette to wait upon them hand and foot, to heave them out of chairs and pick up their glasses when they drop them, in practice the old prefer to have to *ask* you to help them should they desire to be helped, thereby implying you are extremely thoughtless and don't care whether they break their necks or not. This is much more fun for them. They *like* saying: 'Shut the window, dear, you know I can't stand a draught!', and it is a cruel disappointment to them if you remember to keep it closed. It is a moot point, of course, whether it is more fun to be assisted from a chair and to say crossly: 'Thank you, but I'm not paralysed *yet!*' or to be left struggling until one is forced to cry: 'Joan, I really *do* think you might help me!' Both systems have their advocates.

Declining Invitations

After reaching a certain age it is legitimate to throw etiquette to the winds and be frank. In society, and indeed out of it, frankness is considered very bad-mannered, and that is why one has to be of a certain age before one attempts so drastic a measure . . . Then, in a voice nicely balanced between self-depreciation and arrogance, one can cay: 'No, Jane! It is sweet of you, but you know how stupid I am? I simply loathe the country in the winter and nothing on earth will make me come to Norfolk in November! I'm sorry, darling. I love you, but NO' . . .

Remember that to get a name for not going out means that eventually you will not be asked out. This is rather a bore, for the whole charm of life lies in being asked everywhere and going nowhere. When you are a very old lady living in one tiny room with only one tiny frayed aspidistra for company, you may wish you *had* gone to Norfolk after all and kept up with dear Jane, who is still being photographed blowing, with her last remaining breaths, down a hunting horn at local Hunt Balls.

– From *Say Please*.

Dear Back of Beyond

WENDY WOOD

There is no road leading into or out of our glen. A bridle track, in places too rough for a horse, runs five miles through the woods to our nearest road, and ten miles in the opposite direction along the side of the loch, to the nearest railway station. In lieu of a shop, we have a store that collects the rations by boat, and for all else that we require we must send by post (sixpence postage for a shilling's worth of meat!) or take the train for thirty-five miles, which computation does not include the ten miles to the station.

There is no resident nurse, and the doctor can be procured only when the 'phone is working, which is not always, and if the weather permits, which is not always either. The doctor, even in peacetime, is fifteen miles away. There is no pipewater supply, no drainage, no lighting. The rates are low, but if they were low enough to represent the service given, they would be nil.

The first night in the house was exciting. It was a strange feeling to be sole occupiers in a deserted glen after twilight had fallen. The stream sounded now loud and clear, now dull and far, and the white schist rocks on the hills caught the light and jumbled one's sense of distance . . . I was tired and sat idle before the peat fire. Suddenly I heard the pipes! I jumped up and ran to the door.

It was pitch-black outside, it looked like the edge of the world, but I expected to be able to detect the piper from the direction of the sound; instead, the pipes now sounded inside the very room from which I had just stepped! They sounded, not as an echo, but with that birling and bummelling that results from small space, and the tune was 'The Barren Rocks of Aden'. I stepped inside again, and imme-

[320]

diately could have declared that the piper was outside and striding past the window. When I went out, the roaring was in the house again. The pipes did not exactly stop playing, but I ceased to hear them, which is different. I was shaking, not with a nasty kind of fear, but with a realisation of the weirdness of hearing pipes within a few feet of oneself and seeing no piper.

In the morning I made furtive inquiries, and learned that there were no pipes in the glen, except a set with no bag, but that the father and the two sons who had lived in this house were all pipers, and the tune that I had heard was the deceased old man's favourite. I felt a sense of gratitude for this news that seemed a token of welcome, and knew that in future I should not mind being alone in the house at night when necessary.

Our first 'stock' consisted of a cow and a calf. There were ten rocky miles to bring that cow, while her calf was in the rowing-boat coming down the loch to be at this end to meet her. As the affair could not be explained to the cow, she and Mac had a misunderstanding, which developed into a rodeo. She threw him and he threw her, and there was a time when both of them were wallowing in the river up to their waistcoats. They arrived after some hours at the harbour here, having shaken hands, so to speak, and Mac humped the calf in a creel on his back the extra mile and a half from the village.

The calf was a half-highlander, tawny and shaggy, with a snub nose below his French fringe, and with thick-set legs made for hill-climbing and – obstinacy. When he was let loose for exercise, I thought we had seen the last of him. He dashed full-gallop ahead as if he would not pull up before John o'Groats, throwing his hind legs away to left and right as though he had no further use for them.

As he grew older, he became a perfect clown and could often be found wandering about with his food bucket on top of his head and cocked over one eye, like the top-hat of an inebriated *roué*.

As we brought Julie the cow home that evening, I remember the quiet scene. Not a breath disturbed the matted heather, its undulations sweeping up the hills, broken only by the black peat-stacks and slabs of grey rock. From horizon to horizon seemed unusually wide; twice that amount of sky would have resembled eternity. Space seemed power, and the sound of a coming footfall almost a sacrilegious disturbance.

'This will be your new cow,' said a neighbour, passing, and added: 'Well, God's blessing on her.'

The first time I milked was a more thrilling affair than it need have been. I had managed a 'spurt' or two under Mac's surveillance, but I was not ready to take over on the night that he was detained across the hill. I sat anxiously watching the clock. The moon rose; milking-time came. I waited. He would come any minute. The hand of the clock spun round; he was already one hour late! How long could one leave a cow? Why hadn't I asked? I would wait another half-hour. At the end of that time I visualised the cow spraying milk like a fire appliance, so I lit the stable lantern, and, feeling very 'pioneer', I grabbed the milk bucket and cautiously made out the tough track to the byre. It was very lonely in the bigness of the outside dark, with the only details of reality crowded round my feet in the small circle of the lantern's light, and I was quite glad to see the byre and anticipate the company of the cow. I banged my head going in, being unused to low lintels. Mac declares that all the out-buildings here were built by a race of dwarfs, but the hefty job of carrying building stones is the real reason.

Under the thick thatch was the most awful silence. The breathing of that solitary beast (the calf was in another outhouse) sounded like a blacksmith's bellows. The shadow of her horns looked like Auld Nick and jumped about in the flicker of the lantern. Moreover, the cow did not add to my efforts at placidity, for she turned her head round and snorted at me. It was not a reassuring gesture. The milk-stool, when I had descended on to it, seemed uncommonly low, and the bulk of the cow looming above me quite preposterous! I never before realised the vast girth of a cow.

The milk came slowly. I suppose she knew the amateur touch. My wrists ached, I had frequently to take rests, and each time I stopped she turned a pair of huge eyes on me, like a schoolmistress with horn-rimmed spectacles reproaching one's ineptitude. Still, I was getting milk out of a cow. I looked at the pail more than half full of frothy creamy milk, and I thought of the comical little bottles I had so often lifted from the doorstep in towns.

From that time on, I began to take a personal interest in the cow, or, I should say, an interest in the cow as a person, as a smooth-coated producer of milk, milk that gave cream, cream that made butter – not a rationed marble, but a big dishful. I didn't mind churning (I had taken my turn at it at an early age), and I could have been happy all day patting the piles of golden butter, modelling it into mountainous landscapes, and smashing it back into a big solid block.

We are delighted when people bang in on our remoteness, and if they do not do it often enough, then we have to bang out of it. For this variety one goes for the day shopping to 'the Garrison', as Fort William is still called.

Tea is put in the thermos and the calves' food prepared overnight. The alarm is set for 4 a.m. By the light of the candle we reheat the food on the oil stove, and then stagger, still blinking with sleep, out into the wet fields. Always one's eyes search seawards for 'the isles', often lying as if themselves asleep, like a drowsy seabird riding an ocean swell. Frequently there will be a drizzle of rain, and as you search for a footing in the slippery places, you heartily wish you were not bothering to go. The huge declivity that leads the ten miles to the station is a black cauldron of alarming mystery; bed is sensible and warm, and you could have a real breakfast leisurely and late with the milking done. There is no sound at this hour of bellowing calves – they are too sleepy – and the surprised cows are lying down, their big sides rising and falling to a slow rhythm. They have to be harshly prodded with the toe before they will rise. The light of the lantern is not bright enough to keep one properly awake. Automatically we squeeze and pull at the teats, and the ping and splash of the milk into the pails is a lullaby. Dreamily I try to remember that we must hurry: it is after four o'clock, double summer time. What a thought! I stop milking.

'Mac,' I call wickedly, 'do you realise that by the *real* time it is only two o'clock in the morning?' Mac's hands stop too. There is silence, then Mac grunts. It is surprising how much disgust, disapproval, and resignation can be intermixed and conveyed in a grunt. Milking continues, buckets bang, the calves are fed. On the way back to the house we are awake enough to feel the freshness of the air on our faces and in our lungs. The sea is now silver-streaked beside Eigg. The pony whinnies as she is untethered and saddled. Inside the candle-lit house the milk is hurriedly sieved, town clothes are donned and covered by oilskins, town shoes pushed into the haversack, and an empty potato-sack tied on behind the saddle for purchases. Milk for the cats, porridge for the dog, out goes the candle, the door is banged. We're off – and hungry again already.

The pony strives willingly up the steep, rough paths, and whichever of us is walking is glad to grab a stirrup. Up and down, switchback, runs the track, so steep and rocky on the downgrade sometimes that one has to dismount and let the pony pick her own way and do her own slides, while we do ours according to our talents and our tackets. As we turn the corner of Bealach Brec, the loch far below catches the first yellowish light of real day and we hurry – for clocks can be slow and the train might be early. The pony is hastily stabled when we reach the inn, a cheque changed (we have no use for coinage in the glen, except for telephone or church) – a whistle – the train! Run, run, up the embankment, along the sleepers – what an awkward distance apart they place the things! The train is moving – she's away – no – the driver has seen us – she is pulling up again – thank goodness! We tumble in, panting. Arriving in the dining-car is a *ceilidh* in itself. 'Hello, Seumas, have you the verse of that song yet? There's the ambulance lady. There's the man from Mallaig I wanted to see.' So we hop about from seat to seat. As the train puffs across the viaduct at the head of Loch Shiel, we look down upon the statue of the Prince, thinking of a far sunrise. History, here, is ever between the finger and thumb.

The Garrison seems smaller than usual, because it has so many extra people in it. We have a meal. What wee marbles of butter, what a pickle of milk and no cream! We hurry to the shops, enjoying looking at the variety in the windows. We get cow-chains, a bridle-buckle, alum to cure rabbit skins, a rope (it is heavy – it will go on the saddle), a rake (it will catch in every tree on the way home), and two new books. We always get two so that we each have something to read, and we always end by reading one between us at a time.

When I am in a town, even a small one, I realise how much I have absorbed of the country. The intense blue of the isles, the surge of the sea, the sorrow of the seabirds, the mystery of the woods, and the breadth of outdoor darkness. All these things and more become part of one's being when one is a companion in nature's work with them. I do not think it can be acquired by looking on. The train journey home with laughter and song, a happy *ceilidh* at Lochailort Inn, where friendship is no burden and doors no barriers, and out into the black night when the lamps are being lit. When it is so dark that I cannot see the road, Mac and the pony can; when (and the occasion is rare) Mac cannot see, the pony can, so he steps behind, holding on to her tail. At first we sing, feeling awake and fresh, then a silence comes, drowsiness descends, we get slower and not so warm. I walk to heat myself while Mac rides, and so we come after midnight to our half-way rest house, a friend's haybarn. The warm, soft comfort of it, the summer meadowsweet smell of it! The pony rolls in the field; we sleep.

In the morning we are hailed: 'Hello, Mac and Wendy, there's a hot cup of tea waiting for you inside the house.' Again the intense pleasure of meeting people for whom you feel a warm affection – there are few enjoyments in the world to match it.

Early morning finds us at the hill gate, gazing down at our own strath, seeing the brown dots of our cattle on the hill, and the speckle of the brown and white calves bunched on a knoll. The cat comes to meet us, the dog is barking a welcome in the house; the pony whinnies – she, too, is home.

We chew the cud of our visit to the Garrison for two or three days, sizing up the characters we met, turning over the conversations we heard, till we have extracted all the interest, wisdom, and enjoyment possible. It is not exactly a rest, but it certainly is a holiday.

– From *Mac's Croft*.

Victorian Garden

H. E. BATES

Looking back into childhood, I remember August gardens with affection. There used to be a garden enclosed by stone walls above the white cliffs of a stone-pit, which had been planted with fruit trees and was sheltered on the far side with pines. The house was kept by an old lady with a thousand-and-one dogs, and we went there in August at fruit-time. Whenever I read the country stories of Turgenev, with their settings of country houses, dogs, sleepy orchards and the dew of summer on the grass, I think of this house. It comes back to me as a period piece of the year 1840, or perhaps 1850, or 1870; it hardly matters. It was square, stone, flat, unpretentious. There was a verandah, on which the thousand-and-one dogs and the few tortoise-shell cats went to sleep. Venetian blinds of pale coffee colour were lowered on hot August afternoons; a cream and crimson sun-curtain hung at the front door, flapping above red pots of blue agapanthus flowers on the porch. Round the garden there was a high stone wall, and round the walls were fields of corn; but within the wall, and perhaps even more within the walls of the house, there was an atmosphere which went back beyond the American Civil War, the Crimea, the accession of Queen Victoria, and perhaps beyond the beginning of the nineteenth century. It was atmosphere that was not merely a compound of associations; it was an atmosphere in reality, an air, a definite but indefinable odour. It had something to do with mahogany furniture, with moulded white cornices of drawing-rooms, with silver-watered wallpaper, with curtains of heavy straw-berry rep at the windows; it had much to do with the odour of heavy carpets, of paraffin lamps, the smell of linen, the queer but pleasant smell of sun-warmed dust and sun-warmed air of closed rooms; it had something to do with comfort and a modest prosperity; and in August it had, above all, something to do with the fragrance of fruit and flowers that poured into the shadowy rooms from the garden outside. It seemed like an atmosphere which had been constant, perhaps unchanged for fifty or a hundred years; you could not tell; it had, perhaps, not changed since Gilbert White pottered round those prolific August cucumber frames at Selborne.

This garden was much less remarkable for flowers than fruit. Yet its flowers stand out in memory. I see large red satin hollyhocks by the wall, cream roses – perhaps Gloire de Dijon and William Allen Richardson – on the house. There is a greenhouse: a scarlet flash of amaryllis through the glass. There is a green rose on the lawn. And through the trees in August the glorious orange trumpets of vegetable marrows glow underneath the silvery branches of honesty that are hung with papery seeds. Larkspurs are bright blue against the scarlet arches of runner beans; gaillardias are as if cut out of scarlet and orange Indian blankets. Old phloxes, small-flowered, mauvy-pink, dead white, are scattered among blue cornflowers. The colours everywhere are wrong according to correct standards, and yet somehow right. Orange and lemon and tangerine and occasional cream nasturtiums cover the ground under the old Victoria plum trees; African marigolds are like orange sponges, strong and almost harsh in the sun; scarlet geraniums are spilt like blood on the distances. But above everything stand the dahlias: pot-hatted, huge, commanding. In some quarters they are despised. From this garden I recall a great lemon cactus like a giant yellow sea-anemone that had something Chinese about it; I see the stiff Victorian little pompoms, like mauve and crimson and speckled honeycomb; the fat, flamboyant doubles like scarlet suns. The whole garden is a jumble, ill-planned; trees and flowers grow together; the yellow August plums, carved down to the stone by wasps, fall among the pinks, the catmint, the flowerless arabis; sunflowers rise far above the apricots on the high south wall.

Over everything there is a smell of ripened corn and fruit and dead-ripe grass, all the warm juiciness of late summer. In the hollow of the stone-pit, where the trees have struggled up to a great height, there is a smell of pines on heavy days; the pears are columns of gold. There is a small, pure yellow plum, rather square, turning when fully ripe to the reddish-gold shade of an apricot, that comes in with harvest. You split it open with your fingers, and it falls in half as if cut by a knife – clean, running with golden juice, aromatic and sweet like thin honey. Siberian crabs are filling out to the size of cherries, and will later turn even more scarlet; Bramleys and Blenheims strain down heavily against the props under their branches. Everywhere there are fallen plums in the grass, the savage hum of wasps, big peacock butterflies, drowsy on leaves and flowers. There are still a few golden gooseberries that you can crush on your palate like grapes, feeling the spurt of half-sweet seeds on your tongue. There are still a few raspberries, but mostly the birds have torn away the pink flesh, leaving only bare nipples among the leaves. There are still a few red currants and a few white, perhaps, under creamy ragged bird-scares that look as if they had been cut out of the old lady's chemise. The asparagus has a touch of gold; the cucumbers curve like green bananas. If there has been a wind in the night, you crush fallen fruit wherever you walk, and the old lady walks with you, quaking and whittling and muttering what a shame it is, what a shame, and the thousand-and-one dogs walk with the old lady, sniffing in the golden grass among the fallen fruit for the smell of a rabbit. Everything, from the fattest Bramley on the highest bough down to the rottenest honey-combed pear in the grass, is sacred. Everything is precious: everything is wrong. The fruit is glorious, but the wind blows it down. The fruit hangs on, but is eaten by wasps and birds. The weather is dull and the wasps are scarce: you hire a man to shoot the birds; but somehow the boys have been over the wall again, and – oh, dear! what are we going to do?

The old lady is deaf and talks in a whisper. She quakes so much you think her hands will drop off. There is a bit of a moustache on her lip, and she wears a pocket on a black silk cord . . . It is 1915 or 1815 or perhaps even 1715; in that sun-soaked garden in mid-August you could never tell. There is trouble in the world, but it means nothing. All the trouble in the world will not equal the trouble of gathering the fruit, combating the wasps, thwarting the scrumping boys. The old lady quivers and quakes throughout the long tour of fruit-scattered grass, hand to ear, striking sometimes at the dogs with the cord of her purse, shaking her head, bowed down by trouble. Beyond the wall the corn has been cut, and now the rooks are on the corn. No business of hers, of course, but – oh, dear! oh, dear! more trouble. From time to time it is necessary for the old lady to be bellowed at, and this sound hits the air like the echo of a gunshot, startling a flock of starlings from the farthest tree of pears. More trouble! The Lord giveth, but the Lord taketh away.

The old lady and the dogs dissolve at last into mellow distances. A deep August silence, amplified by the sound of wasps that seem to be burning their way everywhere into fallen and unfallen fruit, comes down again, heavy and drugging. It is hot in the hollow against the limestone. On stony ledges, which suit the fruit-trees so well, there are dwarf thistles, mauve scabious, many butterflies. I do not seem to recall a buddleia in the garden, but, if it was there, it, too, would be covered in August with Tortoise-shells, Painted Ladies, Red Admirals, Peacocks. Moths would charge softly through the August dusk as we gave up at last the gathering of fruit and went back to the house, to pick up again that atmosphere of dust warmed by sun throughout the hot day, the smell of dogs, of paraffin and candles; the air of linen and mahogany; the air of comfort that should be trivial but is for some reason persistent and perhaps imperishable. Moths fly into the house, towards the lamp, from the silent garden; they are heavy, fur-brown, dusted; or they are cream, pure milk-white, delicate, like thistledown. The scent of tobacco-flowers is strong on the evening air; the leaves of the house geraniums are strong-odoured. The dogs lie under the tables, quiet after the day, and the white horse that is waiting for us outside, tethered to the verandah-post, begins to look vague, like cotton, as I peer out of the window into the falling darkness. There seem to be many clocks in the house, and they strike ten one after another. There is a dark plum cake on the plush tablecloth under the ornate brass lamp, and a glass of rose-coloured rhubarb wine.

This old, dark house, with the coffee-coloured Venetian blinds and the garden rich with fruit and untidy flowers, probably accounts for my affection for August gardens; and because we never went there

[329]

except when the weather was fine or was going to be fine there remains a constant happy impression of heat and sunlight. It was a large, beautiful, half-wild paradise.

– From *The Country Heart*.

On Brensham Hill

JOHN MOORE

The way to the hill from Elmbury took us through Brensham Village, which was long and straggling and ran in a semicircle more or less coincident with one of the lower contours. The houses were mostly half-timbered, with deep straw thatch, and their gardens were full of old-fashioned flowers, hollyhocks and peonies, sweet-williams and rambler roses, red-hot-pokers and love-lies-bleeding. There was a scent of gillyflowers which I remember still; so that whenever I smell it I think of Brensham.

There was a church with a tall spire, beside which three poplars grew, and spaced through the village at decent intervals there were three pubs, the 'Horse and Harrow', the 'Trumpet', and the 'Adam and Eve'. The 'Horse and Harrow' was locally spoken of as the 'Horse Narrow', which was confusing to strangers and had certainly confused the itinerant artist who had painted its inn-sign; for he had represented with meticulous accuracy a horse and an arrow. Nobody minded; nobody suggested taking the sign down and altering it, or making the artist paint a new one. The thing was a good joke; so much the better. That was the Brensham attitude and, looking back upon it now, I can see that it was typical of Brensham, where the people are humorous and tolerant and crack-brained and wise.

The 'Adam and Eve' also had its painted sign. The artist this time had given full value for money; the tree, the forbidden fruit (undoubtedly a Cox's Orange Pippin), the serpent, the two naked figures, all were there in careful detail. If you looked closely you perceived that Eve's face wore a look of mischievous and disingenuous delight, not to say satisfaction; clearly she had eaten the apple and enjoyed it. But there were some who said that the model for Eve had been the red-

[331]

headed wanton little puss of a barmaid who served in the pub when the artist was staying there.

In the middle of the village was a turning off the road, called Magpie Lane, which led to the cricket-field and also to the Colonel's farm. Along this lane were a lot of little cottages which belonged to the Colonel; and I shall never forget my astonishment when I saw a number of small girls, who were the daughters of the cottagers, curtsy to the Colonel as he passed by on his motor-bike. He waved back, and his blue eyes twinkled. I had never seen a curtsy before; it was an enchanting sight, the small girls in their print frocks clutching the hem and bobbing, and the grotesque and wonderful old man waving back, at some peril to his stability, as he chugged by on his fantastical machine. It seemed to me entirely proper that he should receive these marks of respect; and I tugged hard at the peak of my school-cap as he went by.

Immediately opposite Magpie Lane was Mrs Doan's Post Office and Village Stores, which sold almost everything from fish-hooks to corn-plasters. The only commodities, however, which concerned us in those days were huge and tiger-striped bull's-eyes, so indestructible that you could use them for marbles; and elastic for catapults. Mrs Doan's elastic was very thick, and square in section; surely it must have been made specially for catapults by some manufacturer with the heart of a boy, for I cannot imagine any other use for it. Nor, I think, could Mrs Doan; and since she strongly disapproved of the slaughter of birds, she had to invent an elaborate fiction to the effect that we employed our catapults for the purpose of shooting at tin-cans. 'Now, remember, no *live* targets,' she would say. 'You will get just as much fun shooting at empty bottles; but you must take care not to cut yourselves with the broken glass.' Then she would quote to us a Victorian rhyme:

> If Human Beings only knew
> What sorrows little birds went through
> I think that even boys
> Would never think it sport or fun
> To fire a nasty horrid gun
> Only for the *noise*.

'Of course,' she would say, 'I know that catapults are silent; but this elastic is *very strong*, and if you hit a poor little fluffy bird with a stone you might hurt it *very badly*.' It was all we could do to keep our faces straight; we whose catapult-handles each bore a score of notches. And I don't think Mrs Doan really succeeded in believing her tin-can fiction. She sold us the stuff reluctantly, rather in the manner of the Apothecary selling the poison to Romeo: 'My poverty, but not my will, consents.' 'It's very *strong*,' she would say hesitantly. And so it was. The Elmbury shops sold nothing like it, and offered us instead strips of narrow pink stuff which might have served, we thought, for a girl's garters. We were shocked and insulted and thereafter we put up with her admonitions and dealt exclusively with Mrs Doan, whose square-sided cattie-lackey was as black as liquorice and so strong that when you pulled it back to have a shot you felt like a longbowman at the Battle of Agincourt.

When you started to climb the hill you left the half-timbering behind; the village still straggled along beside the steep path, but the cottages were built of limestone quarried a few hundred yards away, and the hedges gradually gave place to stone walls. Then you came to the end of the path and to the last cottage, which was inhabited by an old man with a wooden leg and a long beard. He kept in his garden a billy-goat which also had a long beard. We called him Goaty Pegleg, and thought of him as the hill's janitor, for he was almost always to be found leaning on the gate at the road's end. If he were feeling good-humoured he opened the gate for us; and we went through into a rough chalky field full of furze-bushes, ragwort, thistles, and rabbits. A stony cart-track led upwards towards the quarries, the banks covered with scrub and bramble, the hanging woods of oak, sycamore, and ash, and the larch plantation on the hilltop, with the round pre-posterous tower of Brensham Folly just showing above the feathery top of the conifers.

This was the unexplored jungle, the unclimbed mountain, the unmapped hinterland!

There were no hoopoes nor golden orioles, it is true; but there was a pair of merlin falcons, and before our amazed eyes a *brown* jackdaw flew away among the black ones which with loud clacking and chatter rose from the old quarries. We saw no fire-crested wrens, but plenty of goldcrests in the larch-plantations. And there also, while we watched and waited for we knew not what, we heard a patter as light as falling leaves, and held our breath while three dappled shadows cantered by, paused among the bracken, became for a moment substantial in the sunlight as they twitched velvet ears and noses, and then suddenly in a panic and flurry of delicate legs rejoined the trees' lacy shadows and so vanished. The Mad Lord's fallow-deer still roamed Brensham Hill.

The Mad Lord, whose wife had died, had a daughter of about our own age, a pale-faced, wide-eyed, flaxen-haired child called Jane, whom we encountered from time to time during our walks on the hill. She soon became friendly and at ease with us, and one day she informed us, to our great astonishment: 'I have an ancestor who lives in a sort of jam-jar. I only show him to my special friends. You can come and see him if you like.' We followed her down by a rough scrambling path to the Mad Lord's house on the side of the hill, where she obtained from her easy-going nurse a large and important-looking key and led us down the garden to a very peculiar building which she told us was the private chapel. (It had been designed, we learned later, by the second Lord Orris who had made a Grand Tour and had been greatly impressed by Venice.) She unlocked the door and took a candle and a box of matches off the shelf. 'We're going down to the family vault,' she said. 'Hardly anybody goes there except relations'. She held the candle above her head to light our way down some wet slippery steps into a place of cavernous darkness which was full of cobwebs and the rustle of bats and which had a queer damp smell. At the far end of it was an oaken door with a heavy padlock; she nodded towards it and said: 'I've never been through there; but I know what's in it. Can you guess?'

We said we couldn't.

'*Coffins*,' said our young hostess. 'But I expect they're not worth seeing. They are all the dull ancestors. Robert, the exciting one, is here.'

She lifted the candle to show us a small recess in the stone wall, where there stood, not a jam-jar, but a beautiful urn, greeny-bronze in colour and very delicately fashioned. Hanging on the wall beneath it was a framed inscription in neat old-fashioned handwriting:

> This Urn contains the Heart and Viscera of Robert La Bruère who fell at the Siege of Acre in 1191.

Craning our necks we read above it another and later inscription:

> There is a tradition that Robert La Bruère distinguished himself in the Third Crusade, and was at one time a sort of aide-de-camp to Richard Cœur-de-Lion, and eventually met his death in combat with Saladin himself. His embalmed heart and viscera were brought home in 1214 after the failure of the Crusade. Having suffered various vicissitudes they were interred here in 1790.

'What's viscera?' we asked.

Jane gave us a superior look.

'Insides,' she said. 'But his heart's there as well. For all we know it might actually have a hole in it, where Saladin stuck him with his scimitar.'

It was our turn to be superior.

'Scimitars don't stick,' we said. 'They slice.'

'Well, then, with a slice out of it,' said Jane, tossing her head. 'Like a melon. Naturally we haven't looked. But I was allowed to hold the jar in my hands once ...'

We began to think very highly of Jane. 'Well, that's that,' she said, in a business-like tone. 'Good-bye, Robert.' She seemed to be on excellent terms with her ancestor. Then she held up the candle again and a bat's opening wings threw a huge and grotesque shadow on the roof, like that of a vampire; and Jane with scarcely a glance at it led us up the steps which were wet with green slime and showed us the way back through the garden-gate. Another wonder was added to Brensham, which was surely the only village where you could find the heart of a crusader.

– From *Brensham Village*.

Scented Memories

ALISON UTTLEY

Once I was walking in the Pyrenees, on a lower slope of a mountain, when I was arrested by the most ravishing perfume. I could see nothing in the green rocky country where I stood, no flower or tree, and the scent disappeared as I moved away; but I returned at once and searched closely in the grass. I hunted for some minutes, using my nose to find the perfume which was so elusive. Then I found a little flower, a wild mountain pink, a clump of alpines hidden in the rocks. It had a scent I had never experienced before, and I bent down to absorb this delicate fragrance. A few years later I was in a large store in Paris, overwhelmed by the variety of goods around me, and I suddenly had the feeling of the mountains, the pure air, the short grass under my feet, the presence of my companions and the guide; and so vivid was this scene I felt dazed and bewildered. The messenger that brought back the visible sight of the Pyrenees was a cake of soap, scented with *l'œillet*. The wild scented pink has a fragrance quite unlike the carnations and pinks in England, which have no effect of time-travelling on me; but details I had quite forgotten came to me in that great noisy store, and I seemed to stand under a vast sky, with shapes of peaks above me, seeing the rocky ground and narrow green track and the small mountain pink on its harebell stalk. The sense of smell acts so powerfully that it brings in its train not only the sight of objects associated with it and the sounds one heard at that time and place, but an enhanced perfume, as if buckets of fragrance were there. I might have been in a field of wild pinks.

A lily-of-the-valley with its fine perfume can carry the scent of the high valley woods, and the thousands of pale green bells that grew on those slopes under the trees, when we picked bunches of these flowers and carried them home. I grow in my present garden many lilies-of-the-valley and I fill my room with them at Whitsuntide, but only occasionally am I swept away by the scent to those woods of childhood. Other odours come into play of which I am ignorant, and I think the lilies must have the smell of certain trees and moss and grass to give the response and place-memory.

The bitter smell of rue as I rub the herb in my hands brings me the little grey-green bushes at the garden's end, where many herbs grew in a hot herb garden. I am translated to that place, in white pinafore, sitting back against the wall on the oak seat secluded in the green corner, hiding from everybody, while I enjoy the blazing sunshine, the birds and butterflies which haunt that place. Yet more than this is brought by the smell of rue. I feel some of the miseries of childhood, the frustrations and evasions, all mingled with the bliss of sun on bare arms, the song of the blackcaps, and the flight of the honey-bees and butterflies.

Heliotrope, or cherry pie, has its own special fragrance, and the scent of this purple flower first came to me when I was about twelve years old, so it has not the intensity of the earlier associations. The scene brought to my mind is the narrow peeping window that looked out on stable and barn, a window set in the thickness of the wall, with a wooden shutter for winter and no opening. It was very warm, a trap for the sunrays, and on the deep windowsill my mother kept her plants: maidenhair ferns, a white geranium, a scented geranium, a begonia with tiny pink flowers which grew to a large bush, and a wonderful aged tree with gnarled boughs and thick trunk, made into a dwarf by the Japanese. All were gifts from friends, and they came from hall and farmhouse, cottage and greenhouse, to be admired and treasured. We sniffed at the heliotrope, carefully standing away from it, for we had been told that our noses must never touch the tiny mauve blossoms, exquisite as fairy flowers, or the heliotrope would turn brown and die. It was no ordinary plant, but knowledge-able and aloof.

All these things I had forgotten until I bought a small plant one day at a local shop and the whiff of perfume came to sort everything out as if with a magic wand. The window with its geraniums, its maiden-hair like the tresses of a green mermaid, and the strange little ancient tree appeared in their corner, the dog was in his kennel, and the muslin-covered cushions lay on the couch under my hand.

I think it was Maeterlinck who said: 'The impression perfumes make upon us is so strong that if once associated with any remarkable event in life, whether joyful or sorrowful, the same perfume will, after long years, revive all the same sensations we at that time experienced.' It may be that a remarkable event is needed to make this association, but for me the most trivial incident of everyday life, forgotten and lost, is recalled by a scent, with all the potency of the first impression of that timeless world.

The scent of a hayfield, common enough in country places, never seems to lose its power of bringing to life other hayfields, and it always gives the sight of summer and little fields on the hills, of wooden rakes with long teeth, and the call of the distant men with the leading-cart. This smell of summer with its accompanying scene can be conjured up by the drying of a few flowers of the white woodruff, which is called 'new-mown hay'. The dead herb carries hayfields distilled in its withered petals and stalk. In the streets of a town, the sudden whiff of a country smell is a delight, and once I met a haycart in London, carrying its scent to hundreds of people as it lumbered along.

The smell of an unseen brewery always fascinates me, and on my first visit to Marlow, as I drove down the broad High Street to the Thames, I received this heavy rich odour, with no warning: so that for a timeless moment I was in a pony-trap instead of a car, sitting outside the stone fortress walls of the brewery, with ferns and running water by the side of the road, and the brewery behind the big doors near the water-wheel, and the smell of malt and hops permeating the country air.

The smell of roasting coffee is one of the pleasant aromas that brings no picture in its train. The smell of a good cigar has a childhood floating scarf attached to it, of an empty room, and cigar smoke lingering, and myself breathing it in with curiosity. Nobody smoked in our family, and this luxurious odour was treasured up, with the scent of the cedar-wood boxes.

[338]

The smell of Pears' soap, when I suddenly come across it, has the power to bring back a long series of associations, ordinary scenes, which are intensely alive; and indeed soap is a stimulus of the senses, even more potent than flower scent. Some years ago I had just arrived on a visit at a strange house, a Hall in the depths of the country, where I felt shy and diffident with people I scarcely knew. I was taken to my bedroom, and there I stood, gazing from the wide windows at the parkland and woods. It was an old-fashioned house, and a fire burned in the grate, for it was winter and the large bedroom was chilly. On the washstand stood a copper can of hot water with a towel draping it. I picked up the soap and began to wash my hands. Suddenly I was flooded with warmth and sweetness, a feeling invaded my senses so strongly that I felt no more discomfort. I knew something was near, I waited for it to reveal itself. In that moment of vision as I stood there, a door opened with a flood of golden light. Voices greeted me, dogs barked, a horse whinnied, and all came to life. I ran upstairs noiselessly to my bedroom, where a fire was burning, and I poured water from a little can swathed in a towel, and I washed my hands, smelling the Pears' soap, the lavender of the linen towel, the soft rainwater with its distinctive odour of moss and leaves decayed in the rain barrel. The room where I stood completely captured my senses, I was in two rooms at once, and I realised I was breathing in the same mixture of odours: Pears' soap, lavender in the towel, hot rainwater in which moss and leaves had been brewed, and wood on the fire; for this country house, many years later in a different county, carried the fragrance that I had known from childhood to adult life. All apprehensions vanished in that moment of timelessness. I was completely accepted by this house of strangers, whose walls held so much tradition.

The strong odour of home-made bread is one of the pleasant smells of life, and the smell of linseed cake for cattle is extremely agreeable. I have always enjoyed this smell which I seldom come across in a more urban life. As children, we sniffed the dark crinkled slabs of cake which stood in the barn waiting to be broken up, and often a few crumbs went into my pocket after I had given some morsels to a favourite cow, whispering to her, touching her wet nose, and scratching behind her silky ears.

The smell of newspapers, freshly printed, is another good smell, and although it comes every morning it never loses its charm. Even as one passes a newsboy with a pile of papers at the corner of a London street, the pungency of newspapers seems to overcome the smells around. It has no memory for me, it brings no vision; for we had no daily paper, and the weekly paper had no individual smell after its burial under many things in the basket.

The smells of leather, of boots and bags and saddles, are aromatic, especially the faint scent of a morocco-covered prayer book. A saddler's shop is one of the happiest places to loiter, and saddlers can still be found in most country towns. When I see one I make an excuse to enter, and I finger the long straps, and admire the saddles and whips, while I buy a dog-lead. The saddler has tales of his customers, his trade and his fine leather-work, but the odour of the leather is the attraction.

The smells of shops, the composite aroma of village shops, bring messages of a disagreeable nature, for I am transported to murky little interiors, with windows filled with articles in mixed profusion, with counters spilling over to the wooden floor, with barrels and boxes and shelves overflowing, while a jangling bell warns the lady in the cottage behind to be quick. It was a nerve-racking business to go along to a shop, to walk down a step and lift the latch and set the bell ringing as one stumbled in the dusk. The most up-to-date grocer's shop has remnants of the same smell, modified but bringing the strong mixture to the senses of vinegar and bacon, pickles and salt, without the addition of paraffin and mice.

A modern chemist's shop has quite different smells from the old druggist's, and the cosmetics and powders, scented soap and perfume give a frivolous fragrance that would have shocked the dour druggist with his embrocations and horse medicines and ointments. Only a medicine cupboard, opened after it has been closed for a long time, brings a whiff of the chemist's shop of old. The reverse is true of the post-office, which used to have a clean fresh smell of notepaper and writing-pads, of rose-scented and violet paper for a boudoir, and small bottles of perfume, in addition to the stamps and telegram forms and good brown paper parcels. A modern post-office often smells of disinfectant and humanity.

Sweet and harsh, beautiful and repulsive, the various smells come to pervade one's senses. Wet dog, bruised bracken and trampled grass, candle smoke and river mud, unbleached calico and wet blankets and wool have disagreeable smells through the years of time; but each has the power to transform one's time and place to another, to bring back the even stronger dislike one felt in youth. I am glad I had the lost pleasure of the scent of musk, which grew in every cranny of garden and stone path, and in flower-pots of cottage window-sills. It filled the air with its own delicate fragrance, but I cannot recover this scent by any mind messenger, and no effort of imagination will bring back the perfume.

– From 'The Pleasures of Smell' in *Here's a New Day*.

Country Notebook

ADRIAN BELL

The Patter

For some reason, as I was carrying armfuls of logs through the house, I thought of the patter of children's feet up in the nursery that used to be the background noise to all my comings and goings. The nursery is now the spare bedroom; the house is quiet for months on end, and I have long since ceased to expect that stir, that slight pleasant rumbustiousness from overhead. These wintry days the little ones would have been playing in the nursery, or getting ready to go for a short, sharp walk. Whatever they were doing, or preparing to do, seemed to occasion a constant running to and fro; six little feet patter, patter, patter on the boards, mingled at moments with high-pitched laughter. It was a cheerful background to life. Noisy? Bless you, we were only too grateful for the noise, as betokening health. All those ailments yet uncaught; the whooping-cough (that was noise enough of the wrong sort), measles, mumps, chicken-pox, flu – they plague generation after generation; yet there was that germ moratorium between babyhood and school age, and the feet in the little shoes went patter, patter, patter.

What made me recall those times to-day, I wondered, even as I was passing through the hall silently in gum-boots, bearing an armful of logs? I opened the sitting-room door, and paused, and smiled to myself.

'Well?' said Nora, looking up from her knitting.

'I was remembering,' I said, 'the patter of children's feet which used to sound from upstairs.'

A curious look came over Nora as I said this, as though the memory were almost too poignant.

'It's foolish,' I went on, 'but I could almost swear I heard ghostly feet. . . .'

Nora had risen and gone quickly past me out of the room. I stared at her knitting lying tangled on the floor, baffled by her sudden access of feeling.

'What, my dear?'

Nora was yelling at me from the top of the stairs. 'Go and turn the main water-cock off,' she shouted. 'We're being flooded. Quick!'

My Inner Self

Several times a day I go into my stable for poultry food or some tool. As I no longer keep a horse I suppose it should no longer be called a stable. The gig-house has become the garage, but somehow 'stable' is still the name for this building, though it now houses bicycles, potatoes, a motor scythe and that great number of jam jars and paint pots which family life seems to collect.

Every now and then somebody lifts up a paint pot and shakes it, decides that whatever paint is inside it is now useless, replaces it on the shelf, and goes and buys a new pot for the job he wants to do. He who vainly shakes the paint pot also takes up a paint brush. The saucer in which it lies comes up with it: it is cemented to it with a dark substance that looks like toffee. 'Pity it wasn't washed,' mutters the seeker after a paint brush, especially if he is the head of the family, and he replaces the combined brush-and-saucer on the shelf, and makes a note on his shopping list: 'Paint brush.'

I make more New Year resolutions about the contents of that stable than anything else. It is there and not in church that the enervation of my moral nature is brought home to me. That place is the true picture of my inner self. It undoes all the mottoes on which I was brought up. It displays 'stitches' never in time, things badly begun and not half done. How many visionary chickens counted before they were hatched inhabit that smoke-blackened brooder? How many a stone might have been left unturned to the benefit of the blade of that scythe? Here is a work-bench at which no work is done, a vice in a condition that is a comment on itself. There are nails of the sizes I never need, and pig-rings that puncture my fingers as I rummage after screws. There are bulbs dug up and not replanted, desiccated roots, a flail all touchwood but still hanging on the wall as an emblem of former industry.

Why are these things not thrown away, you may ask? The answer is that my eyes are so used to these things that I cease to see them. It is only now when I make a resolution about the stable that I become aware of them again. Otherwise they melt into their environment. Thus it is that a person may be seen sometimes standing in the stable with a haunted look, knowing that the thing he is seeking is no doubt there, and that he may be looking at it and not seeing it for having seen it so long.

Mrs Gayely's Garden

One of the most brilliant little gardens I ever saw was tended by Mrs Gayely, who prepared poultry for private customers. I used to see her digging holes beside daphne bushes, and tipping in gory basinfuls. She was a small woman with a lovely wild-rose complexion. She used to pass by, singing, driving her cows. Any Victorian poet would have composed at sight of her. ('Will no one tell me what she sings?') But not if he had seen her slaughtering turkeys under her flowering-currant bush.

Turkeys are not easy birds to kill – I mean when you really want to kill them. They are ready enough to die at any previous stage. My brood of turkeys was almost like Queen Anne's children. Not quite: I had just one left by Christmas.

I looked at it: it looked at me. There was only one way to kill it that I knew – to wring its neck. It takes a strong man to wring a turkey's neck.

Mrs Gayely passed by with her cows. I made a sign towards my turkey, and (doubtfully) at my biceps. Mrs Gayely paused in her singing. 'Bring it to me,' she said.

I took it down to her house.

'A lovely bird,' she murmured as she felt it in her arms. 'Come back at tea-time.'

As I departed I saw her advancing towards her flowering-currant bush with the turkey and a knife. I returned at tea-time. My bird was transformed from one of God's creatures to a viand.

When she was young, Mrs Gayely looked like Persephone. And she sacrificed cocks and hens and turkeys under her daphne and flowering-currant bushes. Such a show of daphne and flowering currant she had.

Marmalade

The house smells of marmalade, hot marmalade. It travels up the chimney from the kitchen, out of the chimney-pot and down the chimney beside it, which is the chimney of my room. I put my hand to the fireplace, which is empty because I have an electric stove on, and I can feel the marmalady draught. The fog so depresses the hot vapour that as soon as it pops out of the chimney, true to its Sevillian origin it hates our weather and pops indoors again down the nearest flue. At first I said to myself: 'What a long time breakfast is going on down there.' Then there came a waft of meat cooking, then a breath of onions, then marmalade again. I began to visualise a complex cooking operation.

Sure enough, there was something odd about the day. The ghostly pallor of the window, the huge seagull that brushed past in the fog, and then a bell ringing lustily down there.

That bell was for me. I started up guiltily. Ever since I was twenty-one that bell has summoned me. It is a big brass handbell. My mother bought it to summon me. There were two hundred acres of land, and I might be anywhere on that two hundred acres when somebody arrived and wanted to see me on business. They did, and my mother rang the bell: it could be heard all over the parish. . . . Nowadays it fetches me out of 'The Green Man' at the climax of the argument. 'So long, chaps,' I say, and scuttle.

It means dinner or some emergency. I hurried downstairs to-day. Nora was in the kitchen playing with a child's wooden spade, toddler's size. She seemed happily preoccupied, digging with the spade in a seething cauldron. The odour of marmalade down there was like all the breakfasts you had ever had rolled into one. 'I can't leave this,' Nora said, 'or it will boil over. So I rang the bell for you to come and collect your elevenses.'

'What has happened to your wooden spoon, the one the cat gave you for Christmas?' I asked. 'Surely it has not been worn away to a knob already?' When I look at those wooden spoons their heads reduced to the size of buttons, I think what a lot of wood she and I must have consumed in twenty years of marriage.

'This spade is handier,' she said. 'It is so long it doesn't slip into the pan.'

The pan is buckled, dented beside the handle. 'Yes, you used it once for draining the car radiator in a frost, then forgot and ran over it. I can't fill it higher than the handle now; it leaks.'

There was something fascinating about the seething marmalade. But I glimpsed something else.

'Tell me, you aren't by any mistake boiling my vest in marmalade, are you?'

'That is a bag containing the pips.'

'Do we have to eat the pips?'

'No, but there's jellification in pips.'

'How is that?'

'Don't ask me: all I know is they help it to set – the something that boils out of the pips.'

That afternoon Nora said: 'Are you going out?'

'Yes,' I said, 'I thought I would go for a walk.'

'I'll come with you,' she volunteered. I was pleased. I do not often have her company on walks these days. 'As far as the grocer's,' she added. 'I want another five pounds of Seville oranges. You can carry them home for me.'

By seven o'clock that evening, the news by chimney-flue was that marmalade was finally subdued by savoury omelette. So I came downstairs. On the kitchen table was a glass beer-mug full of light ale.

'Now, this *is* good of you,' I exclaimed, as I picked it up.

'Stop!' cried Nora. 'It's marmalade. I had just too much for my jars.'

I held it to the light. 'What a perfect imitation of half a pint of bitter. Who, in a thirsty moment, would notice that it was semi-solid? What a terrible practical joke this might be. Half a pint in the face, down the neck. Let us mention no names. No, let us not even contemplate it, or I shall begin to think of someone.'

– From *A Suffolk Harvest.*

Florist of the Old School

MISS MITFORD

. . . Matthew is an old bachelor of fifty-five, or thereaway, with a quick eye, a ruddy cheek, a delightful benevolence of countenance, a soft voice and a gentle manner. He is just what he seems, the kindest, the most generous, and the best-natured creature under the sun, the universal friend and refuge of servants, children, paupers, and delinquents of all descriptions, who fly to him for assistance and protection in every emergency, and would certainly stun him with their clamorous importunity, if he were not already as deaf as a post.

Matthew is one of the few very deaf people worth talking to. He is what is becoming scarcer every day, a florist of the first order, and of the old school – not exactly of Mr Evelyn's time, for in the gardening of that period, although greens were, flowers were not – but of thirty or forty years back [*i.e.*, about 1780] the reign of pinks, tulips, auriculas, and ranunculuses, when the time and skill of the gardener were devoted to produce, in the highest imaginable perfection, a variety of two or three favoured tribes. The whole of this large garden, for the potatoes and the cabbages have been forced to retreat to a nook in the orchard, dug up in their behoof – the whole ample garden is laid out in long beds, like those in a nursery ground, filled with these precious flowers, of the rarest sorts and in the highest culture; and as I have arrived in the midst of the hyacinth, auricula, and anemone season, with the tulips just opening, I may consider myself in great luck to see what is called in gardening language, 'so grand a show'. It is worth something, too, to see Matthew's delight, half compounded of vanity and kindness, as he shews them, mixed with courteous offers of seedlings and offsets, and biographical notices of the more curious flowers: 'How the stock of this plant came from that noted florist Tom Bonham, the B—— tailor, commonly called Tippling Tom, who once refused fifty guineas for three auriculas! and how this tulip was filched (Matthew tells this in a particularly low and confidential tone) 'from a worthy merchant of Rotterdam, by an honest skipper of his acquaintance, who abstracted the root, but left five pounds in the place of it . . .'

Perhaps the tulips, especially this pet root, are on the whole Matthew's favourites; but he is a great man at pink shows and melon feasts, and his carnations, particularly those of a sort called the 'Mount Etna', which seldom comes to good in other hands, as regularly win the plate as Andrew's greyhounds. It is quite edifying to hear him run over the bead-roll of pink names, from 'Cleopatra' to the 'Glory of New York'. The last mentioned flowers are precisely my object to-day; for I am come to beg some of his old plants, to the great endangerment of my character as a woman of taste, I having, sooth to say, no judgment in pinks, except preferring those which are full of bloom, in which quality these old roots, which he was about to fling away, and which he is giving me (with a civil reluctance to put anything so worthless into my garden), greatly excel the young plants of which he is so proud.

Notwithstanding his love for his own names, some of which are fantastical enough, Matthew wages fierce war against the cramp appellations, whether of geraniums or of other plants, introduced latterly, and indeed against all new flowers of every sort whatsoever, comprehending them all under the general denomination of trash. He contrives to get the best and the rarest, notwithstanding, and to make them blow better than anybody, and I would lay a wager – Ay, I am right! the rogue! the rogue! What is that in the window but the *cactus speciosissimus*, most splendid of flowers, with its large ruby cup and its ivory tassels? It is not in bloom yet, but it is showing strong and coming fast. And is not that fellow the scarlet potentilla? And that the last fuchsia? And is there such a plant in the county as that newest of all the new camellia? Ah, the rogue! the rogue! He to abuse my geraniums, and call me new-fangled, with four plants in his windows that might challenge the horticultural! And when I

[349]

laugh at him about it, he'll pretend not to hear, and follow the example of that other great deaf artist:

'Who shifted his trumpet and only took snuff.'

Ah, the rogue! the rogue! To think that fickleness should be so engrafted in man's nature, that even Matthew Shore is not able to resist the contagion, but must fall a-flirting with cactuses and camellias – let the pinks and tulips look to it! The rogue! the rogue!

If the fickleness of man were my first thought, the desire to see the camellia nearer was the second; and Mrs Shore appearing in the porch with her clean white apron and her pleasant smile, I followed her through a large, lightsome, bricked apartment, the common room of the family, where the ample hearth, the great chairs in the chimney corner, defended from draughts by green stuff curtains, the massive oak tables, the tall japanned clock, and the huge dresser laden with pewter dishes as bright as silver, gave token of rustic comfort and opulence. Ornaments were not wanting. The dresser was also adorned with the remains of a long preserved set of tea-china, of a light rambling pattern, consisting of five cups and seven saucers, a tea-pot, neatly mended, a pitcher-like cream jug, cracked down the middle, and a sugar basin, wanting a handle; with sundry odd plates, delf, blue, and white, brown-edged and green-edged, scalloped and plain; and last, and choicest, with a grand collection of mugs – always the favourite object of housewifely vanity in every rank of rural life, from Mrs Shore of Lanton Farm, down to her maid Debby. This collection was of a particularly ambitious nature. It filled a row and a half of the long dresser, graduated according to size, like books in a library, the gallons ranking as folios, the half pints ranging as duodecimos. . . . Half a dozen plain white ones, rather out of condition, which stood on a side-table, were clearly the drudges, the working mugs of the family. The ornamental species, the drone mugs, hung on nails by their handles, and were of every variety of shape, colour, and pattern. Some of the larger ones were adorned with portraits in medallion – Mr Wilberforce, Lord Nelson, the Duke of Wellington, and Charles Fox. Some were gay with flowers, not very like nature. Some had landscapes in red, and one a group of figures in yellow. Others again, and these were chiefly the blues, had patterns of all sorts of intricacy and involution without any visible meaning. Some had borders of many colours; and some, which looked too genteel for their company, had white cameos relieved on a brown ground. Those drinking vessels were full of the elegance and grace of the antique. I stood admiring them when Mrs Shore called me into the parlour, where the plant I wished to see was placed. The parlour – Oh, how incomparably inferior to the kitchen! – was a little, low, square, dark box, into which we were shut by a door, painted black, dimly lighted by a casement window, quite filled by the superb camellia, and rendered even more gloomy by a dark paper of reds and greens, with an orange border. A piece of furniture called a beaufette, open and displaying a collection of glassware, almost equal to the pewter for age and brightness, to the mugs for variety, and to the china for joinery, a shining round mahogany table, and six hair-bottomed chairs, really seemed to crowd the little apartment; but it was impossible to look at anything except the splendid plant, with its dark shining leaves, and the pure, yet majestic, blossoms reposing on the deep verdure, as a pearly coronet on the glossy locks of some young beauty. Ah! no wonder that the pinks are a little out of favour, or that Matthew stands smiling there in utter oblivion of striped tulip or streaked carnation! Such a plant as this would be an excuse for forgetting the whole vegetable creation, and my good friend Matthew (who always contrives to hear the civil things one says of his flowers, however low one may speak, and who is perfectly satisfied by my admiration on the present occasion) has just made me almost as happy as himself, by promising to rear me one of the same sort, after a method of his own discovering, which he assures me brings them to perfection twice as fast as the dawdling modes of the new school. Nothing like an old gardener after all! above all if he be as kind, as enthusiastic, and as clever as my friend Matthew Shore.

– From 'Matthew Shore' in *English Life and Character*.

A Country Brood

LAURIE LEE

Walking downstairs there was a smell of floorboards, of rags, sour lemons, old spices. The smoky kitchen was in its morning muddle, from which breakfast would presently emerge. Mother stirred the porridge in a soot-black pot, Tony was carving bread with a ruler, the girls in their mackintoshes were laying the table, and the cats were eating the butter. I cleaned some boots and pumped up some fresh water; Jack went for a jug of skimmed milk.

'I'm all behind,' Mother said to the fire. 'This wretched coal's all slack.'

She snatched up an oil-can and threw it all on the fire. A belch of flame roared up the chimney. Mother gave a loud scream, as she always did, and went on stirring the porridge.

'If I had a proper stove,' she said. 'It's a trial getting you off each day.'

I sprinkled some sugar on a slice of bread and bolted it down while I could. How different again looked the kitchen this morning, swirling with smoke and sunlight. Some cut-glass vases threw jagged rainbows across the piano's field of dust, while Father in his pince-nez up on the wall looked down like a scandalised god.

At last the porridge was dabbed on our plates from a thick and steaming spoon. I covered the smoky lumps with treacle and began to eat from the sides to the middle. The girls round the table chewed moonishly, wrapped in their morning stupor. Still sick with sleep, their mouths moved slow, hung slack while their spoon came up; then they paused for a moment spoon to lip, collected their wits, and ate. Their vacant eyes stared straight before them, glazed at the sight of the day. Pink and glowing from their dreamy beds, from

who knows what arms of heroes, they seemed like mute spirits
hauled back to the earth after paradise feasts of love.

'Golly!' cried Doth. 'Have you seen the time?'

They began to jump to their feet.

'Goodness, it's late.'

'I got to be off.'

'Me too.'

'Lord, where's my things?'

'Well, ta-ta, Ma; ta boys – be good.'

'Anything you want up from the Stores . . .?'

They hitched up their stockings, patted their hats and went running
up the bank. This was the hour when walkers and bicyclists flowed
down the long hills to Stroud, when the hooters called through the
morning dews and factories puffed out their plumes. From each
crooked corner of Stroud's five valleys girls were running to shops
and looms, with sleep in their eyes, and eggy cheeks, and in their
ears night voices fading. Marjorie was off to her Milliner's Store,
Phyllis to her Boots-and-Shoes, Dorothy to her job as junior clerk
in a decayed cloth mill by a stream. As for Harold, he'd started work
already, his day began at six, when he'd leave the house with an
angry shout for the lathe-work he really loved.

But what should we boys do, now they had all gone? If it was
schooltime, we pushed off next. If not, we dodged up the bank to
play, ran snail races along the wall, or dug in the garden and found
potatoes and cooked them in tins on the rubbish heap. We were
always hungry, always calling for food, always seeking it in cupboards
and hedge. But holiday mornings were a time of risk, there might be
housework or errands to do. Mother would be ironing or tidying-up,
or reading books on the floor. So if we hung round the yard we kept
our ears cocked; if she caught us, the game was up.

'Ah, there you are, son. I'm needing some salt. Pop to Vick's for
a lump, there's a dear.'

Or: 'See if Granny Trill's got a screw of tea – only ask her nicely,
mind.'

Or: 'Run up to Miss Turk and try and borrow half-a-crown;
I didn't know I'd got so low.'

[353]

'Ask our Jack, our mother! I borrowed the bacon. It's blummin'-well his turn now.'

But Jack had slid off like an eel through the grass, making his sly get-away as usual. He was jumpy, shifty and quick off the mark, an electric flex of nerves, skinny compared with the rest of us, or what farmers might call a 'poor doer'. If they had, in fact, they would have been quite wrong, for Jack did himself very well. He had developed a mealtime strategy which ensured that he ate for two. Speed and guile were the keys to his success, and we hungry ones called him The Slider.

Jack ate against time, that was really his secret; and in our house you had to do it. Imagine us all sitting down to dinner; eight round a pot of stew. It was lentil-stew usually, a heavy brown mash made apparently of plastic studs. Though it smelt of hot stables, we were used to it. And it was filling enough – could you get it. But the size of our family outstripped the size of the pot, so there was never quite enough to go round.

When it came to serving, Mother had no method, not even the law of chance – a dab on each plate in any old order and then every man for himself. No grace, no warning, no starting-gun; but the first to finish what he'd had on his plate could claim what was left in the pot. Mother's swooping spoon was breathlessly watched – let the lentils fall where they may. But starveling Jack had worked it all out, he followed the spoon with his plate. Absent-mindedly Mother would give him first dollop, and very often a second, and as soon as he got it he swallowed it whole, not using his teeth at all. 'More please, I've finished' – the bare plate proved it, so he got the pot scrapings too. Many's the race I've lost to him thus, being just that second slower. But it left me marked with an ugly scar, a twisted, food-crazed nature, so that still I am calling for whole rice puddings and big pots of stew in the night.

The day was over and we had used it, running errands or prowling the fields. When evening came we returned to the kitchen, back to its smoky comfort, in from the rapidly cooling air to its wrappings of warmth and cooking. We boys came first, scuffling down the bank, singly, like homing crows. Long tongues of shadows licked the curves of the fields and the trees turned plump and still. I had been off to Painswick to pay the rates, running fast through the long wet grass, and now I was back, panting hard, the job finished, with hay seeds stuck to my legs. A plate of blue smoke hung above our chimney, flat in the motionless air, and every stone in the path as I ran down home shook my bones with arriving joy . . .

Indoors, our mother was cooking pancakes, her face aglow from the fire. There was a smell of sharp lemon and salty batter, and a burning hiss of oil. The kitchen was dark and convulsive with shadows, no lights had yet been lit. Flames leapt, subsided, corners woke and died, fires burned in a thousand brasses.

'Poke round for the matches, dear boy,' said Mother. 'Damn me if I know where they got to.'

We lit the candles and set them about, each in its proper order: two on the mantelpiece, one on the piano, and one on a plate on the window. Each candle suspended a ball of light, a luminous fragile glow, which swelled and contracted to the spluttering wick or leaned to the moving air. Their flames pushed weakly against the red of the fire, too tenuous to make much headway, revealing our faces more by casts of darkness than by any clear light they threw.

Next we filled and lit the tall iron lamp and placed it on the table. When the wick had warmed and was drawing properly, we turned it up full strength. The flame in the funnel then sprang alive and rose like a pointed flower, began to sing and shudder and grow more radiant, throwing pools of light on the ceiling. Even so, the kitchen remained mostly in shadow, its walls a voluptuous gloom . . .

Meanwhile Jack had cleared some boots from the table and started his inscrutable homework. Tony, in his corner, began to talk to the cat and play with some fragments of cloth. So with the curtains drawn close and the pancakes coming, we settled down to the evening. When the kettle boiled and the toast was made, we gathered and had our tea. We grabbed and dodged and passed and snatched, and packed our mouths like pelicans.

Mother always ate standing up, tearing crusts off the loaf with her fingers, a hand-to-mouth feeding that expressed her vigilance, like that of a wireless-operator at sea. For most of Mother's attention was fixed on the grate, whose fire must never go out. When it threatened to do so she became seized with hysteria, wailing and wringing her hands, pouring on oil and chopping up chairs in a frenzy to keep it alive . . .

But tonight the firelight snapped and crackled, and Mother was in full control. She ruled the range and all its equipment with a tireless, nervous touch. Eating with one hand, she threw on wood with the other, raked the ashes and heated the oven, put on a kettle, stirred the pot, and spread out some more shirts on the guard. As soon as we boys had finished our tea, we pushed all the crockery aside, piled it up roughly at the far end of the table, and settled down under the lamp. Its light was warm and live around us, a kind of puddle of fire of its own. I set up my book and began to draw. Jack worked at his notes and figures. Tony was playing with some cotton reels, pushing them slowly round the table.

All was silent except for Tony's voice, softly muttering his cotton-reel story.

'. . . So they come out of this big hole see, and the big chap said Fie he said we'll kill 'em see, and the pirates was waiting up 'ere, and they had this gurt cannon and they went bang fire and the big chap fell down wheeee! and rolled back in the 'ole and I said we got 'em and I run up the 'ill and this boat see was comin' and I jumped on board wooosh crump and I said now I'm captain see and they said Fie and I took me 'achet 'ack 'ack and they all fell plop in the sea wallop and I sailed the boat round 'ere and round 'ere and up 'ere and round 'ere and down 'ere and up 'ere and round 'ere and down 'ere . . .'

Now the girls arrived home in their belted mackintoshes, flushed from their walk through the dark, and we looked up from our games and said: 'Got anything for us?' and Dorothy gave us some licorice. Then they all had their supper at one end of the table while we boys carried on at the other. When supper was over and cleared away, the kitchen fitted us all. We drew together round the evening lamp, the vast and easy time . . . Marjorie began to trim a new hat, Dorothy to write a love-letter, Phyllis sat down with some forks and spoons, blew 'Ah!' and sleepily rubbed them. Harold, home late, cleaned his bike in a corner. Mother was cutting up newspapers.

We talked in spurts, in lowered voices, scarcely noticing if anyone answered.

'I turned a shaft to a "thou" today,' said Harold.

'A what?'

'He said a "thou".'

Chairs creaked awhile as we thought about it . . .

'Charlie Revell's got a brand new suit. He had it made to fit . . .'

'He half fancies himself.'

'Charlie Revell!'

Pause.

'Look, Doth, I got these bits for sixpence. I'm going to stitch 'em all round the top here.'

'Mmmm. Well. Tccch-tcch. S'all right . . .'

'Dr Green came up to the shop this morning. Wearing corduroy bloomers. Laugh! . . .'

'Look, Ma, look! I've drawn a church on fire. Look, Marge, Doth! Hey, look! . . .'

'If x equals x, then y equals z – shut up! – if x is y . . .'

'O Madeline, if you'll be mine, I'll take you o'er the sea, di-dah . . .'

'Look what I've cut for my scrapbook, girls – a Beefeater – isn't he killing?'

'Charlie Revell cheeked his dad today. He called him a dafty. He . . .'

'You know that boy from the Dairy, Marge – the one they call Barnacle Boots? Well, he asked me to go to Spot's with him. I told him to run off home.'

'No! You never!'

'I certainly did. I said I don't go to no pictures with butter-wallopers You should have seen his face . . .'

'Harry Lazbury smells of chicken-gah. I had to move me desk.'

'Just hark who's talking. Dainty Dick.'

'I'll never be ready by Sunday . . .'

'I've found a lovely snip for my animal page – an old seal – look girls, the expression! . . .'

'So I went round 'ere, and down round 'ere, and he said FIE so I went 'ack, 'ack . . .'

'What couldn't I do to a nice cream slice . . .'

'Charlie Revell's had his ears syringed . . .'

'D'you remember, Doth, when we went to Spot's, and they said Children in Arms Not Allowed, and we walked little Tone right up the steps and he wasn't even two? . . .'

Marge gave her silky, remembering laugh and looked fondly across at Tony. The fire burned clear with a bottle-green light. Their voices grew low and furry. A farm-dog barked far across the valley, fixing the time and distance exactly. Warned by the dog and some hooting owls, I could sense the night valley emptying, stretching in mists of stars and water, growing slowly more secret and late.

The kitchen, warm and murmuring now, vibrated with rosy darkness. My pencil began to wander on the page, my eyes to cloud and clear. I thought I'd stretch myself out on the sofa – for a while, for a short while only. The girls' muted chatter went on and on; I struggled to catch the drift. 'Sh! . . . Not now . . . When the boys are in bed . . . You'll die when you hear . . . Not now . . .'

The boards on the ceiling were melting like water. Words broke and went floating away. Chords of smooth music surged up in my head, thick tides of warmth overwhelmed me. I was drowning in languors of feathered seas, spiralling cosily down . . .

Once in a while I was gently roused to a sound amplified by sleep; to the fall of a coal, the sneeze of the cat, or a muted exclamation. 'She couldn't have done such a thing . . . She did . . . Done what? . . . What thing? . . . Tell, tell me . . .' But helpless I glided back to sleep, deep in the creviced seas, the blind waters stilled me, weighed me down, the girls' words floated on top. I lay longer now, and deeper far; heavier weeds were falling on me . . .

'Come on, Loll. Time to go to bed. They boys went up long ago.' The whispering girls bent over me; the kitchen returned upside down 'Wake up, lamb . . . He's whacked to the wide. Let's try and carry him up.'

Half-waking, half-carried, they got me upstairs. I felt drunk and tattered with dreams. They dragged me stumbling round the bend in the landing, and then I smelt the sweet blankets of bed.

It was cold in the bedroom; there were no fires here. Jack lay open-mouthed, asleep. Shivering, I swayed where the girls undressed me, giggling around my buttons. They left me my shirt and my woollen socks, then stuffed me between the sheets.

Away went the candle down the stairs, boards creaked and the kitchen door shut. Darkness. Shapes returning slow. The window a square of silver. My bed-half was cold – Jack hot as a bird. For a while I lay doubled, teeth chattering, blowing, warming against him slowly.

'Keep yer knees to yerself,' said Jack, turning over. He woke. 'Say, think of a number!'

' 'Leven hundred and two,' I groaned, in a trance.

'Double it,' he hissed in my ear.

Double it . . . Twenny-four hundred and what? Can't do it. Something or other . . . A dog barked again and swallowed a goose. The kitchen still murmured downstairs. Jack quickly submerged, having fired off his guns, and began snorkling away at my side. Gradually I straightened my rigid limbs and hooked all my fingers together. I felt wide awake now. I thought I'd count to a million. 'One, two . . .' I said; that's all.

– From *Cider with Rosie.*

Fox in the Moonlight

HENRY WILLIAMSON

I pulled the chair nearer the fire, put my feet up, and thought of
nothing.

Stealthy footfalls outside. Whispered boyish voices came through
the open silver window.

'My Gor, look at thaccy!'

'Gordarn, what be it?'

'I'm afraid.'

'Let's tell Mis'r Wisson.'

I looked down on the upturned faces of Tikey and Mustard.

'Look Mis'r Wisson, quick, look, what be thaccy up auver your
steps?'

The garden I had moved to after my marriage was a 'made' garden,
many hundreds of loads of soil being dumped on the slope of rock,
and held in by a mortared wall of stone. The garden was level with
the wall top, which was six or seven feet above the lane. Steps led
up from the lane just under the window. At the top of the steps I
had made a small rockery for Alpine plants; this was known locally
as the Dog's Grave. Tikey and Mustard were pointing at the Dog's
Grave. Moon-shadows from the lumps of rock made it look like
a cubist picture; and staring at an unfamiliar halo of dimness at the
top of the steps, I suddenly started: for there an animal stood, or
rather crouched, its bushy tail half-curled about its hindquarters, its
ears sharp as the fixed look of its eyes.

'Keep still! Don't move!' I hissed. 'It's a fox!'

Mustard and Tikey stood obediently still in the lane below. For
nearly half a minute I was as frozen as the fox in the moonlight.

'Now don't move, boys,' I said quietly as I could, 'whatever you do, don't move. I want to get my wife to see it. Most extraordinary! It thinks we haven't seen it – natural colour protection – it will stay there so long as no one disturbs – now don't make any sudden movement – keep still.' I fancied I saw a glint from one of the fox's eyes.

'Not a movement – keep very still ——' I implored.

'Oh, sir,' whispered Mustard.

'What?'

'Please sir, will it hurt us?'

'No. Don't be frightened, boys. It's more scared than you are. Please don't move.'

'No, sir,' whispered Tikey.

'No, sir,' whispered Mustard.

Somehow I dragged my wife, holding a feeding bottle and baby's napkins, and protesting that milk would boil over, to the window. The fox had not moved. Other children were below, about a score, all standing still watching our window. We stared at it. Tikey and Mustard and the children stared at our moonlit faces. Momentarily they glanced at the fox; but their interest was upon our faces. All the children were staring at us, expectantly.

'It's not alive,' said my wife. 'The milk, I left it ——'

. . . A devastating and united yell came upon me from below like many missiles. The only thing to do was to wait until it stopped, and then to congratulate the promoters of the joke. Have you ever been chased by a family of weasels, animals smaller than rats? It is a disintegrating experience; you are actually hunted; the world has turned upon you.

'Please don't let them make such a noise,' said a voice at my side, scarcely audible. 'The baby —— '.

Below in the road, the children gathered round. I handed the stuffed fox – a sorry object when scrutinised, the abandoned nursery of many generations of moths – to Mustard, its owner.

'Us, put'n first by the stream,' explained Mustard, 'and when "Champion" Hancock came by, he saw it, and cried: "It be an otter – get me a stick, bigorr!" Then with the stick he ran to give it a dapp. That's why the head be broke.'

[361]

I learned that the farmer called Champion had been angry – his tactics of avoiding the hunt. He had disappeared into the Lower House, where over his beer he would be able to laugh about it.

– From *Tales of a Devon Village*.

Doing the Rounds at Belvoir

DIANA COOPER

When we reached home after the Sunday drive a large crowd of tourists would have collected on each side of the last hundred yards of the approach, and my grandfather would uncover his head and bow very slightly with a look of pleasure and welcome on his delicate old face. He loved his tourists. They represented to him England and liberty and the feudal system, and were a link between the nobility and the people. The house was open to them three times a week and on all bank holidays. They would arrive in four-in-hand charabancs from all over the country. Bedrooms and one drawing-room, one study and a dining-room were excluded from their tour. Otherwise, from morning to dark, armies of sightseers tramped through that welcoming house. No efforts were made to improve it for them. There were no signed photographs of royalty or of the family, no special flowers or Coronation robes draped casually over a chair, coronet to hand, no tables laid or crumpled newspapers. Nor could they have any idea of how we really lived. In the summer my mother arranged for us children to picnic out and not to return until the hordes had departed, for in truth the atmosphere – the smell – was asphyxiating. Not that one could get away with one's picnic – they all brought picnics too and were encouraged to eat and sleep and take their boots off and comb their hair in the garden, on the terraces, all about and everywhere. They paid no admittance and two or three elderly ladies in black dresses – Lena the head housemaid, the controller of a regiment of maids and the terror of our chapel choir (she sang loud and false to poor Miss Thursby's pedal-sore harmonium), and Mrs Smith the housekeeper, sparkling with jet arabesques, or a pensioned retainer – would shepherd them round.

On Sundays the family, its guests, its governesses and nurses, my grandfather's gentlemen secretaries, his chaplain, Mrs Knox and their child, made a tour of the demesne. Soon after lunch church clothes were changed for equally long close-fitting costumes. The pony chaise was ordered for my grandfather, and a groom to lead it. We would make first for the stables. Mr Durrance, the head groom, would be standing there in blue and silver, carrots in hand, to receive us. The gigantic Princes, Belvoirs and Wellingtons that drew the carriages, lined up hind-end foremost, were given a pat on the withers by my grandfather's withered hand, and a carrot was proffered to each twitching muzzle. Next the sore backs of the hunters were looked at reprovingly. An apple for my Shetland pony, and the doors closed on the champing, the ammonia smell and the exquisitely-plaited selvedge of straw. A minute's glance at the harness-room's gleaming crests of peacocks on blinkers, another at the carriages, dog- and tub-carts and the sleigh.

After the stables came the gardens. Mr Divers, the head gardener, had a black W. G. Grace beard covering his chest, a black cut-away coat, Homburg hat and a bunch of Bluebeard keys. It was impossible to imagine a spade in his hands. He would cut us off a fine bunch of white grapes from the thousand hanging clusters in the vinery, pick us a camellia apiece and offer some not-up-to-much apples to munch on the walk. My grandfather would congratulate him on his last-won horticultural medal and pretend to understand the Latin names of his flowers. I liked the poultry yard better because there was a muster of peacocks, and best perhaps the dairy and Miss Saddlebridge the dairymaid (whose face was not her fortune), who filled the dishes with creamy milk and churned yellow butter-pats crested with peacocks. The kennels next, but they smelt of dead horse, and hounds are not trained to know the difference between men and doorposts, so ladies often weakened on this last call. It was an exhausting walk and my legs were very short. I got a lift sometimes on my grandfather's lap in his chaise, but it was hard on the polite and reluctant men and women who trudged a good three miles, the ladies gathering up their long skirts in their little frozen hands . . .

·   ·   ·   ·   ·

We were chiefly at Belvoir in winter, I suppose, for I think of the tobogganing down slopes worthy of a world's fair, and my fear of the horse-pond ice breaking and drowning Letty, and of day-and-night prayers for snow. The elders outprayed me in their petitions for thaw and for the Meet of the Belvoir Hounds at the Castle door. Bright and beautiful as meets were, I would rather have had snow. Meets were two a penny, and following the hunt in a pony-cart frankly bored me. The ladies wore top hats or billycocks with very black veils drawn taut across their cold noses, and fringes and buns. The men were in pink, with glossy white 'leathers', swigging down cherry brandy from their saddles to keep out the cold. Hounds making a faint music of excitement were dexterously and mercilessly being whipped into a pack by Ben Capel and his underlings. The Master, Sir Gilbert Greenall, was popular though seldom seen, and in his place would be his redoubtable wife surrounded by the horses pawing and twitching and foaming at the mouth, some incorrigibles sporting red bows on their tails that said 'I kick'. Then they would be off, with a flinty clatter of hooves and suppressed oaths and the language horses are thought to understand, through the bare woods to the open Vale, the second horsemen following demurely. They would hack home cold, weary and fulfilled in the twilight, generally caked in mud and smelling of horse, and fall upon the tea and boiled eggs, and discuss the runs and falls and scandals until the gong rang for dressing-time, getting louder and louder as it approached down the unending passages.

The gong man was an old retainer, one of those numberless ranks of domestic servants which have completely disappeared and today seem fabulous. He was admittedly very old. He wore a white beard to his waist. Three times a day he rang the gong – for luncheon, for dressing-time, for dinner. He would walk down the interminable passages, his livery hanging a little loosely on his bent old bones, clutching his gong with one hand and with the other feebly brandishing the padded-knobbed stick with which he struck it. Every corridor had to be warned and the towers too, so I suppose he banged on and off for ten minutes, thrice daily.

Then there were the lamp-and-candle men, at least three of them, for there was no other form of lighting. Gas was despised, I forget why – vulgar, I think. They polished and scraped the wax off the candelabra, cut wicks, poured paraffin oil and unblackened glass chimneys all day long. After dark they were busy trimming wicks up or down, snuffing candles, and de-waxing extinguishers. It was not a department we liked much to visit. It smelt disgusting and the lamp-men were too busy. But the upholsterer's room was a great treat. He was exactly like a Hans Andersen tailor. Crosslegged he sat in a tremendous confusion of curtains and covers, fringes, buttons, rags and carpets, bolsters, scraps (that could be begged off him), huge curved needles like scimitars, bodkins, hunks of beeswax to strengthen thread, and hundreds of flags. The flags on the tower-top, I suppose, got punished by the winds and were constantly in need of repair. I never saw him actually at work on anything else. There were slim flags for wind, little ones for rain, huge ones for sunshine, hunting flags, and many others.

The water-men are difficult to believe in today. They seemed to me to belong to another clay. They were the biggest people I had ever seen, much bigger than any of the men of the family, who were remarkable for their height. They had stubbly beards and a general Bill Sikes appearance. They wore brown clothes, no collars and thick baize aprons from chin to knee. On their shoulders they carried a wooden yoke from which hung two gigantic cans of water. They moved on a perpetual round. Above the ground floor there was not a drop of hot water and not one bath, so their job was to keep all jugs, cans and kettles full in the bedrooms, and morning or evening to bring the hot water for the hip-baths. We were always a little frightened of the water-men. They seemed of another element and never spoke but one word, 'Water-man', to account for themselves.

If anyone had the nerve to lie abed until eleven o'clock, which can seldom have happened, there were many strange callers at the door. First the housemaid, scouring the steel grate and encouraging the fire of the night before, which always burned until morning, and refilling the kettle on the hob until it sang again. Next the unearthly water-giants. Then a muffled knock given by a knee, for the coal-man's hands were too dirty and too full. He was a sinister man, much like his brothers of the water, but blacker far and generally more mineral. He growled the single word 'Coal-man' and refilled one's bin with pieces the size of ice-blocks.

The carpenter's shop was an excitement. It smelt good. One could use the lathes and coax Mr Ricketts to frame a picture or make a box with one's name fretted into it. Then too there was Betsy, the little old stillroom help. She was ninety when I first remember her. She had been born in the Castle, no one quite knew how, and for seventy-five years she washed and dried the plates for the lesser meals. She was felt to be one of the Castle's treasures, together with the Benvenuto Cellini ewer and basin. The visitors were always shown her. She had never learned to read or write – no disgrace, I think, to the family, as what child of her class did learn to read before Waterloo? But maybe she was the happier for her ignorance, for she was always laughing, lived to over a hundred and had a grand funeral.

Lastly there were the watchmen, who frightened many a new-comer to death. There was a little of the water-men about them, but they were dreadfully silent and they padded. All night they walked the passages, terraces, and battlements, yet no one really saw them. One would leave a paper with a request (as one put a letter to Father Christmas in the grate) on the floor of the passage. The paper would disappear and the request would be granted by this remote, unseen power. Always if one woke in the night, as the fire flickered to its death, one would hear a padded foot on the gravel outside and a voice, not loud enough to waken but strong enough to reassure, saying 'Past twelve o'clock. All's well.' . . .

As soon as the Castle became my father's property the old order began to change. Bathrooms were carved out of the deep walls, rooms and passages were warm without the coal-man's knock, the water-men faded away into the elements. . . . The watchmen still guarded the fort, but no longer cried 'All's well'.

The children at Belvoir became the Castle guides for the Quality. The unfortunate guests, after the Sunday walk and a tremendous tea, were handed over to Letty and me (the novice) to be instructed about our family history and heirlooms and any legend we had picked up, or the facts about the authenticity of the Benvenuto Cellini ewer, or the strange panel representing Henry VII and his minions Empson and Dudley. I cannot tell how irritating or disarming we were, babbling and embroidering truths and suppressing nasty rumours, about the Gainsborough being a replica.

– From *The Rainbow Comes and Goes.*

The Unfeathered Nest

HENRY DAVID THOREAU

Near the end of March 1845 I borrowed an axe and went down to the woods by Walden Pond, nearest to where I intended to build my house, and began to cut down some tall arrowy white pines, still in their youth, for timber. It is difficult to begin without borrowing, but perhaps it is the most generous course thus to permit your fellow-men to have an interest in your enterprise. The owner of the axe as he released his hold on it, said that it was the apple of his eye; but I returned it sharper than I received it. It was a pleasant hillside where I worked, covered with pine woods, through which I looked out on the pond, and a small open field in the woods where pines and hickories were springing up. The ice in the pond was not yet dissolved, though there were some open spaces, and it was all dark-coloured and saturated with water. There were some slight flurries of snow during the day that I worked there; but for the most part when I came out on to the railroad, on my way home, its yellow sand heap stretched away gleaming in the hazy atmosphere, and the rails shone in the spring sun, and I heard the lark and pewee and other birds already come to commence another year with us. They were pleasant spring days in which the winter of man's discontent was thawing as well as the earth, and the life that had lain torpid began to stretch itself. . . .

I hewed the main timbers six inches square, most of the studs on two sides only, and the rafters and floor timbers on one side, leaving the rest of the bark on, so that they were just as straight as and much stronger than sawed ones. Each stick was carefully mortised or tenoned by its stump, for I had borrowed other tools by this time. My days in the woods were not very long ones; yet I usually carried my dinner of bread and butter, and read the newspaper in which it was wrapped, at noon, sitting amid the green pine boughs which I had cut off, and to my bread was imparted some of their fragrance, for my hands were covered with a thick coat of pitch.

I began to occupy my house on the 4th of July, as soon as it was boarded and roofed, for the boards were carefully feather-edged and lapped, so that it was perfectly impervious to rain, but before boarding I laid the foundation of a chimney at one end, bringing two cart-loads of stones up the hill from the pond in my arms. I built the chimney after my hoeing in the fall, before a fire became necessary for warmth, doing my cooking in the meanwhile out of doors on the ground, early in the morning; which mode I still think is in some respects more convenient and agreeable than the usual one. When it stormed before my bread was baked, I fixed a few boards over the fire, and sat under them to watch my loaf, and passed some pleasant hours in that way. In those days, when my hands were much employed, I read but little, but the least scrap of paper which lay on the ground, my holder, or tablecloth, afforded me as much entertainment; in fact, answered the same purpose as the Iliad.

Before winter I built a chimney, and shingled the sides of my house, which were already impervious to rain, with imperfect and sappy shingles made of the first slice of the log, whose edges I was obliged to straighten with a plane.

I have thus a tight shingled and plastered house, ten feet wide by fifteen long, eight-feet posts, with a garret and a closet, a large window on each side, two trap-doors, one door at the end, and a brick fire-place opposite. The exact cost of my house, paying the usual price for such materials as I used, but not counting the work, all of which was done by myself, was . . . twenty-eight dollars twelve and a half cents.

To what end, pray, is so much stone hammered? In Arcadia, when I was there, I did not see any hammering stone. Nations are possessed with an insane ambition to perpetuate the memory of themselves by the amount of hammered stone they leave. What if equal pains were taken to smooth and polish their manners? . . . Most of the stone a nation hammers goes toward its tomb only. It buries itself alive. As for the Pyramids, there is nothing to wonder at in them so much as the fact that so many men could be found degraded enough to spend their lives constructing a tomb for some ambitious booby, whom it would have been wiser and manlier to have drowned in the Nile, and then given his body to the dogs.

. . . My food alone cost me in money about twenty-seven cents a-week. It was, for nearly two years after this, rye and Indian meal without yeast, potatoes, rice, a very little salt pork, molasses, and salt, and my drink water. It was fit that I should live on rice, mainly, who loved so well the philosophy of India. I learned from my two years' experience that it would cost incredibly little trouble to obtain one's necessary food even in this latitude; that a man may use as simple a diet as the animals, and yet retain health and strength. I have made a satisfactory dinner, satisfactory on several accounts, simply off a dish of purslane (*Portulaca oleracea*) which I gathered in my corn-field, boiled and salted. I give the Latin on account of the savouriness of the trivial name. And pray what more can a reasonable man desire, in peaceful times, in ordinary noons, than a sufficient number of ears of green sweet-corn boiled, with the addition of salt? Even the little variety which I used was a yielding to the demands of appetite, and not of health. Yet men have come to such a pass that they frequently starve, not for want of necessaries, but for want of luxuries; and I know a good woman who thinks that her son lost his life because he took to drinking water only. . . .

Bread I at first made of pure Indian meal and salt, genuine hoe-cakes, which I baked before my fire out of doors on a shingle or the end of a stick of timber sawed off in building my house; but it was wont to get smoked and to have a piny flavour. I tried flour also; but have at last found a mixture of rye and Indian meal most convenient and agreeable. In cold weather it was no little amusement to bake several small loaves of this in succession, tending and turning them as carefully as an Egyptian his hatching eggs. They were a real cereal fruit which I ripened, and they had to my senses a fragrance like that of other noble fruits, which I kept in as long as possible by wrapping them in cloths. . . . It would seem that I made it according to the receipt which Marcus Porcius Cato gave about two centuries before Christ. – 'Make kneaded bread thus: Wash your hands and trough well. Put the meal into the trough, and water gradually, and knead it thoroughly. When you have kneaded it well, mould it, and bake it under a cover,' that is, in a baking-kettle. Not a word about leaven. But I did not always use this staff of life. At one time, owing to the emptiness of my purse, I saw none of it for more than a month . . .

I saw that I could easily raise my bushel or two of rye and Indian corn, for the former will grow on the poorest land, and the latter does not require the best, and grind them in a hand-mill, and so do without rice and pork; and if I must have some concentrated sweet, I found by experiment that I could make a very good molasses either of pumpkins or beets, and I knew that I needed only to set out a few maples to obtain it more easily still, and while these were growing I could use various substitutes beside those which I have named. 'For,' as the Forefathers sang, –

'We can make liquor to sweeten our lips
Of pumpkins and parsnips and walnut-tree chips.'

Finally, as for salt, that grossest of groceries, to obtain this might be a fit occasion for a visit to the sea-shore, or, if I did without it altogether, I should probably drink the less water. I do not learn that the Indians ever troubled themselves to go after it. . . .

My furniture, part of which I made myself (and the rest cost me nothing of which I have not rendered an account) consisted of a bed, a table, a desk, three chairs, a looking-glass three inches in diameter, a pair of tongs and andirons, a kettle, a skillet, and a frying-pan, a dipper, a wash-bowl, two knives and forks, three plates, one cup, one spoon, a jug for oil, a jug for molasses, and a japanned lamp. None is so poor that he need sit on a pumpkin. That is shiftlessness. There is a plenty of such chairs as I like best in the village garrets to be had for taking them away. Furniture! Thank God, I can sit and I can stand without the aid of a furniture warehouse. . . .

I would observe, by the way, that it costs me nothing for curtains for I have no gazers to shut out but the sun and moon, and I am willing that they should look in. The moon will not sour milk nor taint meat of mine, nor will the sun injure my furniture or fade my carpet, and if he is sometimes too warm a friend, I find it still better economy to retreat behind some curtain which nature has provided, than to add a single item to the details of housekeeping. A lady once offered me a mat, but as I had no room to spare within the house, nor time to spare within or without to shake it, I declined it, preferring to wipe my feet on the sod before my door. It is best to avoid the beginnings of evil.

– From *Walden.*